Patriarch and Prophets

PATRIARCH AND PROPHETS

Persecution of the
Russian Orthodox Church Today

Michael Bourdeaux

MOWBRAYS
London & Oxford

This edition published in Great Britain 1975 by
A. R. Mowbray & Co. Ltd, The Alden Press,
Osney Mead, Oxford OX2 0EG

© 1970 in London, England by Michael Bourdeaux

Printed in Great Britain by
REDWOOD BURN LIMITED
Trowbridge & Esher

ISBN 0 264 66296 2

KESTON BOOK No. 2

To the people of Czechoslovakia, who will find a reflection of
their own spirit in the finest traditions of Christian Russia

Contents

Abbreviations and Russian terms

ABBREVIATIONS

CP(SU)   Communist Party (of the Soviet Union).

CRA   Council for Religious Affairs (the Soviet Government's ministry dealing with the churches from 1966).

CROCA   Council for Russian Orthodox Church Affairs (merged with the Council for the Affairs of Religious Cults to form CRA in 1966).

KGB   Committee of State Security (secret police).

LRA   Law on Religious Associations, 8 April 1929.

MGB   see KGB.

MVD   Ministry of Internal Affairs (an earlier name for the secret police).

NKVD   People's Commissariat of the Interior (secret police).

RFR   *Religious Ferment in Russia* (the companion volume to this work).

RSFSR   Russian Soviet Federated Socialist Republic (the geographical area including Greater Russia and Siberia).

RUSSIAN TERMS

Dvadtsatka   'Council of Twenty' (the basic group of believers in a parish which must seek registration for a congregation to make it legal).

Kolkhoz   collective farm.

Komsomol   Communist Youth League.

Pioneers   communist organization for school-children.

Soviet   policy-making and administrative council under the Communist Party.

Sovkhoz   state farm.

NOTE ON TEXTUAL LAY-OUT

Omissions in the text are indicated by . . . ., whereas the presence of dots in the original is indicated by . . .

Where complete texts are given, this fact is noted.

All translations are given in the standard typography, whereas comments and linking passages are in smaller print.

Addenda

Since the preparation of the text of this book, a number of important new documents relating to the subject have become available:

1. Letter dated 9 May 1968 by Fr. Sergi Zheludkov supporting Anatoli Marchenko's book, *My Testimony*, and quoting an extract on people imprisoned for religious reasons. Zheludkov's letter was addressed to the World Council of Churches, the Archbishop of Canterbury and others. Russian text in *Russkaya Mysl* (Paris), 26 June 1969.

2. Letter from workers of the city of Gorki to Dr. Eugene Blake, General Secretary of the World Council of Churches. Copy also sent to U Thant, with covering letter dated 4 November 1968. 1,500 people have petitioned for the opening of another church in the city. Russian text in *Russkaya Mysl*, 19 July 1969.

3. Letter of an anonymous group of Orthodox intellectuals to the editors of *Vestnik* (undated), thanking them for providing the new members of 'the Russian religious renaissance' with inspiration and suggesting topics of interest. Russian text in *Vestnik* 89–90, 1968, pp. 1–3. Excerpts in English in *Frontier* (London), May 1969.

4. Story by Solzhenitsyn, *The Easter Procession*. Describes an anti-religious demonstration by young people at an Easter service. Russian text in *Posev* 2, February 1969, pp. 45–7. English translation in *The Observer*, London, 6 April 1969.

5. The latest document on the Pochaev affair (August 1967). Petition to the Patriarch of Constantinople by the Monks Sergi (Solomko) and Apelli (Stankevich). Russian text in *Vestnik* 89–90, 1968, pp. 46–8.

6. 'Christ and the Master' by Anatoli Levitin. Commentary on Mikhail Bulgakov's novel, *The Master and Margarita*. Russian text of Part I in *Grani* 71, 1969, pp. 162–95.

7. The 'Chronicle of Current Events' (see pp. 341–4) has now been continued to seven consecutive issues. Reference in *Posev* 4, April 1969, p. 7. No. 5 is due to appear in English in *Survey* 73 and it lists a number of religious documents circulating in the Soviet Union, most of which have been included in this collection. No. 7 refers to the release of a Baptist prisoner and to persecutions of the Ukrainian Uniates.

8. Very important speech by 'a Christian' at the funeral of A. Ye. Kosterin, 14 November 1968. Russian text in *Posev* 4, April 1969, pp. 60–1.

9. Book of 250 pp. by Fr. Zheludkov, *Why I too am a Christian*. Extracts published in *Vozrozhdenie*, Paris, No. 210, June 1969, pp. 101–7.

Preface

This book is a companion to my *Religious Ferment in Russia*, published in 1968. Both works were conceived together, their genesis being the savage policy which the Soviet Government introduced against religion in the later years of Mr. Khrushchev's rule. The earlier work treated of new directions of thought on state policies emerging in the Evangelical Christian and Baptist Church, which resulted in a schism that still persists between the reformers and those who, apparently at least, accept the *status quo*. We now turn to a very similar movement in the Russian Orthodox Church, potentially of much greater importance because it could affect by far the largest religious group in the Soviet Union. The cross-fertilization between the two movements, which we postulated in the Epilogue of *Religious Ferment in Russia*, can now be proved. Never before in history has an Orthodox archbishop held up an initiative taken by the Baptist Church as an example to be followed.*

The title of this work is symbolical. In the Old Testament there was a long conflict between the established cultic religion, as personified by the priest, and the explosive calls to repentance from the prophet. This was not a dramatic, 'either-or' choice between good and evil, but a creative tension in which both elements were necessary to the formation of Jewish religious consciousness. So in Russia today we have the Patriarch, his staff and most of the bishops, who have reached a *modus vivendi* with the atheist regime, on the one hand and the new, impassioned voices of those seeking fresh ways forward on the other. The title is not *Patriarch OR Prophets*. We believe that this conflict, too, is a creative one and that ultimately both the Baptists and the Orthodox will come to see that neither attitude must totally exclude the other if the church is to play a full part in the developing society.

The problem of balance in the presentation of the two positions

* See p. 245.

has been impossible to solve. This book presents the new voices at length, because they have had only an inadequate platform elsewhere, while officials from the Patriarchate have been able to speak at great conferences of churchmen all over the world. Nevertheless, in the very nature of the situation, the Moscow Patriarchate has not been able to use this privileged position for any adequate discussion of internal developments in church life. To have attempted to do so would have threatened the very basis of its own relations with the state. Exactly the same applies to the publications of the Patriarchate. Therefore it is useless to search in them for any accounts of the events which the documents presented in this book describe or for any justification of Patriarchal policies. Indeed, the *Journal of the Moscow Patriarchate* has printed much less of relevance here than has the parallel Baptist publication, *Bratsky Vestnik* ('Fraternal Herald').

To sum up this argument, the facts in these documents expose the practical consequences of the Soviet State's atheist policy and do not always exonerate the Moscow Patriarchate from complicity in what has happened. Against this latter point, however, we must constantly place the probability that at least some members of the Patriarchate are using behind-the-scenes means of negotiating with the authorities on behalf of believers. If any details should be revealed, there would be a breakdown in this process. There is here a whole area of enquiry which it is at present impossible to document. This, then, is an interim report presenting as many facts of the persecution as are known to us.

Because the writers we quote are so explicit in their presentation of these facts, it was found possible to adopt a different method from that used in the companion work. Here, after my introduction, the documents are allowed to stand on their own feet. They are grouped thematically into chapters for the convenience of the reader, but many of them are so rich in content that they contain much of relevance to other sections also.

My thanks are due to the London School of Economics and Political Science, whose generous offer of a Visiting Fellowship gave me the opportunity of bringing this work to a conclusion.

The following have given invaluable help and advice: Messrs. Peter Reddaway, W. D. McAfee, Constantine Brancovan, Brian Cooper, Dr. Francis Thomson and Miss Kathleen Matchett. Acknowledgement is also made to the following publications for permission to use translations which have been adapted for use here: *St. Vladimir's Seminary Quarterly, Religion in Communist Dominated Areas, Current Developments in the Eastern European Churches, Encounter.* Miss Xenia Howard-Johnston has helped at all stages with the preparation of the manuscript and my wife has patiently typed it and compiled the index, reorganizing her family life to do so.

Chislehurst   MICHAEL BOURDEAUX
November 1968

Introduction : Church and State

From whichever angle we set out to document the present-day life and thought of the Russian Orthodox Church, we come up against an age-old imponderable factor: the work of the Holy Spirit, which so often triumphs where the human odds are stacked impossibly against it. Waves of persecution have swept over the Christian Church from time to time in the past; they will do so again. Never since the third century, however, has there been anything remotely comparable to the official atheist campaign which the Soviet Government has been waging now for over fifty years. Although tactical concessions were made to the church during the Second World War, the mass media, under stringent control, have remained unremittingly hostile to it and more violent methods have often been used. In physical terms, this sordid struggle has left behind it a wake of broken bodies and ruined masterpieces of architecture, a trail of wilful destruction which can never be repaired. Yet at the end of all this time and with no reversal of the process, the state ideology of communism has few – if any – corresponding spiritual gains to show over against its adversary. Rather the reverse. Through the steadfastness of millions of ordinary believers and the uncompromising stand of its greatest leaders, the Christian faith in the Soviet Union unquestionably holds a stronger moral position now than at any other time since the 1917 Revolution. In purely physical terms, this is inexplicable. The note of faith and its triumph over adversity is rarely absent from the writings of those Russian Orthodox Christians whose work we introduce here.

We, however, adopt the approach of concerning ourselves only with those facts which can be documented, believing that the dimension of faith is strong enough to reveal itself where it will. We shall set the scene by establishing the general framework within which religion is legally permitted to operate, before moving on to consider some of the salient points in the life of the

Russian Orthodox Church over the last decade.

The Constitution, which is the basic law of the USSR, guarantees certain limited religious freedoms. §124 proclaims the separation of church and state and grants 'freedom of religious worship
and of anti-religious propaganda'.[1]* §125 guarantees these basic
freedoms: speech, the press, assembly (including the holding of
mass meetings), street processions and demonstrations. It further promises full use of printing presses, paper, premises, the
streets and means of communication for the practical expression
of these freedoms.[2] None of the rights guaranteed by this latter
article in practice applies to the church, because §125 is introduced
by the limiting clause, 'In conformity with the interests of the
working people and in order to strengthen the socialist system. . . .'
Therefore the church is disqualified from exercising any public
activity outside the four walls of the building registered for worship, a point made explicit in 1929, when the right to 'religious
propaganda' was excluded from the original Constitution of 1918.[3]

The year 1929 is very important for the history of religion
under the Soviet regime, for it was then that the main legislative
acts concerning religion were codified. They have remained in
force ever since, with only insignificant modifications. As one
would expect from the date, these laws are Stalinist in conception
and in their restrictive purpose. Furthermore, from the strictly
legal point of view they cause considerable headaches, for some
of their provisions remove even part of that limited freedom
guaranteed by the Constitution. To put it in its simplest terms,
the basic law of the Soviet Union is contradicted by the body of
legislation on religion. One of the most important themes expounded in *Religious Ferment in Russia* is that certain Baptists have
become sharply aware of the implications of this and have sought
to have the position clarified and liberalized (for which they have
had to suffer severe repressions). This book will show that the
new unofficial spokesmen of the Russian Orthodox Church,
unlike the Baptists, have not yet gone so far as formally or publicly to demand a reform of the 1929 law,† but they are acutely

* See pp. 345 ff. for Notes.   † With one exception: see p. 315.

aware of the rights which ought to be theirs through the separation of church and state.

The following outline of the legal position of religion in Soviet
society can only be provisional, for there are two problematical
factors which at present inhibit a full consideration of the subject.
These are the proven existence of secret instructions to local
authorities, which further reduce the guaranteed freedoms,[4] and
the tendency of the communist authorities in local situations to
disregard the law in order to follow central party directives on
the combating of religion. The latter is a highly variable factor,
not only in time (following the 'soft-' or 'hard-line' pronouncements of the moment), but also geographically. It is certain, for
example, that, even during the height of the Khrushchev campaign against religion, the disposition of local communist officials
made life for Christians more bearable in some areas than in
others.

SOME LEGAL RESTRICTIONS

1. The basic constitutional principle of the separation of church
and state is almost comprehensively violated by the 1929 law.
Every 'religious association' (to use the Soviet term) must apply
for and be granted registration before it can meet at all.[5] Further,
it must supply lists of members' names to the local authorities,[6]
which obviously gives them a tool which may be (and often is)
used for discrimination against the believer at his place of work
or in the allocation of housing, for example. Communist Party
control over the activities of registered religious associations is
made explicit in the rules on surveillance[7] and in the right of the
registration agencies 'to remove individual members from the
executive body'.[8] This right stretches sometimes, in practice and
with encouragement from secret instructions, to the actual appointment of members to the executive body of a religious
association by an atheist local authority[9] – a situation which has
the profoundest significance for our study.

2. The religious education of children is banned in any form,

except that parents may privately instruct their own families (even this is not explicitly stated).[10] This is one of the principal issues at stake in the campaign which the reform Baptists have been waging. They have not sought the introduction of religious instruction into the school curriculum, but the opportunity, which is allowed in most other communist countries, of organizing such classes in the home or on church premises. The possibility of arranging theological courses 'with special permission', which was guaranteed in 1929,[11] is now denied in practice, except for three existing Orthodox, two Catholic seminaries and one centre each for Armenians, Georgian Orthodox, Muslims and, on paper, Jews. Even these are severely restricted in size and scope: for example, it cannot seriously be claimed that adequate rabbinical training is available in the USSR.[12] The Baptists received permission to set up a correspondence course in 1967,[13] but Methodists, Seventh-Day Adventists, Old Believers, Buddhists and many other groups have no courses of any description.[14] At times secret laws have operated which even restrict the presence of children at worship and have denied Orthodox children the right of receiving communion.*

3. The Constitution is explicit in limiting evangelism. There are even restrictions on preaching inside church buildings[15] – a factor which affects the Protestant Churches more than the Orthodox, where so much of the emphasis is on worship through the liturgy. §142 of the Penal Code of the Russian Republic now bans 'the performance of deceitful acts with the aim of arousing religious superstitions among the public',[16] which obviously renders highly dangerous such traditional Orthodox practices as going on pilgrimages and venerating sacred wells, but which is so imprecise in its wording that it could be bent to apply to almost any religious activity. Under the threat of five years' imprisonment or exile, §227 seeks to protect the 'health of citizens' and to prevent any other encroachments upon their rights with which believers might threaten them 'under the guise of teaching

* See pp. 160–1, 168–9 and RFR, p. 20 (probably a reflection of a secret instruction).

religious doctrine and carrying out religious rites'. A similar penalty is threatened for 'prompting citizens to refuse to participate in social activity or fulfil their civil obligations' and for 'enticing minors' into a religious group.[17] Under this article, a priest with a young person in his congregation who refuses to join the *Komsomol* could be jailed for five years.

Priests and pastors are not permitted to be active anywhere except among their own congregations.[18]

4. Religious literature is *de jure* permitted, except where it calls for an infringement of the law.[19] In fact, the amount produced since 1917 is negligible. There have been occasional printings of the Bible in wholly inadequate editions and partly for export; the Orthodox Church has issued a very small number of theological books, several of which were used mainly to 'prove' the freedom of religion in the USSR, and since 1943 the *Journal of the Moscow Patriarchate* has appeared monthly. The only other regular Russian-language publication is the Baptist journal, *Bratsky Vestnik*, which appears every other month, while other churches are restricted to occasional calendars and service-books. From time to time, depending on local conditions, some of the churches in the republics have issued a journal. Imports are banned and people who try to take religious literature with them into the Soviet Union run the risk of arrest, as in the case of Anthony Hippisley, who, when discovered at the Soviet frontier in 1966 with four hundred Bibles, had them confiscated and suffered expulsion.[20] Special punishments are given to prisoners who request religious literature or say their prayers.[21]

5. No welfare or relief work of any kind may be undertaken by the churches.[22] Beyond performance of the ritual or service, no parish activities whatsoever are permitted. Thus, the Soviet system has banned features which in other countries are considered to be a 'normal' part of religious activity, such as prayer groups, women's meetings and communal excursions.[23]

6. Church buildings cannot be owned by communities, but only leased to them.[24] This confronts the church with one of its most serious legal difficulties, for in practice such buildings are

often not leased, in connection with refusal of registration. Furthermore, this arrangement facilitates the liquidation of churches which are already functioning (a point which should be borne in mind as background to Chapter 4).[25] Any religious group wishing to meet elsewhere must obtain separate permission on each individual occasion,[26] which is often not granted.

7. There is a further contravention of the principle of separation of church and state in the necessity to obtain permission to hold any local, regional or national religious assembly.[27] Such permission for national assemblies has been granted only in rare instances (for example, the Orthodox Church in 1945, the Baptists in 1963 and 1966), while some religious bodies, such as the Jehovah's Witnesses, Old Believers and Jews, have never held a convention of any description. The Uniates (Greek Catholics) met in 1946 only to abolish themselves!

8. Nowhere in the legislative acts is it stated which religious denominations are legal and which are not. Therefore the total ban in practice on such sects as the Jehovah's Witnesses and Dukhobors can only reflect a secret instruction. Occasionally certain sects are stated to be illegal.[28] This ban is not confined to sects which would be considered extremist in any society, but also includes Uniates, reform Baptists (*Initsiativniki*), True Orthodox Christians, Pentecostals, the Salvation Army and many others whose ideology would be accepted in any country where true freedom of religion exists. Other groups find themselves in the penumbra, precluded from any form of national organization, but finding it possible, under certain favourable local conditions, to obtain registration. Included here are the Seventh-Day Adventists (their national organization was disbanded in 1960[29]), Mennonites and Methodists – to which one could add even such major groups as the Jews and the Roman Catholics.

*   *   *

Any infringement of §142 of the Penal Code of the RSFSR entails a fine of up to fifty roubles for a first offence and imprisonment of up to three years for subsequent ones, according to the revision of March 1966.[30] Formerly a fifty-rouble fine or a one-year prison sentence could be imposed for any breach, but there was no increased penalty for recidivists. However, in practice many religious activists have been imprisoned for much longer periods of time for alleged infringement of passport (residence) regulations and the so-called 'parasite laws', relating to gainful employment.[31] §227 of the Penal Code still prescribes a maximum sentence of five years for those who infringe it. The 1966 revision does seem to have resulted in a clarification, but cannot be interpreted as instituting greater leniency.[32]

Apart from Albania and China, from which reports came in 1966–67 about the abolition of all institutional religion, no other communist country at present imposes anything like such severe restrictions on religious freedom as does the Soviet Union. Even the laws which do exist in the other countries have been interpreted in recent years in a much more liberal spirit. To quote a random example, the very small Baptist Church in Poland organizes residential summer courses and numerous other activities for young people.[33] In Czechoslovakia the Dubček regime promised guarantees of full religious freedom very early in its life and soon legalized the Uniate Church, which had been proscribed after the communist take-over.[34]

SPECIAL POSITION OF THE RUSSIAN ORTHODOX CHURCH

These legal restrictions are the essential background against which one must view all forms of religious activity in the Soviet Union today. For our study of the Russian Orthodox Church it is also necessary continually to bear in mind its individual history, especially since 1917. However, it would be quite impossible, for reasons of space, to embark on any study of it at this point. In lieu of this we would refer the reader to the following. The first two chapters of the present author's *Opium of the People*[35] contain a very generalized and non-technical account. More specialized recent studies are contained in two books by William C. Fletcher, *A Study in Survival*[36] and *Nikolai*,[37] while Nikita Struve's *Christians in Contemporary Russia*[38] and William B. Stroyen's *Communist Russia and the Russian Orthodox Church, 1943–1962*[39] also contain much useful material.

We cannot, however, understand the last decade of the life of the Russian Orthodox Church without turning back to a key moment. In 1927, after a bitter struggle in the church and more heart-searching than he was ever able publicly to reveal, Metropolitan (later Patriarch) Sergi pledged his own loyalty and that of his followers to 'the Soviet Union as our civil motherland'.[40] In his book on this period, *A Study in Survival*, William Fletcher sets out the one-sided nature of the bargain then achieved, showing how close the Russian Orthodox Church came to extinction as an organized entity before the tide rapidly turned during the Second World War. Though much bitterness had been caused in the church by Metropolitan Sergi's compromise, the eventual consensus was that the arrangement could work.

After the Second World War the Russian Orthodox Church began playing an energetic role in foreign affairs, helping the Soviet Government first of all to freeze its cold-war attitudes and then later to thaw them when policies began to be less intransigent after Stalin's death. In return, the church was allowed to organize its domestic life comparatively unmolested, though almost always within the severe established limits which we set out above.

The church did not betray its trust. The state did. It deliberately broke the unwritten terms of the *modus vivendi* with a high-level decision to intensify the anti-religious campaign during the later years of Mr. Khrushchev's rule. This was not to be just a war of words, though for five years (1960–64) the Soviet press did print a torrent of blasphemy against all forms of religious activity. It can only be described as a calculated, state-inspired persecution, designed to complete the plan of the period of the Stalin purges and secure the physical liquidation of religion. As Khrushchev's ideologist, L. F. Ilichov, put it: 'We cannot be complacent and expect that religion, as an anti-scientific ideology, will die by itself, without any effort or struggle. It is imperative to oppose religion with militant, progressive scientific-atheistic propaganda.'[41] The laws were used as a tool where convenient; often they were disregarded. We discussed the broad outlines of this campaign in the companion volume, *Religious Ferment in Russia*,[42] and examined its effects on a minority church. Here we complement this by giving some of the basic governmental texts in Chapter 1* and we follow this up by recording its effect on a church of (perhaps) forty million people. These official statements are unambiguous in their intention, but they leave open the question of why at that particular moment in history the Soviet Government should have found it necessary to reopen an offensive from which it had gained so very little in the past. As yet, we have only a minimal insight into the way the mind of the Kremlin functions in formulating such policies.

A further crux is why the Russian Orthodox Church, apparently so much stronger in 1959 than in 1927, did not protest more loudly at the Soviet Government's bad faith and even seemed to accept this re-emergent Stalinism. Metropolitan Nikolai, more than anyone else, had personified the *modus vivendi*. William Fletcher, in his study of this outstanding church politician, rightly emphasizes that the seeming passivity of the Moscow Patriarchate did not come into being without a severe hidden crisis.[43] We do not know its exact nature, but its first visible sign was the excommunication of the priest Alexander Osipov.[44] This teacher at the Leningrad Theological Academy defected to the atheist camp in December 1959 and immediately became a key figure in the state's new offensive against religion.† Although Osipov's excommunication was technically an ecclesiastical act, it could also be seen as a challenge to the state. The church used its only defensive weapon at the earliest stage of the new campaign.

This was followed by the unceremonious deposition of Metropolitan Nikolai, after which rumours of his unnatural death began

* Pp. 38–41. † See pp. 46–50.

to circulate. Although in fact he did not die until the end of 1961, the circumstances remain mysterious.[45] He was replaced by the 30-year-old Archimandrite (now Metropolitan) Nikodim as head of the Foreign Relations Department of the Moscow Patriarchate. At the same time, V. A. Kuroyedov replaced G. G. Karpov as head of the government Council for Russian Orthodox Church Affairs.[46] These two substitutions were the prelude to the onslaught which immediately descended upon the church. Once Metropolitan Nikolai's resistence was broken, events moved with great speed. The Patriarchate appeared powerless to forestall them and even gave the impression to many loyal Russian churchmen of acquiescing.

A key date in the recent history of the Russian Orthodox Church is 18 July 1961, when a Synod of Bishops met at the Holy Trinity Monastery, Zagorsk. According to Archbishop Yermogen,* it was irregularly convened. The bishops were invited to assemble to honour St. Sergius together at the monastery which he founded. The fact that there was to be a synod was not revealed until less than 24 hours before it began. At it, a document was rushed through to approval in a single day which was to have a lasting damaging effect on parish life. It is Archbishop Yermogen's contention that these '1961 Regulations' were passed with indecent haste and that the circumstances were so irregular that they can have no canonical authority. Most of the influential figures whom we quote in this book, Frs. Eshliman, Yakunin, Shpiller and the writer of the Open Letter to Fr. Rodzianko, are united in their opinion that this change has had a baneful effect on the life of the church and they argue with Archbishop Yermogen that the 1961 decisions must be annulled.† Because this issue is central to our theme, we quote in Chapter 1 the relevant parts of the Regulations, in both old and new versions.‡

Although the language of these documents is technical, the basic point at issue is simple. The 1945 Regulations set out unambiguously the central place of the priest in his own parish. He was responsible not only for the spiritual welfare of all those under

* P. 245.   † Pp. 245-7.   ‡ Pp. 43-6.

him and the reverent conduct of services, but also, as head of the parish executive body, for all the relevant material needs, 'the preservation of the buildings and properties of the church'. The 1961 Synod of Bishops entirely removed the latter responsibility from the priest by removing him from the executive body. The 1929 law does not explicitly bar the priest from this function, yet from 1961 he was relegated merely to the conduct of worship and the spiritual welfare of the parish.

The motives for this were, on the surface, unimpeachable: the intention of relieving the priest from his routine chores, leaving him free to concentrate on that which he was ordained to do and at the same time giving the laity heightened responsi- bility.* Such measures, in a Western context, would be roundly applauded as progressive by many Christians. In the context of Soviet society, however, they take on sinister tones. In a situation where institutional religion is fighting for its very survival, they must be judged not by their intentions, however laudable, but by their practical results.

This book supplies an accumulation of evidence on what in fact occurred: a mass closure of churches, following which over half of the total parishes of the Russian Orthodox Church were forcibly disbanded in the space of some three years. In retrospect, bearing in mind what we have set out above about the possibility of atheist pressure on – or even infiltration into – the executive body,[47] it can be deduced that there was a direct connection between the passing of the new ecclesiastical legislation and the dire consequences which immediately followed. This suspicion is backed up not only by the testimony of Archbishop Yermogen and others, but also by an analogous event in the life of the Baptist Church. The *New Statutes* and *Letter of Instructions* were promulgated by the All-Union Council of Evangelical Christians and Baptists a year earlier, in 1960,[48] and *Religious Ferment in Russia* demonstrates that their effect on the life of the Baptist Church was disastrous. They were not only used by the Soviet courts as a test of loyalty to the regime, but they also resulted in

* Pp. 44–6.

a schism from the parent church by those who would not accept them. Though these regulations were later annulled, the schism persists.

A question inevitably presents itself: was there a direct connection between the adoption of new regulations by the Baptist and Russian Orthodox Churches in 1960–61? In other words, was this the visible result of pressure which had been applied by government atheist agencies on the highest administrative organs of these churches? We have no direct proof of this in either instance, but the circumstantial evidence suggests an affirmative answer. We note the temporal coincidence of both with the more active atheist policy of the Khrushchev regime (the 'Parasite Laws' and §227 of the Penal Code were introduced in 1960–62); the ease of implementing this campaign as a result of the new internal ecclesiastical measures; crystallization of opposition within the churches to the leadership for having adopted these measures. Even if we are correct in this assumption, however, this does not impute collaboration with atheism to the leadership as a whole of either church. A few individuals may have cooperated with the authorities; others may have been intimidated into believing they were taking this step to save themselves or their churches; others (as was obviously the case with the majority of the Orthodox bishops, according to Archbishop Yermogen's evidence) were forced to act precipitously and vote on a block of proposals without time to consider their full implications.

We fully realize that it is no light thing to state all this about the leadership of a very large religious body. Yet in all honesty we cannot avoid saying it – if for no other reason than because of the evidence which freely reached us from Czechoslovakia in 1968 on the administration of church affairs. This is how the situation of the Slovak Lutheran Church evolved under communism – and we must stress that our source is not an émigré newspaper nor even a church publication, but a Communist Party journal published in Bratislava after the lifting of press censorship:

'The foundation of the life of the Lutheran Church was crippled and its activity almost totally incapacitated. This was brought about not by some administrative prohibition, but by structural reorganization. Outwardly it appeared as if nothing had happened. There was some talk about elections, conventions were held, there even existed an association of ministers which would occasionally meet and the church press produced a few pages of printed material. But over all there ruled the "hand", which forcibly held the reins of church life and mercilessly whipped and eliminated from further activity anyone whom it found, by itself or through a widespread network of well-rewarded confidential agents, expressing any freedom of mind or trying to oppose the machinery. Only a man predetermined by the approval of the state could be elected. . . . A congregation could either formally "elect" a candidate who had been designated for that particular office by the state or church authority (there was no great difference between the two), or . . . . it could accept an alternative minister, which basically meant one and the same thing. . . . The church as a whole has been in prison since 1950. . . . This means that all "elections" and decisions of the captive church since then are, in fact, invalid.'[49]

This is what a communist regime has been able to impose on Christians in Czechoslovakia, on men who have known democracy, in under twenty years, What, by analogy, could be imposed on the church in fifty years in the Soviet Union, a country which has never developed a democratic tradition?

Our editorial attitude to this highly sensitive question can, we hope, be justified. The crisis in the Russian Orthodox Church in 1960 was so muted that it failed to impose itself on the mind of Western Christendom. (Perhaps it should be noted that William Fletcher suggests that the present author, who was living in Moscow at the time, was himself insensitive to it and failed to recognize what may have been a tentative appeal through him from Metropolitan Nikolai to public opinion in the West.[50] If there is any substance in this, it is hoped that this book will be a partial atonement.) It took time for the crisis to come more into the open and for the main lines of argument to become evident. Now that they have, the subject is being much more freely

discussed in the West. Yet the internal church opposition to the
policies of the Patriarchate can be wrongly used (and in some,
though relatively few, émigré groups this has already happened).
To put it crudely, Eshliman, Yakunin and Levitin have been used
as a stick with which to beat the Patriarch's back. Therefore, to
put the record straight, we consider it essential to make conveniently available some of the basic texts, so that the reader can judge
them for himself. Most of them have so far been printed in
Russian only and are widely scattered in obscure journals.

As in the companion volume on the Baptists, our decision to
reproduce material which is highly critical of the church leadership has not been lightly taken. By now dubbing those who make
these accusations the 'prophetic' voice, we are endorsing not the
criticisms themselves, but the bravery of those who have taken
a carefully considered stand against state policies, despite the
likely consequences. The Russian Orthodox Church alone can
resolve the issues raised, but we believe it would be a service to
the Ecumenical Movement to demonstrate the type of pressure
from within his own church to which a Russian leader can be
subjected. One's sympathy goes out to those who are under
attack, for they are unable to defend themselves without departing
from their adopted position of trying to prevent an open confrontation with the state.

In 1966 the Baptists were able to bring in a new statute which
specified that 'only members of the church' can be on the staff of
the Moscow headquarters.[51] It is perhaps ominous that there is
no similar provision in the internal regulations governing the
Orthodox Church.

At a lower level, certain types of infiltration into the church
can be proved and we reproduce evidence on this.* Much of this
is amateurish and easily discerned by believers, who have sometimes allegedly acted forcibly against it.† It remains an open question whether the priests whose defections were given so much
publicity were planted by atheist agencies at the outset, whether
they were originally sincere but wilted later under severe pressure

* Pp. 50–8.   † See Pp. 55–6.

from the secret police, or whether they changed the basis of their lives from genuine conviction.

THE DOCUMENTS

Having established a framework for the recent life of the Russian Orthodox Church, we do not need to spend time in the Introduction filling in the content: this is contained in the documents. We have made as widely representative a selection as possible of these, but have had to confine ourselves to the merest fraction of Soviet press references giving similar facts from a different point of view. These two sources cohere together and prove beyond question that the campaign against the church under Khrushchev was conducted on a scale second only to the Stalin purges of the 1930's and without parallel in other countries in recent years (China and Albania excepted).

There are no statistics on the number of priests imprisoned, martyred and removed from office in 1960–64. We have merely chosen, in Chapter 2, a few of the best-documented instances. For a more systematic examination we would refer the reader to the work of Nadezhda Teodorovich[52] and Nikita Struve.[53] The former lists 25 bishops, priests, monks and nuns whose arrest can be supported by reference to the Soviet press, but we know that this can represent only a minute proportion of those affected. There are other references to trials of large groups of priests together and provincial newspapers not available in the West must have carried very many more such reports. As it is, Dr. Teodorovich cites 180 examples from the Soviet press and radio recounting the arrests of individuals or groups of all denominations for the period 1956–65; she backs this with a list, almost as long, of references to published attacks against the clergy where trials are not specifically mentioned. The tone of all these articles, as will readily be seen from the few quoted, takes us back to the period of the purges. They employ the well-tried Soviet method of character assassination, in which all manner of false accusation is

B

flung at the victim in the hope that some may stick. Embezzle-
ment, sexual misdemeanours, collaboration with the Nazis,
'anti-Soviet activity' in general – any accusation will do. The
probability is that very few, if any, of them are true. The life-
history of a faithful Russian priest who would not accept the
compromise of Metropolitan Sergi is illustrated by the laconic
curriculum vitæ of Bishop Afanasi which prefaces Chapter 2.*

On the attempt to suppress the monasteries, there is massive
documentation from the appeals of believers themselves (particularly concerning the Pochaev Monastery in the Ukraine), as
well as a great deal of information from the Soviet press. In 1958
the Moscow Patriarchate was able to claim: 'In the Soviet Union
at present there are 69 monasteries and convents.'⁵⁴ Within six
years the number had fallen sharply to ten at the most, with only
a handful of monks or nuns in each.⁵⁵ Among these was the
Pochaev Monastery, which the Soviet authorities may well have
decided to allow to remain open because of the worldwide publicity given to its energetic defence by a group of dedicated and
selfless Christians. Recently, the Patriarchate has made pointed
references to the normality of monastic life there.† The near extinction of monasticism in such a short time was undoubtedly
aided by the fact that in the laws on religion monastic communities are nowhere mentioned, so it was not necessary to resort to
any legal subterfuge to disband them, as was the case with the
parish churches.

In the same period the number of theological seminaries was
reduced from eight to three.⁵⁶ We lack detailed documentation on
the processes used by the Soviet authorities to achieve this, but
some scattered information will be found on it in the documents
and elsewhere.⁵⁷ We have no comprehensive statistics for the
total number of students in training or the annual number of
graduates for any year, either before or after these closures.⁵⁸ One
document clearly sets out the massive obstacles to being accepted
as a theological student.‡

Although we lack precise data, a Soviet source gives the total

* Pp. 65–9.   † P. 116.   ‡ Pp. 117–18.

number of churches at 20,000 to 22,000 before 1959 and goes on to state that this number had dropped to 11,500 by the beginning of 1962.[59] Another source infers that the number had dropped to 7,500 soon afterwards.[60] This backs up the claim of Frs. Eshliman and Yakunin, who stated that ten thousand churches were closed in the Khrushchev era.* The several examples from the Soviet press which we reproduce in Chapter 4 add up to overwhelming evidence. Even the *Journal of the Moscow Patriarchate* itself was able to throw a hint at what was happening,† despite numerous assurances from official church representatives that there was no persecution.

Much more important than any of these single references, however, is the case-study of an individual diocese, that of Kirov (a region five hundred miles north-east of Moscow), carried out by a layman, Boris Talantov.‡ Because of his painstaking work, the clarity of his exposition of it, his unqualified bravery in opposing anti-religious repressions and in bringing the results of his labours to the attention of others, he is one of the key figures in our study. Here we include substantial portions of the major document which he wrote in 1966, showing the exact methods used by the atheist authorities to close the parish churches, which could never be revealed in the Soviet press. In the Epilogue to this work, we reproduce the most recent appeal of his to have reached us. We put it in this position because it draws together more of the relevant themes in our study than any other available document.§

The mass physical destruction of many of the finest examples of Russian architecture was not carried out without widespread protest. We do not just mean the processions and petitions of which Talantov talks. It was reflected, though too late to save irreparable damage, at very high official level by the founding in 1966 of a Society for the Preservation of Historical and Cultural Monuments.[61] This has become a rallying point for those who care about Russia's past (and very likely also for those in official positions well-disposed to Christianity); consequently, a very large number of articles have appeared recently in the Soviet press,

* P. 200.　　　† Pp.119–20.　　　‡ Pp. 125–52.　　　§ Pp. 332–9.

publicizing the country's cultural heritage and begging that all necessary measures should be taken to preserve it at its best.[62] In connection with this, there came the first report of a criminal prosecution for the neglect of an ancient church. In 1966 two architects were sentenced to a year's hard labour each for failing to seal the leaking roof of a church under their care at Yaroslavl, as a result of which three hundred square yards of seventeenth-century frescoes were destroyed.[63]

These indications of a change in official attitudes had the effect of significantly curbing the rate of wanton destruction, though it has evidently not ceased. An ancient church in Galich was destroyed only two months before the prosecution mentioned above.* Another church was burnt down in Belorussia in 1968.† Believers themselves were held to be responsible for this through their own negligence, but there is a very strange element in the case. Why should events of January be reported to *Izvestia* by telephone two months later? It could well be that the article was inserted to counter the circulation of certain persistent rumours containing other versions of the destruction of the church. This is speculation – but we are on firm ground when we say that the whole episode has overtones reminiscent of the Khrushchev era. Although the physical destruction of churches is no longer an officially encouraged policy of the Soviet Government, the Russian Orthodox Church has so far won back no more than a handful at most of the shrines of its glorious heritage which were seized from it in 1960–64.

Though we are appalled at the fate of Russia's churches, it is the human victims of the recent Soviet purges against religion who command the greatest sympathy. We have spoken of the situation of the clergy: that of the laity is as bad. They have in many cases been coerced into giving up their old religious traditions (we quote but one of countless articles on this subject which have been published over the last few years).‡ Popular resistance to these encroachments of atheism has been spirited and to typify it we quote the case of the woman who would not act as nanny for

---

* P. 123.   † P. 123.   ‡ P. 156.

a child unless it was baptized.* In another instance, family traditions proved stronger than other pressures from outside.† But those who have defended their faith within their own family circles have often been forced into a direct confrontation with the state apparatus. This has led to untold misery for parents and even more for children, who have been forced in school to repudiate absolutely what they have been taught at home.‡ This has often put them into an impossible psychological position, where the only way they have been able to integrate themselves into the educational system has been to betray parental ideals.[64] Parents who resisted too openly have, in very many instances, even been deprived by the courts of their rights,§ after which their children have been forcibly removed to boarding schools.[65] We devote much space to the brave stand of Feodosia Varavva, for her case, due to her own initiative, is exceedingly well documented.‖ We believe that what she has done is not untypical of the constancy towards the faith displayed by other parents. Following this welter of material proving that the Soviet Union has been consistently denying the basic human right of allowing parents to bring up their children according to their own beliefs, we include a much less dramatic document, but one of no less importance, by Vadim Shavrov, which shows how one man came to accept the faith in adulthood after a typical atheist education.

The question now arises how far this anti-religious campaign was repudiated by Mr. Khrushchev's successors.

We demonstrated at the outset that there has been no basic change in the legal position of religion. All the restrictions on practical activities remain fully in force, but we wish to establish whether there has been any redress in the numerous instances where the law has been disregarded in the attempt to abolish religion quickly. We noted above that expropriated churches and monasteries have not been returned in any significant numbers. One bishop who was imprisoned has been rehabilitated¶ and many other clergy, some of whom have probably quietly resumed

---

* P. 157. † Pp. 157–8. ‡ Pp. 166–70.
§ P. 160. ‖ Pp. 164–82. ¶ P. 73.

their ministry, will have been released at the end of their sentences. Since 1965, as the important article by G. Z. Anashkin amply demonstrates,* there has been some reappraisal at the top of the methods to be used in the atheist campaign and it is now possible, in certain circumstances, to admit that there have been illegalities. However, according to several recent authoritative statements, the basic aim of totally eliminating religion from Soviet society remains unchanged.[66] The application of measures of physical coercion has been much more selective and the Baptist reformers, at least two hundred of whom were still in prison in 1968, have borne the brunt of a pointed attack.[67] We do not exclude the possibility that the state made an example out of them as a severe warning to any other Christians who should be evolving new ideas about a systematic defence of their rights.

Be that as it may, 1965 saw a vital development in the life of the Russian Orthodox Church in precisely this direction. Up to then, reaction to the persecutions had certainly been vigorous, as every earlier document which we quote demonstrates. However, the defence had lacked a focal point of leadership, it was geographically diffuse and it had cited individual instances at the expense of putting the whole question into a broader and more legal dimension. Only Anatoli Levitin, the church publicist, at this time seems to have aimed at a more general perspective.[68] These deficiencies were remedied once and for all in the summer of 1965 by Archbishop Yermogen, then of Kaluga, who led a delegation of eight Russian Orthodox bishops to the Moscow Patriarchate to request a reconsideration of the regulations adopted at the 1961 Synod of Bishops.† His dismissal from his diocese and enforced retirement into a remote monastery formed the immediate occasion which persuaded the two Moscow priests, Frs. Nikolai Eshliman and Gleb Yakunin, to compile their lengthy and systematic Open Letters to the Patriarch and the Soviet authorities.† Although these documents quickly reached the West and received much publicity, it was not until 1968 that writings of Archbishop

* Pp. 41–3.   † Pp. 221–3.

Yermogen himself relating to the case became available.* Now we have enough information to present the essential facts through the testimony of these prominent churchmen themselves. We are also able to state the official view of the Patriarchate over the banning of the priests from office and the continued refusal to reinstate Archbishop Yermogen.†

One point is not made absolutely clear in the documents: the extent of the influence which the small Baptist Church has had on the huge Russian Orthodox Church. Did it play a role in crystallizing the diversified opposition to state policies and to the Moscow Patriarchate's official position? We hazarded such a speculation in *Religious Ferment in Russia*.[69] We still do not know whether Eshliman and Yakunin themselves knew of the approach to Mr. Brezhnev made by the Baptist leaders, Gennadi Kryuchkov and Georgi Vins, earlier that year,[70] but we now have direct proof that Archbishop Yermogen holds up the example of the Baptists who persuaded the government in 1963 to allow them to organize a national congress.‡ The principle of such a congress every three years has now been established.[71] Further, Boris Talantov is fully aware of the Baptists' initiative of appealing to the United Nations in defence of their rights.§ We should not, however, forget that up to now the main thrust of argument in the two churches has been different. While the Baptists have requested a basic reform of the 1929 law, the Orthodox, with one small qualification, have confined themselves to the demand that the constitutional principle of the separation of church and state should be upheld (although if this were done much of the 1929 law would become obsolete). The dissentient voices here consider the 1929 law as being excessively conditioned by the historical circumstances in which it was promulgated.||

Our final consideration must be to ask how widespread is the support for Archbishop Yermogen and the two Moscow priests in their demands for reform. We have as yet no evidence of the impact of their thinking on the ordinary believer (probably many

* Pp. 238–54.   † Pp. 228–30, 247–8.   ‡ P. 245.
§ P. 337. || P. 315.

have heard about these developments only by hearsay, without having access to the documents, although these clearly circulate in large numbers). We have details of support for what we may broadly term the 'reform' position from Boris Talantov and a significant group of lay Christians from the Kirov diocese,* Anatoli Levitin,† and the Moscow parish of Fr. Vsevolod Shpiller.‡ These are people of diverse views and they do not seem to have joined together in a unified movement in the way that the reform Baptists did. This would naturally be more difficult in a church with such a tradition of authority. Nor do we have evidence that such a huge geographical area is affected as it is with the Baptists.

Levitin has been the most energetic publicist for the reformers and the writings of his which we reproduce here are a very small, though we hope a balanced, selection from what he has produced during a decade of activity. Whole books have now been published in the West devoted to his works.[72] He himself is an intensely interesting, though controversial, figure, about whom opinions are sharply divided in the Soviet Union.[73] There can be no doubt of his intrinsic importance, however. His activity has now clearly become a pivot between the general literary and political dissent and that in the Russian Orthodox Church.[74] The longest Pochaev document§ was included in the underground literary publication, *Phoenix 1966*, and at the ensuing trial of the latter's editor, Yuri Galanskov, Levitin appeared as a defence witness.[75]

Visible on the horizon of Russian Orthodox Church life there broods a cloud of uncertainty – a cloud which could at any moment rapidly fill the whole sky and burst out in a storm. If the church should soon be called upon to elect a replacement for its aged Patriarch (who is already over ninety), this may well be the moment at which the whole controversy comes much more out into the open. Certainly Archbishop Yermogen in his article celebrating the fiftieth anniversary of the re-establishment of the Patriarchate is carefully preparing the church for an election in the conviction that a false step at this point could cause a crisis of

* Pp. 237–8.   † Pp. 289–90.   ‡ Pp. 305–29.   § Pp. 98–115.

the first magnitude, both in the church's internal life and in its relations with the state.* The failure of the Baptist Church to initiate reforms radical enough to satisfy those who demanded them led to a schism which has not yet healed. Perhaps it is phrasing it too baldly to state that the central issue confronting the Russian Orthodox Church today is one of reform or schism. Orthodoxy has a much more tightly-knit hierarchical structure than the Baptist Church, which itself is the result of the schisms of the Reformation. As Fr. Shpiller amply demonstrates,† the danger of schism terrifies the Orthodox mind and responsible churchmen could not go as far as that unless they were forced to it as a last resort. If current policies continue unchanged, those in a far fuller possession of the facts than we can ever be will decide on the correct course of action. We hope, nevertheless, that the present work will shed light on some of the relevant issues. However these problems should be resolved, we are sure that the evidence collected here is a convincing testimony to the continued vitality of the Russian Orthodox Church among both young and old, both the little-educated and intellectuals, in circumstances which would have crushed a purely human agency devoid of the gift of the Holy Spirit.

* Pp. 244–7. † Pp. 321–9.

1 Outline of the Atheist Campaign

STATE POLICY

SPEECH OF Z. T. SERDYUK, SECRETARY OF THE CENTRAL COMMITTEE OF THE CP OF MOLDAVIA, AT ITS NINTH CONGRESS, 28 JANUARY 1960

A basic element of communist education is the struggle to overcome religious prejudices and superstitions. Unfortunately, we quite often find instances where party organizations are passive in the war against them and conduct atheist propaganda without conviction and merely because of official dictates.

While developing scientific atheist propaganda in every possible way, we must at the same time decisively waylay every attempt by ministers of religion to use the church and the sects for ends hostile to the Soviet people. The Council of Ministers and local party and Soviet agencies must not allow a single infringement of Soviet law by the priesthood to go unpunished.[1]

N. S. KHRUSHCHEV'S SPEECH AT THE TWENTY-SECOND CONGRESS OF THE CP OF THE USSR

Communist education assumes freeing the consciousness from the religious prejudices and superstitions which still hinder individual Soviet people from fully realizing their creative potential. We need a considered and well-balanced system of scientific atheist education which would embrace all strata and groups of the population and prevent the spread of religious views, especially among children and adolescents.[2]

MEASURES TO STRENGTHEN THE ATHEIST EDUCATION OF THE POPULATION

The Ideological Commission of the Central Committee of the CPSU has worked out its programme, *Measures to Strengthen the Atheist Education of the Population.* . . .

Scientific solution of the problems of atheism and the preparation of anti-religious specialists

The decision has been taken to create an Institute of Scientific Atheism in the Academy of Social Sciences under the Central Committee of the CPSU. The task of the Institute will be to lead and co-ordinate all scientific work in the field of atheism which is being conducted by the institutes of the USSR Academy of Sciences, the higher educational establishments and the institutions of the USSR Ministry of Culture. It will also prepare personnel with advanced qualifications, solve complex vital problems of scientific atheism and organize all-union scientific conferences and theoretical seminars. On the academic council of the Institute of Scientific Atheism there will be representatives of the Ideological Department of the Central Committee of the CPSU, the central scientific and ideological foundations and social organizations. . . .

Atheist Courses for personnel

From the 1964–65 academic year there will be a compulsory course (with examination) in 'The Fundamentals of Scientific Atheism' at universities and in the medical, agricultural and pedagogical institutes of the higher educational system. In other higher educational establishments an elective course will be taught. . . . Syllabuses and text-books are being prepared which take into account the special needs of the students. A compulsory course of seminar studies is envisaged in teaching plans and programmes, as well as the preparation of extended essays and taking examinations in practical atheism. The atheist content of courses in the natural sciences and the humanities will be strengthened. . . .

The introduction of seminars on questions of atheist education is recommended. These will be for party, *soviet* and trade union workers and activists, for teachers, doctors, Pioneer leaders and assistants in pre-school establishments. . . .

Using all means of ideological coercion in atheist education

Together with the Central Committee of the *Komsomol*, the Trades Union Council and the USSR Ministry of Culture, the All-Union *Znanie* ('knowledge') Society will hold a consultation on questions of improving the organization and content of scientific atheist propaganda in lectures. . . .

The government committee for cinematography of the USSR Council of Ministers envisages an annual output of films on atheist themes: artistic, popular-scientific, documentary and cartoons. It is intended to show atheist films on television and free of charge in institutes of cultural education and in schools. . . .

It is intended to improve the methods of publishing atheist literature, to broaden its thematic content, to use various literary genres and to elevate its ideological, political and publicistic level. The government committee on the press of the USSR Council of Ministers is entrusted with the task of formulating an outline plan for the future publication of atheist literature, including an increased quantity in the languages of the nationalities and also special works for children and adolescents. . . .

The All-Union Trades Union Council, the USSR Ministry of Culture and the *Znanie* Society are recommended to strengthen the material and technical basis of the atheist campaign in lectures and in the programme of cultural education. They should also activate the atheist campaign in museums, especially those devoted to historical and regional studies, in planetaria, mobile exhibitions and motor clubs, and they should increase the production of filmstrips, etc. . . .

In order to inculcate non-religious festivals and rituals more deeply upon the life of Soviet people, it is intended to hold a meeting of party, *soviet*, *Komsomol* and trades union officials, together with ethnographers, propagandists and ZAGS (marriage-registry) representatives.

The atheist education of children and adolescents

The anti-religious emphasis of school curricula is to be strength-ened, especially in social studies. Methodological text-books on anti-religious education in schools will be issued for teachers. It is suggested that various forms of extra-curricular and after-school activity (atheists' clubs and corners, lectures, talks, parties, excursions, cultural expeditions to the cinema and theatre, etc.) should be widely used for the atheist education of schoolchildren. . . .

Controlling the observation of Soviet legislation on religion

So as to prevent illegal activity among the clergy, religious groups and individual believers, there is to be an increase in the control over safeguarding children and adolescents from their influence and from parental compulsion to carry out religious rites. . . .

The commissions controlling the observation of the laws on religion under the district or town executive committees of the *soviets* of Workers' Deputies are to be more active in their work.

The organization of the atheist campaign

Local party organizations are obliged to appoint communists who will be responsible for the organization of the atheist campaign and to unite round them groups of public-spirited people concerned with propaganda and the organization of active atheism in factories, on building-sites, in *kolkhozy* and *sovkhozy*, in institutions, schools, Pioneer organizations, etc. . . .[3]

FREEDOM OF CONSCIENCE AND THE APPLICATION OF THE LEGISLATION ON RELIGIOUS WORSHIP
(G. Z. Anashkin)

'Enticing minors into this group'[4] means enlisting them into a sect which engages in fanatical activity and causes injury to the health of citizens or in some other way encroaches upon the person or rights of citizens. . . . The bringing up of children in a religious spirit, when done by parents and other relatives, does not constitute a crime, since the decree of the Council of People's Commissars (23 January 1918) proclaimed that 'citizens can teach and be taught religion privately'. . . .

In some places, educational work among believers is replaced by crude administrative methods which evoke only their displeasure and resentment.[5] This is exploited by foreign reactionary circles for anti-Soviet propaganda and, in the final analysis, contributes not to the struggle against religious survivals, but to the strengthening of religious fanaticism. . . .

In 1964 only a few persons were convicted of violating the laws on the separation of church from state and of school from church. Convictions for encroaching upon the person and the rights of citizens under the guise of performing religious rites were also few in number. Attention is called to the fact that there were less than a third as many convictions for these crimes in 1964 as in 1962.

The study of the cases and court statistics shows that instances of the prosecution of citizens for violation of the laws on religious worship are extremely rare – no more than a handful. Only those persons are prosecuted who have maliciously violated the Soviet laws on freedom of conscience and on the separation of church and state. This is why the assertions about the 'persecution' of believers in the USSR which one comes across in the bourgeois press are completely unfounded. . . .

Certain investigators and judges have an incorrect understanding of the provisions contained in §227 of the Penal Code of the RSFSR and the corresponding articles in the penal codes of the other Soviet republics. Thus the Gorokhov District People's Court (Volhynia region) wrongly convicted B. under §209, par. 1, of the Ukrainian Penal Code basically merely because he belonged to a sectarian organization: he had committed no acts forbidden by law. This gross violation of legality was corrected by the Collegium for Criminal Cases of the Supreme Court of the

Ukrainian Republic. The verdict was quashed and the case dropped because evidence of a crime was lacking. . . .[6]

The fact that the religious community to which a person belongs is not registered cannot, under this article, be regarded as a ground for initiating criminal prosecution against that person.

. . . . According to the meaning of Soviet law, the refusal of local authorities to register a given religious group can deprive it only of those rights which are enjoyed by registered communities. . . .

The exiling of individual active or fanatical adherents of various sects to other regions of the country is not always justified and is sometimes even harmful. Atheist indoctrination is not always carried out among the exiled persons; as a result, they sometimes begin preaching their 'doctrines' in these new localities. There have been odious instances when the exiles have attracted individual citizens, permanent residents of the place of exile, to their faith. . . .[7]

CHURCH REORGANIZATION

REGULATIONS OF 1945*

Part IV: Parishes

35. The parish priest stands at the head of every parish association of believers. He is appointed by the diocesan bishop for the spiritual guidance of the faithful and to govern junior clergy and the parish. . . .

40. The parish priest, as a result of his office, is an incontrovertible member of the parish association and he is the president of its executive body, the 'church council'. . . .

41. The executive body of the parish association of believers is under the direct guidance and supervision of the incumbent

* See pp. 204-12, 245-7, 325 for commentary and explanation.

of the church and is responsible to the civil authorities for the preservation of the buildings and properties of the church. . . .[8]

ACTS OF THE SYNOD OF BISHOPS OF THE RUSSIAN ORTHODOX CHURCH (18 JULY 1961)

1. The Russian Orthodox Church parish consists of not less than twenty Orthodox believers under the canonical guidance of a bishop; it is created by the voluntary agreement of believers in order to satisfy their religious and moral needs, under the spiritual guidance of a priest who is selected by the congregation and blessed by the diocesan bishop. The parish is registered by the local civil authority and receives from it free use of a church and objects necessary for worship. This is done by individual agreement and the parish is answerable before Soviet law for the safety of all such property. . . .

3. For the management of parish affairs, according to the general church principle of conciliar administration, there are two bodies: the parochial church meeting which makes decisions (the *dvadtsatka* [council of twenty] which founded the parish) and the parochial church council as an executive body. The latter consists of three people: an elder, his assistant and a treasurer. They are elected by the congregation from among its members who are capable and of good Christian morals.

For the perpetual oversight of the condition of church property and the regulation of finances. . . . an auditing committee of three is elected and submits its findings and recommendations for review at the general parochial meeting.

If any abuse or discrepancy is found in the property or funds, the auditing committee prepares a report and forwards it to the local town or village *soviet*.

4. A parochial meeting, composed of those who concluded the agreement for the use of the church and objects for worship, is called when necessary – with the permission of the local town or district *soviet* (in the country). It decides all matters concerning the administration and life of these congregations.

5. The executive body of the parish congregation of believers is responsible for its activities to the general parochial meeting; it administers the financial life of the parish between these meetings. It is responsible to the civil authorities for the protection of church buildings and property. It directs the management of the church and concerns itself with the income, heating, lighting and repair of the church and property; it also sees that the church is supplied with everything necessary for worship. . . . The executive body is the responsible decision-maker in the financial affairs of the parish. . . .

8. The executive body of the religious congregation has its own stamp and seal registered with the appropriate civil authority.

9. The parish priest and other clergy (where there are any) are pastors of the parish, to whom the bishop entrusts the performance in the parish church of the public services and other necessary offices; they give the sacraments according to the rubrics and they guide the people in the Christian life. They are responsible before God and their bishop for the well-being of the parish, from the point of view of its spiritual condition and moral attainments.

10. The parish priest, remembering the words of the Apostle: 'But we will give ourselves continually to prayer, and to the ministry of the word' (Acts 6:4), is responsible for the spiritual guidance of his parishioners; he sees to it that worship in the church is performed zealously and with splendour, according to the rubrics; and that all his parishioners' religious needs are duly and thoroughly satisfied. He has responsible oversight of the discipline of the members of his staff and intercedes for them for promotion with his spiritual head. To this end, he first of all gives a good example in his own personal conduct in the parish. He also ensures that the furnishings for divine worship are kept in exemplary condition and he duly brings to the attention of the executive body of the congregation the needs which arise out of the normal performance of worship, the offices and the sacraments.

11. The executive body does not interfere with the conduct of worship and in the relationship of the staff to each other. In case of

any abnormality here, it refers to the bishop, who is exclusively competent to deal with it.

When cantors, sextons, servers and others who variously participate in divine worship are invited to perform their duties, this is done by the executive body which agrees with the priest over the individuals.

12. Strict adherence by the clergy and the parish congregation to civil legislation on the church, as well as to ecclesiastical discipline, is essential. The general well-being of the Russian Orthodox Church – and of the parish in particular – depends on this. . . .⁹

INFILTRATION AND BETRAYAL

REJECTION OF RELIGION – THE ONLY CORRECT COURSE
(A. A. Osipov)

Yes, I, Professor of Old Testament and Classical Hebrew at the Leningrad Theological Academy and Seminary, formerly Inspector there, Master of Theology and Archpriest, have broken with the church and with religion. I have publicly professed my atheism, attained logically by study and scientific method after a considerable and protracted inward struggle and a complete reconsideration of my outlook on life.

I have abandoned my former world, which I now believe to be one of illusions, of retreat from reality, sometimes even of conscious deceit for the sake of financial gain. I walked out, carrying 48 years on my shoulders, and for almost 25 of these I had occupied positions of intermediate responsibility in the Orthodox Church.

Osipov recounts his early doubts and how he tried to overcome them before beginning his study of theology.

In January 1931 I became a student in the Orthodox department of the theological faculty at Tartu University. I took a room from the local deaconess in the clergy house. There I first all of became acquainted with the terrible milieu of the priestly caste, with all its squalor, the baseness of everyone's interests, the prevalence of uncontrolled petty passions. . . .

The outbreak of nationalist feeling in Estonia in 1936 compelled me to leave the university. I was given a Russian parish in Tallinn. I taught on private Russian theological courses and continued writing and publishing. All this time a deep dissatisfaction brooded in my soul.

The war, service in the army and work as a priest in Perm and Tallinn preceded his transfer to the reopened Leningrad Academy, where he was appointed Inspector.

I hated the sloth, the narrowness and the dullness of the priestly caste and I wanted to educate the young church servants of the future thoroughly so that they should become mature preceptors, far removed from superstitious fanaticism. I wanted them to lead good, active lives of high moral quality. Under my jurisdiction students frequented theatres, regular film entertainments were held, the reading of secular literature was encouraged, there were lectures on political and general subjects and evenings of questions and answers were arranged.

As a result, there was extreme unpleasantness. I was supposed to be following too Soviet a line and paying too little attention to fasts and vigils. . . . The students should have been living in strict accordance with the precepts of patristic literature and their cultural and scientific development should have been on a level with that of the notorious 'Church Fathers' in the first five centuries A.D. I retired from the position of Inspector.

I have not recorded that on my return to Tallinn after its liberation from the Germans I did not find my family. Frightened by fascist propaganda and receiving false news of my death, my wife and two daughters had left for Germany. Later I learnt that she had divorced me, married again and taken my children overseas. In 1951 I married a second time. For this I had to suffer many reproaches from fanatics. There were church leaders who had seriously said to me: 'What do you want with marriage? Live

with whom you like. You're not an old man. You will be for-
given, but everything must be done discreetly. Don't break canon
law, that's all! . . .' But I wanted to be an honest man even in my
private life. I did not want to join myself to those, so numerous
in the priestly milieu, who have been heroes of despicable roman-
tic adventures. Apparently the Patriarch himself understood this.
I put in an application to be removed from holy orders. But, alas,
even this did not save me from the cassock. The Patriarch, not
wanting to give others a bad example by removing someone
from holy orders, perferred to leave me in the Academy as a
professor, under perpetual ban from serving as a priest, but still
wearing a cassock. At lectures I was obliged to continue wearing
this yoke of backwardness and degeneracy. . . .

Everything fell into place for me. I realized that the history of
religion up to the present day was a single process in the development of false ideas and superstitions, a projection of human relationships in the empty heavens. . . .

I had a series of articles printed in the *Journal of the Moscow
Patriarchate*; they defended peace, always my personal favourite
subject. However, I was soon obliged to cut short this undertaking, for the editors demanded from me as much oiliness as
possible, and for this I have less aptitude. . . .

I was coming to realize more and more clearly that only a
complete break with religion could reconcile me with my conscience and give me the right to call myself an honest man. . . .
I thought: 'You should be brave enough to announce your decision as openly and publicly as you have been preaching what you
now admit to be false and deceitful. You knew how to teach: you
must now learn how to expose the falseness of what you have
taught.'

One seemingly trivial experience forced me to pause and
reflect. It was the morning of 7 September (1959). I arrived at the
Academy to invigilate examinations. I went into the conference
hall. A very nice person of naïve childish faith, Dr. Mirolyubov,
was discussing with one of the tutors articles on religion in the
newspapers. The Inspector of the Academy, Professor Parisky,

came up to them. Mirolyubov asked him: 'Should one discuss such articles with the students?' Parisky answered abruptly, raising his voice: 'Under no circumstances. I have given instructions to the library that newspapers and journals in which any such articles appear should not be displayed there. There's nothing for us to say about such stuff. We should ignore them, as if they didn't exist.' Mirolyubov: 'But if they ask? The articles include purely scientific matters, you know.' Parisky: 'They contain no science at all.'

The Rector, Archpriest Dr. Speransky, came up and said: 'But all of them are not purely controversial. Some are very serious articles with a scientific basis.' Parisky exploded: 'They're unscientific!' Everyone fell silent. The Rector moved away. I felt unbearably heavy at heart. I was physically oppressed in this world of scholasticism, where science amounts to no more than ossified dogmatic formulae and teaching about obligatory censing and genuflections.

I started looking for a concrete way out of the impasse. On 2 December I officially sent in my resignation from teaching to the Rector of the Academy and included a letter in which I clearly set out my reasons for leaving the theological department, asking him to read it out to my former colleagues and to the pupils who had studied under me.[10]

Despite his eight years of intense atheist activity, rumours became current during Osipov's last days that he had undergone a death-bed conversion. *Nauka i Religia* countered these by the following (rather equivocal) article.

THE FORTITUDE OF AN ATHEIST
(A. A. Osipov)

Not long before the death of Alexander Alexandrovich Osipov a programme in the series *Science and Life* was broadcast on Leningrad radio. . . .

I only had to fall ill and rumours like this went the rounds: 'God has punished him and will bring him to his senses', 'Osipov is already repenting', 'He's lying in hospital and never lets go of his prayer book.'

At Pochaev in the Ternopol region the 'spiritual fathers' have already thought up a complete story. I received a letter which said that one of them in the monastery had told a believer: 'Osipov has fallen ill, he's written three letters to the Patriarch and the latter replied: "All right, if he kneels in the entrance of all the Leningrad churches before the believers, then I will make him a church caretaker.'"

They've already sent a woman to save my soul in hospital. She burst in, shouting along the whole corridor that it was time Osipov came to his senses, that God would not perhaps punish him any more. The nurses beat her off. Another came along on the sly; she had no mercy towards the memory of my dead mother and spun a yarn about a so-called commission from her to save my soul. . . .

My way of suffering which led to spiritual freedom can't be changed like a suit of clothes. My atheism is the light of my life. I shall be true to it while my eyes are open and while I have breath in my body.[11]

ANALYSIS OF THE ANTI-RELIGIOUS CAMPAIGN
(A. Krasnov-Levitin)[12]

Before us there is a little book. The cover is orange (the colour of betrayal) and it is intersected by two black horizontal lines with white stripes, just like the marks of dirty boots. On the cover there is a strident title in black and white letters: *Why I Stopped Believing in God*. The author's name stands above – Yevgraf Duluman.

. . . . Let us acquaint ouselves with his biography or, as he grandiloquently expresses it, with his 'confession'. We begin to read it and straight away we are bewildered. In the foreword the author vaunts himself as having been 'deeply religious' in the past; but in the most decisive way he refutes the admirers of his talent from the *Molodaya Gvardia* ('Young Guard') publishing house. He relates that he 'never thought of religion' until he was sixteen and did not even properly know what it was. Completely by chance (thanks to his acquaintance with a priest) he entered the Odessa Theological Seminary in the autumn of 1945. The author tersely remarks:

'. . . I entered the Odessa Theological Seminary when I was seventeen, in secret from my friends and acquaintances. I was helped by the enquiries of a priest, which bore no relation to reality, about my "deep religious conviction" ' (p. 11).

Let us pause a little over this. First of all, one is amazed that the author was accepted into a seminary when he was only seventeen, because according to our laws religious education for minors is categorically forbidden. Theological colleges are strictly bound by the law, so we can forthrightly state that we are here dealing with the only exception in post-war years. How can it be explained? This can be done in only one way: Duluman committed yet another falsehood when he entered the seminary, which misled its directors. This was not the end of it, however. Everyone who joins a seminary has to be tested; he is examined in a number of specifically religious disciplines. Thus our modern Julien Sorel from the Odessa region read prayers and tropes aloud before his examiners, he answered questions on the Holy Scriptures and publicly pronounced the Creed. He constantly crossed himself and sought the rector's blessing – all the time, as he himself says, being a complete atheist. . . .

It is true that within a year the author became, in his own words, a sincerely religious man. '. . . I was deeply religious', he writes on p. 12. First of all, this very fact (may the author forgive us) fills us with most serious doubts. People change their convictions very often, especially when young, but the chief prerequisite for working out any personal philosophy is sincerity. . . . He became a Christian approximately in 1946 (p. 15), by the end of which year, however, he had lost his faith. . . 'My religious exaltation', he writes, 'lasted about two years.' Rather little for a 'deeply religious man', don't you think, my good editors and publishers?

Moreover, even in these two years, according to the author's account, it was not a question of a deep religious attachment, but of a few religious moods. We begin with the fact that church rituals were instrumental in the 'conversion' of our seminarist. As he puts it:

'The practice of religion, which enmeshed every step of my life in the seminary like an octopus, was the chief cause of the deepening of my religious conviction' (p. 14). . . .

From this it follows that the none-too-clever youth, who had neither a philosophy of life nor moral principles, fell for a time under the power of religious emotions because of the influence of the atmosphere and the beautiful rituals surrounding him. Can one call this deep religious conviction? Of course not. Real religious conviction is based on an inner certainty of the existence of God and on the moral regeneration of the individual, while the ritual aspect plays a completely secondary role.

. . . . There is nothing suprising in the fact that these emotions quickly disappeared and Duluman again became an all-out deceiver, just as he had been at the outset. . . .

At this time (1949) he became convinced that he had made a big mistake in having turned to religion with the aim of 'finding the truth. . .' He attempted to leave the theological academy, but did not hold firm in the face of three hundred roubles[13] which they added to his grant – so he remained . . . (p. 33). One is strongly reminded of the lady in Chekhov's story, *An Enigmatic Nature*, who also 'became disillusioned with life after a torture of doubts and questioning', and she did not hold out against 'the rich old man', either. Having yielded to his 'rich old man', the Rector of the Moscow Theological Academy,[14] our mischievous lad continued his course of study. Soon he defended his thesis for the degree of Candidate of Theology. We beg the reader to reflect on these words. A thesis is a manuscript which consists of three to four hundred type-written pages, approximately sixty to eighty thousand words.

Eighty thousand words – and not a single one of them sincere, all of them false and lying, deeply repellent to their author! After defending his thesis, the newly-fledged Candidate is appointed as a lecturer at the Saratov Theological Seminary. Here he teaches moral theology. The whole course is founded exclusively on patristic and ascetical works. Every day, for five or six hours at a stretch, he drums into young heads literature, about which he wrote three years ago that there was nothing in it 'except premeditated, unintelligible obscurity'. He defends religion stubbornly, though several years ago he had described it as a 'falsehood'! (p. 33). Night and day he labours to make dozens of young people deeply religious, although three years ago he wrote in his diary: 'Profound religious conviction is madness' (p. 33).

We have already noted that the teaching in theological seminaries is characterized by a deep religious conservatism, together with complete political loyalty.* The slightest attempt to introduce any wind of change is branded as 'Orthodox modernism' and is immediately suppressed. In this, the Saratov Seminary was in no way different from all the others: its Rector and Inspector of that time were perhaps even more orthodox in theological questions than their colleagues. Yet our atheist managed to please even them and once was thanked by no less than the Patriarch himself. What is most remarkable of all is that he recounts all these 'achievements' without the slightest blush and with an expression of self-contentment, as if it were a most ordinary affair. 'I received 3,900 roubles,[15] plus free board and lodging', he notes with a certain satisfaction. One does not know what to be more amazed at: this 'atheist's' brazenness or the simple-mindedness of the publishers, who attempt to represent this 'hero' as an 'eminent idealist' and even a 'deeply religious man'.

It is true that in 1952 Duluman left the seminary and openly proclaimed his atheist convictions. From any point of view this move was to be welcomed. The man had at least stopped lying and there was one less deceiver in the church. 'Having told everyone about my break with religion, I went to work on a *kolkhoz*,' he writes, still maintaining the same cheap pose. . . .[16]

Having analysed the brochure, *Why I Stopped Believing in God*,

* Cf. p. 47-8.

we thought we could say farewell to Duluman – but lo and behold! he has forced himself upon our attention once again. On p. 3 of *Komsomolskaya Pravda* ('*Komsomol* Truth'), No. 83 (9 April 1959), an article entitled 'Frankly Speaking' by Duluman and Darmansky* has been printed.

Now we shall permit ourselves to recount a little episode in which Duluman figured four months ago. On 23 December 1958 he delivered a standard lecture at Zagorsk,[17] after which a man well known both in Moscow and Zagorsk came up to him.

This person is an invalid of the Second World War, decorated with four orders and eight medals for outstanding military distinction, and after the war he became a deeply religious man. Our friend came up to Duluman at the end of the lecture and asked to be given the chance of objecting publicly. Duluman, however, categorically refused, using every excuse to evade the issue and avert a discussion in front of an audience of three thousand. He said: 'Go to church and speak there . . . I'll go myself to the Academy and we can debate there . . .' He gave his opponent literally no chance to utter a single word. Moreover, when Mr. Sh.† said that he would await Duluman at the club entrance to discuss with him after the dispute, our famous propagandist slid away from him like a coward through a side door (you certainly would have received no orders or medals for military distinction if you had been at the front, my dear Duluman).

How should believers react to Duluman? The writer is neither a professional 'churchman' nor a 'fanatic' (although he is a religious person); however, if he were a 'churchman', he would suggest that Duluman should be paid not four thousand (which he was receiving at the Saratov Seminary), but eight thousand a month.

Even the most ardent 'churchman' and 'fanatic' would not be able to devise a better means of conjuring up aversion to antireligious propaganda than Duluman's lectures. Thus from this point of view no believer can do more than thank Duluman and wish him success in his useful activity.

However, there is one more light in which we should review

* See p. 64.   † Vadim Mikhailovich Shavrov. See pp. 182–8.

what Duluman is doing. Anyone who is acquainted with the press of Tsarist times immediately feels when he reads Duluman's articles that some dim, half-forgotten memory is stirring within him. Alas, this is soon clarified: of course! that was how the 'publicists' of the Black Hundreds wrote (in the newspapers, *Russkoye Znamya* ['Russian Banner'], *Zemshchina* and other filthy rags which any decent person would be ashamed to pick up).

There is the same impudent, reckless and brazen lying, the same over-familiar tone of bare-faced insolence, the same unenlightened ignorance, with pathetic attempts to be witty.

The aim of the Black Hundred pen-pushers was to incite a hysterical hatred of people, to sow discord among nations and to ignite foul anti-semitic prejudice.

What are Duluman's aims? To be frank, we do not believe that he has any aim at all beyond the narrow one of his own personal career. Nevertheless, whatever his intention, the effect is almost the same as with the Black Hundreds: the kindling of religious strife, the stirring up of hatred, enmity and mutual estrangement between religious and non-believing elements of the population.

What can embitter people, fill them with indignation and offend more than lying, slander, prejudice and unscrupulousness? Yet this is the *leitmotiv* of all Duluman's public utterances.

And you give a place to such illiterate, Black Hundred rubbish on the pages of your newspaper, designed to educate young people!

(On 12 April 1959 I gave this rebuttal to the then editor of *Komsomolskaya Pravda*, Adzhubei.[18])

'HOLY MEEKNESS' THIRSTS FOR BLOOD
(A. Chistyakov)

People who are certain of the correctness of their views eschew violence and act only from the strength of conviction. Thus N. S. Petukhov, a former Candidate of Theology, acted in his atheist work. He exchanged a black cassock for a doctor's white coat and in the last three years has given more than two hundred lectures and written more than a hundred articles. . . .

Suddenly the door opened. A ginger-haired man with a narrow forehead came in, reeling drunkenly. He went up to the table, raised a knife above the doctor's head and said slowly and sensuously, 'For the cross and the faith. . . .'[19]

Following this the intruder killed the doctor.

An unusual type of infiltration is described below. Alla Trubnikova, a journalist, disguised herself as a pilgrim and insinuated herself into a convent. She described her experiences in a booklet published in 1963.[20] No less a person than Alexander Osipov finds this type of subterfuge distasteful.

BESIDE THE POINT OF THE ARGUMENT
(A. A. Osipov)

I know A. Ya. Trubnikova personally and I have always considered her a talented and energetic journalist. But her atheistic work has evoked great misgivings in me, which, alas, my broad experience as a lecturer and also my correspondence with believing people have confirmed.

What troubled me when I read the essays of A. Ya. Trubnikova?

The fact of the matter is that even during the time of my work in the Leningrad Theological Academy and Seminary I constantly heard conversations of believers alleging that 'the communists are infiltrating their agents into the church in order to corrupt it . . .' When I became an atheist and began to give lectures over practically the entire country, from time to time I would receive notes on the same subject: 'Is it true that they infiltrate?' 'Are there now among the clergy many communists with special assignments?' – and so on.

I always refuted these fabrications with indignation, saying that our party struggles against religious ideology are armed with the truth and nothing but the truth.

People believed me, understanding the correctness of my words. Now suddenly comes the news of A. Ya. Trubnikova's trip to a convent disguised as a pilgrim . . . Just imagine how the spreaders of malicious rumours rubbed their hands! Of course, not everyone understands that this was just the unfortunate device of one journalist. . . .

To talk of this has become more difficult. People are accustomed to believe the printed word. And in the booklet the account is printed in black and white of how a journalist entered a convent by deceit, masquerading as a pilgrim.

It was a bad business that A. Ya. Trubnikova accomplished with her 'heroic' trip to the convent![21]

This brave sermon of the Patriarch demonstrates how aware the church is of the danger of infiltration.

ALLOCUTION OF PATRIARCH ALEXI OF MOSCOW AND ALL RUSSIA

(on the occasion of the presentation of the episcopal crosier to the newly-consecrated Bishop Nikodim of Kostroma and Galich,[22] Holy Trinity Church, St. Sergius Monastery, 10 August 1961).

How much attention and prudence we must use in exercising the right of election and consecration entrusted to us bishops by the church!

It need hardly be said that at this very moment certain persons are trying particularly hard to penetrate into the precincts of the church, with self-interested, evil and even perfidious motives. Or need we be reminded that the whole weight of the sins of such people falls on those who let them participate in the ministry of the church's sacred office?

With particular circumspection and – might one say – reverence for the sacred nature of the church's work of sanctification, exercise zeal and foresight, beloved brother, in preventing regrettable and blameworthy consequences from arising out of the election and ordination of irreverent and unspiritual persons. Do not make yourself an accomplice in the sins of others. 'Keep thyself pure' (I Tim. 5:22)[23].

POLICE METHODS

SILHOUETTES
(A. Krasnov-Levitin)

As an example, let us take the activity of the Department for the Affairs of the Russian Orthodox Church, which comes under the Committee of State Security (KGB). It pays zealous attention to the recruiting of agents within the confines of the Theological Academy at Zagorsk.* The procedure is as follows: usually the student is summoned to the military call-up office, where an avuncular figure with the rank of major addresses him as follows:

'You're a completely Soviet person whom we know and trust. You've got many foreigners at the Academy, among whom are spies. If you notice them, could you help us to unmask them?'

'Oh, yes, of course I'll help you.'

'In that case, sign.'

A paper is pushed in front of the bewildered youth, in which there is an obligation, couched in general terms, to help the security organs.

It very often happens that a young man who is inexperienced, frequently of low literacy and come up from the depths of the provinces, signs this document. Then they arrange a meeting with him. The rendezvous is usually a hotel, but sometimes it is else-where – by a pleasure-garden, for example (perhaps the 'Aquarium' park).

The young man is invited into a car. Here they turn on a tape-recorder and an interrogation begins – not now about spies, but fellow-students. This is the first stage of the work.

It should be noted that the secrets which these recruited agents (primitive and semi-literate people) can impart to the contacts (mostly themselves just as primitive and semi-literate) are not worth a brass farthing. The disguising of these agents is carried out in a ham-handed and unsubtle way . . . . and they are usually seen to be what they are the day after their recruitment . . .[24]

* Cf. p. pp. 117–18.

TO THE WORLD COUNCIL OF CHURCHES, ODESSA,[25]
THE ORTHODOX CHRISTIANS OF RUSSIA,
THE UKRAINE AND BELORUSSIA
(By a group of believers)

We would like to talk to you of one more important subject and acquaint you with the extraordinary way in which the web of surveillance over our fellow-Christians from abroad has been developed. Every foreign delegation is accompanied by a 'guardian angel', usually a priest (unfortunately there are many of them working in the Foreign Relations Department).* After every meeting with the foreigners, the man accompanying them has to write a detailed report on all the questions addressed to him and on the answers he gave. A similar report is drawn up by the interpreter, if there was one (interpreters are usually appointed directly by the MVD and not by the Patriarchate). The two reports are then sent to the MVD where they are compared. If there is the slightest discrepancy the priest is immediately summoned and interrogated, so that the truth can be established. If it becomes evident that the priest has said something out of place, he immediately loses the parish which he was looking after in addition to his work in the Foreign Relations Department. Unfortunately, there are agents paid by the MVD among the clergy, although they are very few in number. . . .

We cannot keep silent over the way foreign guests are hoaxed in the Academies. All are lavishly treated, regaled with very strong wine so that they will ask fewer questions, think and observe less. They are given valuable presents and those whom they especially wish to flatter are made honorary members of the Academy or are given some diploma. Thus, by pandering to the vanity of certain individuals, our people achieve their goal. They are good at pulling the wool over the eyes of foreigners.

The students at the Academy are mostly young people who are sincere in their faith. But amongst them there are also agents recruited by the MVD and sent to corrupt the Academy . . .

* See p. 321.

These individuals spy on their fellows. They are also ordered to accompany any foreign visitors to the Academy. Many janitors, librarians (who report on the kind of books which interest the students), cleaners and night-watchmen are in the service of the MVD, too. . . .

Do not listen to the lying words which certain church representatives will speak to you. Try to talk directly to believers. Of course, many are afraid and will not dare speak the truth. Look at what you are not shown rather than what you are shown. . . .[26]

2 February 1964

TO HIS HOLINESS, PATRIARCH ALEXI OF MOSCOW
AND ALL RUSSIA
(By believers of the Kirov diocese)

In December 1963 Bishop Ioann* transferred Archimandrite Klavdian Modenov, incumbent of the church in the village of Ankushino, without adequate reason to the village of Korlyaki. He left Ankushino without a priest, even though there were candidates who would have liked to be instituted there. Therefore, I. Ye. Kazakov, the warden of the village church, sent several complaints to the Patriarchate in 1964 about the illegal activities of Bishop Ioann.

These remained unanswered, while Bishop Ioann became angry with the warden. When Kazakov went to Bishop Ioann on 17 February 1965 to see about the appointment of a priest, the bishop spent two hours threatening to attack him with his fists and crying, 'I'll send you to the NKVD!'

Then the bishop went to the flat of the believer, B. V. Talantov, whom he apparently suspected of being an accomplice in the writing of complaints. Here, in the presence of many people, he threatened Talantov with the law and acted just as if he was an NKVD investigator making an arrest during the *Yezhovshchina*.[27]

He was publicly trying to demonstrate that he was not only a bishop, but also an influential figure of the security agencies. In

* Cf. pp 143–4, 152.

truth, 'Every prudent man dealeth with knowledge, but a fool layeth open his folly' (Prov. 13:16).

Thus, though the church is separated from the state, a bishop of the church could be simultaneously a state security agent![28]

June 1966

THE PATRIARCHATE'S REACTIONS TO PERSECUTION

METROPOLITAN PIMEN'S INTERVIEW WITH TASS

I deeply regret the actions of Bishop Antoni of Geneva and Western Europe,[29] who has recently assumed the role of defender of the believers in the USSR. . . . A shadow is cast on the activities of Bishop Antoni by the fact that he long ago deserted his homeland and mother-church and now belongs to a group of churchmen who go under the name of the Karlovtsy Schism.[30] The afore-mentioned bishop does not belong to the hierarchy of the Russian Orthodox Church.

In my view the activities of Bishop Antoni should be regarded rather as an attempt to further hostile attitudes in certain circles in the spirit of the 'cold war', since believers in the USSR have no need of his defence. Their rights are protected by the relevant articles of the Constitution of the USSR. . . .

The assertions about the closure of churches are baseless. Thus, in the city of Minsk not a single parish church has closed since the war. On the contrary, two churches damaged during the Nazi invasion, one of which is the large cathedral, have been restored and are now open for worship.

Only the domestic chapel of the Bishop of Minsk has ceased to exist, in connection with the move of the diocesan administration to different premises.[31]

REPLIES OF PATRIARCH ALEXI OF MOSCOW
AND ALL RUSSIA
to questions from the permanent correspondent in Moscow
of the Italian newspaper, *Corriere della Sera*

Question 1: Do you think that a spiritual renaissance is taking place in the USSR?

Answer: Most impressive successes in the realms of education, science and culture have occurred in the Soviet Union since the revolution. Spiritual values occupy an important place in the life of our people. In this sense one can talk of a constant effort in the spiritual life of our country.

Question 2: Do you consider that, despite this, the Orthodox Church is in decline?

Answer: I consider this question to be incorrectly formulated. The position and life of the Russian Orthodox Church became stabilized long ago. Our priesthood is devoted to its duty, our pious believers have a relationship of deep love to their church.

Question 3: How do you explain the successes of other Christian denominations – the Baptists, for example?

Answer: Insofar as it is not apparent from your question, sir, how you measure success or the lack of it in the church life of our country, it is not possible to give an answer. . . .

Question 6: Do you not consider it necessary to call a Council of the Orthodox Church to renew the liturgy and to review the relations between the priesthood and the Soviet authorities, as a section of the priesthood has demanded?

Answer: In the Orthodox Church the question of 'renewing the liturgy', as you put it, does not necessitate the convening of a special Pan-Orthodox Council. On the relations between the priesthood and the Soviet authorities, or (as you should have said) between church and state, in every country they are regulated in different ways, depending on local traditions and circumstances. In every country these questions come within the competence of the relevant church and state bodies.

Question 7: What are your relations with the Council for

Church Affairs? Is it not necessary, in your opinion, for the Orthodox Church to have greater independence in the appointment of clergy and in carrying out various religious rites?

Answer: Our relations with the Council for Religious Affairs under the Council of Ministers of the USSR are completely normal. In no way does the Council bind the religious authorities in their appointment of clergy to any church office. . . .

Question 8: How do you explain the recent closure of Orthodox churches and monasteries?

Answer: The number of churches and monasteries in any Orthodox Church, including the Russian, is naturally subject to changes. Certain parishes can discontinue their existence or become so attenuated in their support that they may be closed. On the other hand, parishes can spring up again where they had previously been or where they can be reconstituted – in which case churches open.[32]

On some occasions churchmen have spoken more frankly, as Bishop Yuvenali's words below demonstrate. No other pronouncement in recent years, however, has been as decisive as the excommunication of Alexander Osipov.

INTERVIEW WITH THE BISHOP
(Bishop Yuvenali of Zaraisk)

The number of atheistically-minded people is increasing as a result of growing materialist outlook on life. This means a dwindling number of worshippers among the youth.

Another reason for the drop in the number of believers in our country is that our religious communities do not attract young people to the church by artificial means such as dances, sport or other purely worldly attractions, as is practised in the West. . . .

Our youth have the opportunity of choosing freely between worship and atheism.

I wouldn't say that many young people go to church in our country, but you can rest assured that those who do are utterly devoted to Christ, to religion.[33]

EXTRACT FROM THE DECISION OF PATRIARCH
ALEXI AND THE HOLY SYNOD, No. 23
(30 December 1959)

At its session the Holy Synod, under the chairmanship of His Holiness, Patriarch Alexi, decreed:

The former Archpriest and Professor of the Leningrad Theological Academy, Alexander Osipov, the former Archpriest Nikolai Spassky, the former priest Pavel Darmansky and other clerics who have publicly reviled the Name of God are to be defrocked and excommunicated. . . .

Yevgraf Duluman and other former Orthodox laymen who have publicly reviled the Name of God are to excommunicated.[34]

2 The Persecution of the Clergy

BISHOP AFANASI

Bishop Afanasi opposed Metropolitan Sergi's 1927 declaration of loyalty to the state. We include this section to demonstrate that recent persecution of the clergy is merely a continuation of the original Stalinist policy towards the churches. Even the *Journal of the Moscow Patriarchate* alluded to Bishop Afanasi's hardship and the complete disruption of church life. His autobiographical notes were found among his papers after his death. The writer of the Open Letter to the BBC* later appended them to his document.

OBITUARY

. . . . Archimandrite Afanasi was consecrated bishop of Kovrov on 27 June 1921.

It is now difficult to ascertain how long Bishop Afanasi remained in charge of his see, but we do know that he was exiled in connection with the considerable disorders in the church caused by the Living Church schism, which created an administrative centre for itself in the Vladimir diocese. He did not return from exile until 1954, when he began living at Petushki, in the Vladimir region.[1]

DATES AND MILESTONES OF MY LIFE

2 July 1887 I was born.
1896–1902 Shui church school. . . .
18 June 1921 Superior of the Bogolyubovo Monastery.
27 June 1921 consecrated Bishop of Kovrov.
17 March 1922 arrested and brought before a revolutionary tribunal.
18 March 1922 released.

* Pp. 230–6.

30 March 1922 (Wednesday of Holy Week) arrested (with Metropolitan Sergi, Archbishop Pavel, Bishop Vasili).

27 May 1922 accused at show trial in connection with the confiscation of church treasures.

28 May 1922 amnestied, after having been condemned to one year.

15 July 1922 arrested (with Bishop Serafim. . . .).

25 July 1922 released.

10 September 1922 arrested (with Archbishop Nikander. . . .).

14 November 1922 sentenced to two years of exile in the Zyryanka region. Prisons: Vladimir, Moscow, Tagan (with Bishop Feodosi), Vyatka.

10 September 1922–15 May 1923 *en route* (with Bishops Serafim and Nikolai). Ust-Sysolsk, Ust-Vym and Korchemye in the Zyryanka region (with Metropolitan Kirill, Archbishop Faddei, Bishop Nikolai, Archpriest Bogdanov, Archpriest Neofit).

Re-trial at a people's court on the church treasures charge – one year's imprisonment. . . .

14 November 1924–20 January 1925 in the Zyryanka region in excess of sentence.

February 1925 returned to serve the church at Vladimir.

8 September 1925 arrested at Gavrilov Posad during a journey around the diocese and transferred to Vladimir for establishment of identity on the next day.

10 September 1925 released.

2 January 1926 arrested.

2 March 1926 released.

December 1926 requested either to leave Vladimir or to cease administration of diocese. I refused to leave the diocese entrusted to me.

2 January 1927 arrested.

3 January–30 April 1927 Moscow inner prison.

23–28 April in solitary confinement with Metropolitan Sergi.

May 1927 Leningrad transit prison.

June 1927–2 January 1930 in the Solovki camps according to

sentence for belonging[2] to the group of bishops headed by
Metropolitan Sergi Stragorodsky (with Archbishops Kornili
and Grigori). Solovki prisons – Raznovoloka, Chupa Dock,
Priests' Island, Kem. Watchman, store accountant. . . .

1 January 1930 returned to Priests' Island.

January–February 1930 ill with typhus.

2 January–23 February 1930 beyond term of sentence.
Transferred to Turukhan region for three years.

23 February–23 April prisons: Leningradskiye Kresty, Novo-
sibirsk, Krasnoyarsk transit and inner (with Metropolitan
Kirill).

1930 Krasnoyarsk, Yeniseisk, Stanki, Turukhansk, Melnichnoye,
Selivanikha, Punkovo.

January 1932 arrested.

January–February 1932 (between two and two and a half weeks)
in a Turukhansk police cell.

February 1932 released.

30 April 1930–2 January 1933 in the Turukhan region according
to sentence.

2 January–6 August 1933 beyond term of sentence.

August 1933–18 April 1936 returned to Vladimir; free but did
not officiate as a priest.

18 April 1936 arrested (with Archbishops Sergi Grishin, Filipp,
Yuvenali). Sentenced to five years in the White Sea and
Baltic camps.

November 1936–June 1941 prisons: Vladimir, Ivanovo (inner
and transit), Yaroslavl, Vologda, Leningrad transit, White
Sea camps.

December 1936–January 1937 worked as accountant. Because a
thousand roubles were stolen from me this sum was exacted
from me and one year added to the sentence. Worked as a
lumberjack, laying sleepers for a railway; leader of a brigade
weaving *lapti* (birch-bark shoes).

August–October 1937 arrested (without any accusation being
brought). Saved through God's mercy from any great danger
and put in solitary punishment cell.

End of October 1937 freed and returned to? (*sic*)

Beginning of November 1937 arrested without accusation and put in solitary punishment cell.

December 1937 released.

May holidays 1938 put in solitary punishment cell.

June–July 1941 at the beginning of the war transferred on foot about four hundred kilometres to the Onega camps. . . .

July–November 1942 indefinite exile to Omsk region.

Golyshmanovo *sovkhoz* – night watchman over the vegetable plot.

December 1942–November 1943 Ishim.

7 November 1943 arrested.

November 1943–July 1944 prisons: Ishim, Omsk, Moscow (inner), Lefortovo, Butyrki, Krasnopresnaya.

August–September 1944 Siberian camps: work in the fields.

September 1944–August 1946 work on night brigade.

30 August 1946 arrested.

August–September 1946 Mariinsk transit point, Moscow prisons: inner, Butyrki, Krasnopresnaya. Temnikov camps, weaving *lapti*. Dubrovo camp as invalid without work.

9 September 1943–9 November 1951 in prison according to sentence.

9 November 1951–18 May 1954 in camps beyond term of sentence.

18 May 1954 in the Zubovo-Polyana invalid home – not known until when.

Beyond term of sentence in prison three years, four months, twenty-two days.

27 June 1954 was the 33rd anniversary of my consecration as bishop.

In that time I served 33 months in my diocese.

I was free but not officiating for 32 months.

In exile 76 months.

In prison and doing forced labour 254 months.

It is usual in life that the longer the separation, the weaker con-

nections grow. Christian love reverses such a rule. Those dear
people who cared for me, moved by Christian and not by worldly
love, each year made their concern and solicitude more manifest,
each year increased their alms. Whereas in the first two years and
four months I was sent 72 parcels (thirty a year), in 1954, the last
year, I received two hundred. May God's mercy never leave my
benefactors. I believe that they will hear these words in that day:
'Come, ye blessed of my Father . . . I was in prison, and ye came
unto me.'³

ARCHBISHOP IOV OF KAZAN

HISTORY OF A CAREER (Complete text)
(L. Zavelev)

A few days ago in Kazan the Supreme Court of the Tatar
ASSR sat to hear the case against Archbishop Iov (in secular life,
Vladimir Andrianovich Kresovich). The spiritual pastor was
accused of . . . swindling. During seven years of 'work' in Kazan
he had concealed his real income and failed to pay the state more
than two million roubles income tax. The accusation was proved
and the court sentenced Kresovich to three years' imprisonment
and confiscation of his property.

Such is the inglorious end of Iov's career – the bishop in charge
of the diocese of Kazan and Mari.

This story began almost forty years ago in Volhynia.

After graduating from the Kremenets Theological Seminary
in 1922, Vladimir Kresovich turned up in the village of Rakh-
manovo. For many years he carefully carried out his service: he
read the prayers, baptized, buried, gave communion, heard confessions . . . His ministry in a poor country parish brought him
neither wealth nor power – the only thing he really believed in
and worshipped.

In early autumn 1939 the western regions of the Ukraine were
reunited with the Ukrainian Soviet Republic, finally realizing

the cherished dream of the Ukrainian people. All honourable people of the region greeted this great event with an outburst of rejoicing, but Kresovich did not join in. The new administration removed his hope of realizing his treasured dream – to become rich, famous and powerful.

When the war began and Hitler's men came to the Ukraine, Kresovich met them as liberators and began to serve them. In his sermons Kresovich described 'Bolshevik outrages' which he had himself invented and blessed the fascist aggressors. Kresovich's zeal was noted by the invaders. He was 'in the public eye'. His name became well known to Hitler's 'supreme ruler' of the Ukraine himself and reward soon followed. Putzinger, the representative of the general commissar of Volhynia, ordered Kresovich's promotion. In July 1942 the hastily convened 'Synod of Bishops of the Autonomous Orthodox Churches' elevated this obscure country priest, who had no higher theological education, to the office of Bishop of Lutsk, suffragan of the Volhynia diocese, with the name of Iov.[4]

Much could be said about the base acts of the high-ranking spiritual pastor who was serving the enemies of his people, but we shall let the documents speak.

This, for example, is what the Reverend Archpriest A. Korneichuk, of the Ternopol region, reported to Bishop Nikolai: 'When Bishop Iov took charge of the diocese, he immediately ordered that church bells should be given to the German Government for its war requirements in order to vanquish its enemies. This was carried out.'

'During the German occupation of Volhynia', we read later in the same report, 'Bishop Iov gave strict instructions, for which all monks had to sign, that at services they should proclaim the good health of Hitler and his "valiant army". The stipulation was made: "Whoever shall fail to carry out these instructions will be banned from participating in services and defrocked."'

One would have thought that with the defeat of the Nazis Kresovich's career would have ended too – especially since he did not manage to decamp with the invaders, as others of his colleagues managed to do. However, after the fascists had been driven out of Soviet territory, the Metropolitan 'consecrated' Kresovich to the diocese of Lutsk and Kovel. A little later, in February 1945, Iov was appointed bishop in charge of the Izmail diocese.

No more than a year had passed, but in this short time it became clear that it was impossible to leave Iov any longer at the head of a diocese. The Patriarchate had received hundreds of complaints about the activities of the Bishop of Izmail. Finally Kresovich was dismissed and sent to the Izmail Monastery. But the role of a suffering, repentant sinner caught up in adversity did not suit him. He bombarded the Patriarchate with tearful letters and mercy succeeded their anger. Iov was appointed suffragan bishop in the town of Lyskovo, Gorki region.

Having spent all his life taking the credit for other people's good and growing rich on his parishoners' money, the lascivious Bishop of Lyskovo fulminated in his sermons against 'atheists who have been wallowing in sin'. 'War is inevitable!' he affirmed, and when he was instructed by the Patriarchate to read aloud some documents from a congress of peace supporters, he refused.[5] War begot Iov, so why should he be its enemy?

Again letters flew to the Patriarchate – complaints against Iov, exposing him as an embezzler and debauchee.[6] At the beginning of 1950 the mischievous pastor was 'retired'.

Nevertheless, a year later Iov took over the diocese of Cheboksary. Then he left Chuvashia and moved to Kazan, where a large and profitable episcopal see awaited him. His 'black guard', comrades-in-arms from the time of the German occupation of the Ukraine, people devoted to him from Izmail, Lyskovo and Cheboksary, began to congregate here at Iov's summons from Volhynia and other places.

Administering his diocese, travelling about and preaching occupied a great deal of the enterprising bishop's time, but even then this was not his basic activity. His main task was his personal enrichment. It is difficult to calculate, even in approximation, how much money was transferred from believers to Iov's pocket in the seven years of his stay in Kazan. In any case, there is documentary confirmation that the Kazan diocese paid out no less than a million roubles[7] a year to support its archbishop – for his luxurious villa, cars, drinking bouts and orgies. In 1958–59 alone Archbishop Iov illegally received 840,000 roubles, excluding his 'salary'.

For many hundreds of years Christian preachers have been affirming to believers that religious morality teaches good and restrains people from evil, that religion leads people along the path of truth and virtue. If this is so, why then was Iov among its prominent servants? And is it Iov alone who has been exploiting the trust and backwardness of his flock to acquire the income from their work?

... Kresovich has been sentenced – not for his faith, because he believes neither God nor the Devil. He has been punished for coarse violation of the laws of our country and for criminal machinations. The sentence was greeted with the approval of the workers. A large number of people left the court-room cursing Kresovich and his like for having enmeshed them in his web of barefaced deceit.[8]

SWINDLER IN A CASSOCK
(A correspondent)

Pay-day came round and Iov was brought the register.

'Father, sign for receipt of the five thousand[9] due to you for running the diocese.'

After this another register was put on the table – 7,500 roubles were due for officiating at services in St. Nicholas Cathedral. Then a third register appeared – 7,500 roubles for officiating in the cemetery church.

Then Iov received 35,000 more roubles for various expenses and he did not have to sign for them at all ...

'Excellent, Father Nikolai!' exclaimed Iov. 'But how are the others? They must be supported too. Let's give them new rates of pay: six thousand for priests, five for deacons, two for the cantor and my personal chauffeur. We'll pay the taxes out of diocesan funds.'

But even fifty thousand was too little for the bishop. They paid him 65,000 roubles monthly and his salary amounted, in round figures, to a million roubles a year.[10]

DECISIONS OF THE HOLY SYNOD

We appoint His Reverence Archbishop Iov, formerly of Kazan and now in retirement, as Archbishop of Ufa and Sterlitamak.[11]

This brave and independent act by the Patriarchate demonstrates that in certain circumstances it can support those who have fallen victims of the state. At the same time, it gives us good reason to ask whether the campaign against Archbishop Iov (and others) was not fabricated from beginning to end. It is barely conceivable that the Holy Synod should have reinstated him if he had been guilty of any of the crimes of which he had been accused.

ARCHBISHOP VENIAMIN OF IRKUTSK

THE FACTS SPEAK FOR THEMSELVES
(Complete text)

Archbishop Veniamin of Irkutsk, a very old man, is known for his grandiose way of life. He has three private cars. The seven hundred roubles[12] of his income as archbishop are not sufficient for him. In order to increase it he is implicated in shady enterprises. To act more easily, he has created in his diocese a set-up of nepotism and mutual guarantee. His sister, Anastasia Korzun, controls the material resources of the diocese and his niece, Tatyana Golodinskaya, is director of the candle factory and other enterprises. The sale of candles provides the main income of the diocese.

Last summer Archbishop Veniamin was brought before the people's court accused of illegally acquiring liquid paraffin. The archbishop had bought stolen paraffin at a reduced price in order to sell it to his church for an exorbitant sum.[13]

ANATOLI SHCHUR

TO THE GENERAL SECRETARY OF THE UN, U THANT
from Yefrosinia Vladimirovna Shchur,
1 Graby St., Pochaev,
Ternopol region, Ukraine.

Your Excellency, dear Sir,

I am fully aware of the wide range of your duties and responsibilities and I know how overburdened you must be; but extreme sorrow has induced me to beg you urgently, to consider my complaint.

Although it is a personal one, the grief that afflicts me is more than this. It is the lament, the tears of the entire Christian population of the Ukraine and of all Russia; this is why you should not reject my request.

I was brought up as a Christian and am now the mother of six children. My husband and two sons took part in the Great War of 1941–45. My husband and one son were killed, but the other son returned home.

My youngest son, Anatoli, decided to become a monk and joined the Pochaev Monastery in 1953. Although we lived in conditions of extreme deprivation and suffered from famine, our life passed by more or less in tranquility. We Christians set little store by material gains, knowing that our life is transient; we sought consolation from our saving faith in the Lord Jesus Christ and the bliss of the future life.

But in 1961 this state of apparent calm was broken. They began to drive the Christians away from Pochaev. . . .* They adapted §196 of the Ukrainian Penal Code (infringement of passport regulations) to fit the case of the monks, who now had to live illegally at the monastery.

My son, Anatoli, who by that time had already taken his monastic vows under the name of Andrei and had been ordained priest-deacon, was included in one of these groups. He was sen-

* For a full account of the Pochaev affair see pp. 97–116.

tenced to one year's imprisonment under the above passport law. It must be clear to everyone that the monks could in no way be violating these regulations, since they were confined to the territory of the monastery, never leaving it and always living in one place. The offenders are those who took away their residence permits and demanded that they should leave Pochaev. If one considers the fact that we, his relatives, and in particular I, his mother, reside here in Pochaev, then he in fact has nowhere else to go. But for communists white will always be black and vice-versa. Thus my son languished in a dungeon for a whole year. They kept him in terrible conditions in a stone quarry and he returned more dead than alive.

As a monk, he of course returned to the monastery. Then it all began again – repressions, enforced signature of pledges to leave, fines, investigations and so on. He tried to appeal to higher authorities for justice. He described all the details of the conduct of the militia, the KGB, the volunteer police and so on. He sent his appeal to various organizations in Moscow (also to Brezhnev and Khrushchev). We hoped that an end would be put to this mockery of justice. And what was the outcome? My son's residence permit was not renewed, he was arrested again and he has already been accused of being an enemy of the Soviet Government engaged in religious propaganda and 'slander' against the state.

He was arrested on 10 February 1964, and was held under investigation for six months until 13 July 1964, while the authorities tried to work out how to frame the accusation. On the latter date they demonstrated their 'justice': they sentenced my son again – this time to three years of strict-regime imprisonment. The judge refused to let me have a copy of the sentence so that I could file an appeal, trying to conceal his dirty machinations, since the whole trial was a demonstration of violence against Christians. Most of the Pochaev communists appeared as witnesses, such as Belik, the chairman, Maximyuk, chief of the Pochaev headquarters of the volunteer police, and a number of other people, all of whom are criminal persecutors of the Pochaev Christians.

The trial was a well-acted comedy which had been rehearsed during the six months of investigation.

Maklush stated: 'We are fighting only idlers, vagrants, speculators and their like. We don't forbid prayer.'

Belik: 'We don't revoke anyone's residence permits – we act only under the instructions of Bishop Grigori and Abbot Varfolomei.' They claim that they are not to blame: 'It's the bishop himself who chases the monks away.'

Maximyuk: 'We are fighting the monks because they break Soviet law. They steal firewood which belongs to the school and take it to the monastery, so we stop their lorries and take the appropriate steps.'

Golubeva (member of the *soviet*): 'We've been waging a war against the monks, we've beaten them morally and will continue to beat them to the victorious end.'

Prokopchuk (volunteer policeman): 'In Pochaev we're only after vagrants and those who've committed crimes against the Soviet regime. Christians? We even show our concern for them. They suffer and sleep on the ground near the monastery, so we pick them up and take them to the militia in order to safeguard their health, and so on.'

Judges, counsels for the defence and witnesses were all the same people. . . .

I beg your world organization to influence the communists to grant freedom to the monks and all Christians. My son's case is not an isolated one among the people of Pochaev – it is only one link in the long chain of communist crimes.

The following monks from Pochaev are still languishing in prison: Priest-Deacon Apelli (Stankevich)* has been thrown into prison for the third time, my son and Priest-Monk Dionisi for the second time. Abbot Vyacheslav has also been twice sentenced, while a number of others who have now been released do not have an improved position, in that their residence permits have not been restored and they have no documents.

The repressions continue. This is why I call on Christians of the

* See pp. 77–84.

whole world to resist the communists and never to trust them. All their words are false, being aimed merely at deceiving the nations in order to subject them to slavery. Every Christian must make it clear in his mind that our Lord Jesus Christ has decreed that one may not serve two masters, that it is wrong to make a compromise of thought with atheists and that every effort must be made to defend the truths of the Christian faith.

Forgive me, gentlemen, if I have said anything out of place, for I am a simple, uneducated woman and I do not know how to express myself well. But I feel a very, very deep sorrow as I watch the sufferings of my son and his fellows. The communists threaten that they will lock me up with my son. Let them do it, let them jeer at me. Thanks to the truths of our Lord Jesus Christ I fear nothing, I am prepared for anything; but I want people in the world outside to know what Russian communists are like, since in the international arena they speak as angels of justice. All their words are lies, they are all servants of Satan the seducer and in everything they are like him.

Men of good will, champions of the good and of peace on earth, protect us from the yoke of communism.
25 July 1964.[14]

ARSENI STANKEVICH

This is a small selection of the several legal documents covering this case.

TO THE SUPREME COURT OF THE UKRAINE
(Complete text)
Kiev, 4 Chekistov St.

From Zoya Yevdokimovna Stankevich,
Osovbuda, Mozyr district,
Gomel region, Belorussia.

REQUEST FOR REVIEW OF SENTENCE

My brother, ARSENI YEVDOKIMOVICH STANKEVICH, was sentenced by the People's Court of the Kremenets district,

Ternopol region, on 21 January 1964 to two years' imprisonment under strict-regime conditions.

We disagree with the sentence for the following reasons:

My brother, A. Ye. Stankevich, is a priest of the Russian Orthodox Church and before his sentence he had a permanent place for exercising his office in the Pochaev Monastery, for which he also had a regular residence permit and passport. He never broke the passport regulations and had no intention of doing so, because he never left Pochaev to go anywhere else. But in 1961 officials of the Pochaev militia confiscated my brother's residence permit by administrative means, thus forcing him to transgress the passport rules, and they condemned him to six months' imprisonment.

After completing his sentence, my brother returned to his former place of residence, according to the directive issued by No. 1 Prison in Dnepropetrovsk. Yet his residence permit was not restored and he was again sentenced to one year's imprisonment, on the evidence that, according to Decree 1179 of 24 June 1961 issued by the Bishop of Lvov and Ternopol, he had been excluded from the house register of the Pochaev Monastery.

While he was serving the second prison sentence, on 30 May 1963 His Holiness Alexi, the Patriarch of Moscow and All Russia, gave the order to Bishop Grigori that the decree should be annulled as incorrect and all the monks should be restored to the brotherhood of the monastery.

By Decree 390 of 14 June 1963, Bishop Grigori annulled the former decree. Therefore my brother had every reason, upon his release in August, to return to the Pochaev Monastery. Nevertheless, the local authorities brought him to court for the third time, even though the whole church hierarchy, including the Spiritual Council of the Pochaev Monastery itself, had petitioned for restoration of his residence permit.

The entire hierarchy of the church stands sentenced with Stankevich.

I have petitioned the Ternopol regional court about my brother's innocence, but the result was negative. Are we really criminals because we believe in God? According to Soviet law, religious faith must not be persecuted. Therefore we beseech you to come to a humanitarian decision over our complaint and to quash the sentence in the Stankevich case, because he has committed no criminal offence.[15]

PROSECUTOR'S OFFICE
(Complete text)
4 Oktyabrskaya St.,
Ternopol,
Ternopol region.
Miss Zoya Yevdokimovna Stankevich,
Osovbuda,
Mozyr district,
Gomel region,
Belorussian SSR.

I inform you that your complaint about the groundlessness of the conviction of your brother, A. Ye. Stankevich, addressed to the Ministry of Justice of the Ukraine, has been investigated by the office of the Ternopol region.

A study of the affair has established that A. Ye. Stankevich, having been excluded from the monks of the Pochaev Monastery and struck off its residence list, returned again to Pochaev in August 1963 after having been released from a place of captivity, where he had been serving a sentence for a malicious infringement of the passport rules and for vagrancy. He again began to live there without authorization, even though on his liberation he had been directed from his place of imprisonment to take up residence in the Gomel region.

Despite a warning from the Pochaev district militia and a fine, Stankevich continued to infringe the passport regulations, living at Pochaev without authorization.

Stankevich's guilt in the crime committed has been proved by the testimony of the witness Prokopchuk and other material evidence.

In choosing how to mete out punishment, the people's court

took into consideration all the circumstances: the third conviction of A. Ye. Stankevich for infringing passport rules and the personality of the defendant.

There are no grounds for protesting against the sentence of the people's court, therefore your complaint is rejected.

Enclosure: five pages.

Head of the Department for the Review of Criminal Court Sentences, Junior Legal Advisor,
10 September 1964.   P. Litvinov.[16]

TO THE UNITED NATIONS ORGANIZATION, TO ALL GOVERNMENTS OF THE WORLD, TO THE HEADS OF ALL CHRISTIAN CHURCHES, TO CHRISTIANS OF THE WHOLE WORLD

> From Priest-Deacon of the Pochaev Monastery
> APELLI (A. Ye. Stankevich).
> 10 Vossoyedineniye Square (Monastery),
> Pochaev,
> Kremenets district,
> Ternopol region,
> Ukraine.

COMPLAINT

I, Arseni Yevdokimovich Stankevich, was born in 1929 in a poor peasant family in the village of Osovbuda, Petrikov district, Gomel region, Belorussia, and I am Belorussian by nationality. Our family is a religious one and from childhood I was brought up as a Christian. Our life was very difficult and we lived under extreme deprivations, but despite this we tried to carry out God's commandments.

I desired to dedicate my life to God's service and in 1957 I became a novice at the Pochaev Monastery, which at that time was under the direction of Archimandrite Sevastian (Pilinchuk). I was accepted and joined the brotherhood. Soon I took the tonsure (in 1958) and in the next year I was ordained to the rank of priest-deacon. I was naturally overjoyed and zealously followed the path of obedience set before me.

But this joy was short-lived. In 1961 the Soviet authorities began to persecute the monks and Christians of Pochaev. . . . The summonses recurred repeatedly, as someone was called in every day. The conversation was always identical in character: 'When are you leaving?' the KGB officer would ask initially. He would follow this up with a torrent of obscenities and with threats of physical repressions to follow. Then they would demand to see one's passport; the person concerned would have his residence permit withdrawn and he would be moved out of the monastery. We understood their tactics and would not give up our passports. Then the KGB organs brought pressure on the church hierarchy, especially on Bishop Grigori of Lvov and Ternopol (who had been appointed to this diocese in 1961), under whose jurisdiction the Pochaev Monastery fell. Previously Archbishop Palladi had held this post. Under pressure of the KGB and of Kolomatsky, its chief in the Ternopol region, Bishop Grigori signed a decree dismissing eight of the residents of the Pochaev Monastery, of whom I was one. The order was addressed to the Spiritual Council of the monastery, which, realizing the groundlessness of the decree, shelved it. However, Kolomatsky also received a copy of the above decree and he gave it to the KGB men, who set about driving us out of the monastery. They gave this as the nominal 'basis' for depriving us of our residence permits for living in Pochaev, although in fact this permit was still in our passports and we were inscribed in the register, because a monastery representative, the Secretary of the Spiritual Council, had protested against such a withdrawal of our residence permits and dismissal. In its turn the Spiritual Council of the monastery sent to Bishop Grigori a protest report, giving evidence of our good conduct and saying that the dismissal was incorrect. The bishop did not give a written answer, but replied orally that he had signed the dismissal under pressure from an official; in fact, however, he knew nothing about it because he had only just taken over the diocese. Previously he had been Bishop of Chernovitsy and

Bukovina. In our turn we complained about this decree to His
Holiness the Patriarch and waited for a result. The Soviet authorities did not wait, however. To them this decree was neither here
nor there: they merely intended to close the monastery, so they
arrested us then, sentencing us to various terms of imprisonment
under §196 of the Penal Code of the Ukraine ('infringement of
passport regulations'). . . .

Thus the People's Court of Pochaev sentenced me to six
months imprisonment on 16 October 1961. I served my sentence in Prison No 1 at Dnepropetrovsk, after which I again
returned to the Pochaev Monastery according to the prison's
directive.

I took this directive to the militia headquarters for them to
regulate my passport and residence permit accordingly. Captain
Lysak received me (he was then acting head of the Pochaev
district militia) and I handed him over the documents. But he
flew into a rage and launched into a five-minute tirade of unprintable language, of which he has such a fund. There were no bounds
to his wrath. 'You've got no place in the monastery,' he shouted
' – neither in the monastery nor anywhere in the Pochaev district.' Such was the reaction to my release – the more so because
in 1962 the Soviet authorities intended to close down the monastery altogether. . . .

But my lot was up. I was again summoned to the KGB, the
militia and the juridical authorities; they came to the monastery,
brought pressure upon its leadership and took steps to have me
expelled from it. I appealed to every arm of the Soviet State and
to the press, requesting that my documents should be returned
and my residence given back. But all to no avail. All my complaints were directed to the Ternopol KGB, but the latter came
to Pochaev and put moral pressure on me, calling me a parasite,
a vagrant and other select names. As a result, on 17 August 1962
they issued a second warrant for my arrest and I was sentenced
under two articles of the Ukrainian Penal Code: §196 ('infringement of the passport regulations') and §214 ('vagrancy'). All this
was in spite of the fact that I was a priest of the Russian Orthodox

Church and had worked at the monastery until the very moment of my arrest. Soviet 'humanitarian conduct' manipulated this to mean vagrancy and demanded a second revenge on me, condemning me to a year's imprisonment under strict-regime conditions. I served this sentence in the Lvov prison, P.O. Box 128-20. On 17 August 1963 I completed this sentence, too. On my release I was not given a directive to go back to Pochaev, so as to prevent my rejoining the monastery (although Soviet law states that a prisoner should always be returned to his former place of residence). The Ternopol KGB had telephoned every prison where Pochaev monks were serving their sentences with instructions that they should not be given directives to return to the monastery. Thus, illegally and against my own wish, I was directed to my birthplace in the Gomel region.

Despite this, I returned to Pochaev. Where can a monk go, where are his native land and dwelling-place, except in his monastery? Moreover, at that time the situation in Pochaev had improved ever so slightly to allow this. His Holiness the Patriarch had received our complaints and given instructions to Bishop Grigori, who had cancelled his decree which the KGB had used to arrest and convict us. The Spiritual Council of the monastery had received a petition to reinstate a certain number of the monks who had been evicted and I was among them. I hoped that at last justice would prevail, that our residence permits for the monastery would be restored and that we would henceforth be able to live quietly and peaceably, serving God and man. But my hopes were not to be realized.

On 29 January 1964 a group of monks, including me, were summoned to the Pochaev passport office to 'fill out our residence permits'. I had a passport, for this time it had been given back to me at the prison at the time of my release. I filled out the forms and had only to have the stamp inserted for all to be apparently in order. The head of the passport office came in, Captain Belik of the militia, and five other militiamen were with him. 'You're under arrest. You won't write any more complaints!'

Thus, instead of the sacred precincts, I was yet a third time 'assigned' to a prison. The Kremenets People's Court again sentenced me under §196 of the Ukrainian Penal Code to two years' imprisonment in a strict-regime penal colony. This was the maximum they could give under the relevant article. I served this sentence in the strict-regime penal colony at P.O. Box 128–81, Strizhavka, Vinnitsa region. Thus for the third time I had fallen foul of Soviet 'torture' and experienced Soviet 'humanity', so that I hardly survived. Captain Litvinchuk, the deputy chief of the colony, and the head of the special sector, Lieutenant Shvets, again failed to direct me to Pochaev, my place of residence, providing me neither with my passport nor with an application form for it. On 21 January 1966 I returned to Pochaev without any documents, having fully served my third sentence. But in Pochaev the former situation still obtained and there were only thirty monks left, all of whom were old men and weak (in 1961 there had been 149). . . . The monks lie low and conceal themselves. Since then, I, too, have been living illegally and Captain Belik and Lieutenant Gordeyev, a senior official of the district, have several times come for me. My position is desperate.

. . . . Atheist functionaries have seized total power in the church. Therefore I have decided to address the international organizations of the UN and all the governments of the world to beg for pity on us and intercede for our residence in the Pochaev Monastery, to review our documents and complaints. . . .

Before I joined the Pochaev Monastery I had a residence permit for a forbidden border area in the Murmansk region, because I was working there under conscription, but now they do not want to reinstate me in Pochaev, a country area.

Mine is not an isolated case, for similar circumstances have overtaken many monks in Pochaev and they are still suffering at the present time.

Help us.

10 February 1966.[17]

3 The Suppression of the Monasteries and Seminaries

THE PRESS CAMPAIGN

This chapter contains a small selection from the voluminous evidence on the closure of the monasteries between 1960–64. Very few of the many references from the Soviet press have been included, because we wished to reserve as much as possible of our space for the fully documented accounts of the events at Pochaev and Pskov. Further evidence relating to the closure of the monasteries and convents at Chernigov, Grodno and Polotsk will be found elsewhere.*

'HOLY RELICS' (BEFORE THE JUDGMENT OF SCIENCE)
(I. Brazhnik and M. Kanyuka)

The fact is that during the fascist occupation of Kiev the monastic brotherhood restored the community on the territory of the monastery. It was then, perhaps, that the only 'miracle' of its history occurred. Through the deft hands of the monks, the museum exhibits – the mummified corpses – were again transformed into the 'incorruptible relics of the holy saints'. The old fables resumed their currency. . . .

You could not claim that no-one is alarmed by these illegal actions of the monks who are concerned with religious propaganda. Many times public opinion of the city has demanded the return of the grottoes to the museum preserve of the 'Kiev Caves Monastery'. Unfortunately, however, so far the matter has not progressed beyond fruitless conversations.[1]

It did progress further in the next year (1960) when the monks were evicted.[2]

* See pp. 175–6.

THE MONASTIC WALLS ARE COLLAPSING
(Ye. Mayat and I. Uzkov)

. . . . A few years ago a medical inspection revealed that in St. Cyprian's Monastery ten monks were suffering from venereal diseases. . . .

In pools near convents, in wells and toilets, the bodies of new-born babies have been found, begotten by the 'holy fathers' from the 'brides of Christ'. . . .

In the same monastery (Tsyganeşti), priest-monk Yevarest Kiper raped the daughter of the monk Sergi who had come to see her father. . . .

Open money-grubbing and theft, parasitism and vagrancy, cynical egotism and unconcealed debauchery: these are what characterize the life of the 'holy monks' who preach love for one's neighbour, cleanliness and sinlessness. . . .

Another monastic church has been transformed into the sports room of the local school. Although the cupolas and crosses have already been removed, at times one can see an old nun turn towards the sports room and cross herself. . . .

Let the monastic walls collapse. Let the fresh wind of life blow open the gates of monasteries and the doors of cells, may it free the deceived from spiritual subjugation and bring them to the joy of life and the happiness of free labour.[3]

We have given the briefest selection from this catalogue of monastic 'vices'. As a corrective to what is written here, it is most instructive to read Levitin's defence of monasticism.

LEVITIN'S DEFENCE

MONASTICISM AND THE MODERN WORLD
(A. Krasnov-Levitin*)

I wrote the word 'monasticism' and shuddered involuntarily, thinking what an anachronism it sounds in the ears of the man in

* See pp. 255–63.

the street. 'Monasticism!? – that's something horrible. When did it arise and when did it die out?' Any average person today would ask this question, or something like it.

I would answer: it originated at the dawn of man and will die out when he disappears.

Monasticism is not an institution, foundation or a historical phenomenon, but an element, just as love, art and religion are elements.

Here follows an essay on the general history of monasticism, concluding with an impression of its history in Russia.

What is monasticism like now?

First of all, one should note that monks are now being subjected to a cruel persecution from the local authorities. In recent years a large number of monasteries have been closed with brutal use of force, among which we should mention the Caves Monastery at Kiev, Glinskaya Pustyn (Kharkov region), well known for its strict rule of life and ardently loved by believers, and many monasteries in the Western Ukraine, the Carpathian region and Moldavia. The closure of monasteries is taking place in the face of fierce opposition from local believers, with barbarous affront to the religious feelings of the population. All these acts of the local authorities are being covered up by the bishops who have betrayed their duty and who in a cowardly way are backing up these illegalities with their signatures.*

However, we have no intention of following their example and therefore we will not mince our words in describing the action of the authorities in terms it deserves: it is piracy. This is not abuse, but a statement of the facts: the open infraction of the law in broad daylight and in an organized way is, in legal language, piracy; those who participate in such illegality are pirates.

In the spring of this year we described the siege of the Pochaev Monastery in our article, *The Heart Votes*.[4] Since then the position of the monastery has improved: the local authorities, under the

* Cf. pp. 140–5.

influence of public opinion, have been forced to change their tactics somewhat.*

There follows a brief account of the repressions at Pochaev.†

It would be a mistake to assume that atheist activists always confine their campaign to such methods. Besides the physical siege, there is the ideological one.

When it is permitted to instigate libel illegally against people who are completely defenceless victims, to besmear them with any curses and insults in the press, while being fully guaranteed against having to answer for it – what is this other than ideological gangsterism?

Levitin here includes a poem by Andrei Voznesensky attacking monasticism and adds his own comments.

Monasticism is here criticized from a completely philistine standpoint.

The main atheist journal, *Nauka i Religia* ('Science and Religion'), attacks monasticism on the same premises. As is well known it has a section on Orthodox saints. Atheist campaigners, when they talk of monks venerated by the church, express complete horror of the fact that St. Makari of Kalyazin left his father's house and, despite all his father's entreaties, refused to leave the monastery, or that Alexi the Man of God left his family and his young wife. The most comical aspect of this, which these ill-starred writers fail to notice, is that they almost literally, word for word, repeat the conservative publicists of the end of the nineteenth century who charged the revolutionaries with the same lack of respect towards their parents. . . .

At that time there was an axiom among socialists and democrats that it was necessary to sacrifice one's family for ideals, to suffer and give up one's own happiness for them. The philistines of *Nauka i Religia* do not consider this to be so, which, incidentally, is quite natural. What have they to do with socialism and democracy? Just about as much as with science and religion.

*   *   *

* Cf. p. 116.   † Cf. pp. 97–116.

'Take this candle, brother, and see how yours must be a pure and virtuous life, how you must be a light to the world through your exemplary morals.'

Thus speaks the abbot as he hands over a lighted candle to the newly-tonsured monk. . . .

These words define the social role of monasticism and since a pure and virtuous life and exemplary morals cannot become obsolete, neither can monasticism. . . .

At no time (even in the age of *sputniks* and cosmonauts) can debauchery, egotism and moral laxity be useful. Neither can atheism be, for it is an ideology which looks at the world as an arena of chaotic or moribund forces.

Always, at all times, the monastery has been the best school for educating people to clean living, self-denial and unselfishness. The monastery was the highest ideal for old Russia and it has remained so for many Russian people who have attained the peak of culture.

. . . . In monasteries, as everywhere, there are many short-comings, but by the very fact of its existence monasticism influences for the better those in contact with it.

Restraint and cleanliness demonstrate to the profligate that debauchery is not a norm, but an abnormality; renunciation and voluntary poverty teach scorn of riches; self-denial is the best weapon against egotism. Thus monasticism is a healthy weapon against selfishness, banality and uncleanliness. Naturally, however, the role of monasticism is not exhausted by this.

For monasticism is a holy mystery.

Metropolitan Antoni Khrapovitsky spoke about this in the twentieth century (he was an extreme conservative in politics, but a bold thinker and a profound theologian).

This position exactly corresponds to patristic teaching on monasticism.

But first we must briefly state what a holy mystery is.

Primarily, it is a miracle, a direct act of God's grace, which changes human nature itself. Like any miracle, a mystery demands active participation on the part of man – and this is faith. Without this there is no miracle and without miracle there is no mystery. A mystery, like any miracle, happens instantaneously, but it is prepared slowly and gradually. We see this in the Gospel miracles. The man sick of the palsy had been awaiting healing for decades; the woman with an issue of blood had also been waiting for many years; the father of the boy possessed of a devil had been seeking his son's cure in a state of tension. . . .

Slowly but inexorably, changes in the human psyche mount up, then suddenly there is a leap ahead. Man's whole nature experiences an instantaneous shock and it changes in a moment.

The specific of a holy mystery is that the miracle is here performed through the church. . . .

Levitin enumerates seven mysteries.

The eighth mystery, but perhaps not the last, is that of monasticism.

This is also a great miracle; by the action of the Holy Spirit human nature is changed. Man is endued with power over passions and lusts, a power which is not natural to him. Human nature becomes superhuman and angelic.

Monasticism is an exaltation of man to the angels, a betrothal to purity. . . . It is an imitation of Christ. . . . It is not something sombre, sad or depressing. It is joy and eternal Easter (as we see it in the two great monks, St. Seraphim of Sarov and St. Francis of Assisi). . . . A monk is a fighter for truth, a soldier for Christ's cause, a manly and fearless warrior. . . .

We firmly believe in the coming of a new wave of monasticism in the Russian Church. The future of Russia is with the ardent and zealous young people of our country who, despite opposition, are every day attaining to the faith. New monks will come from among them – zealous warriors for Christ's cause. They will renew and transform the Church of Christ and the Russian land with their purity, self-sacrifice and spiritual ardour.

So be it.

18 October 1963. . . .[5]

THE TRUTH ABOUT THE MONASTERY OF THE CAVES AT PSKOV
(G. Gerodnik)

The author recounts a conversation at the monastery with a friend whom he met there. The extracts we have chosen demonstrate how the monks organized staunch opposition to atheist incursions.

'I am amazed that the local experts and atheists should be inactive. Why aren't they trying to neutralize this citadel of ignorance? Take yourself, Georgi Petrovich. You can recount so much about the past and present of the monastery and the whole Pechory region. You've got some cards up your sleeve.'

'That's true . . . We local intelligentsia, especially the atheists, can be reproached in many ways and we don't exonerate ourselves completely. Until recently many people reasoned like this: the monastery is such an ancient relic of the past that in Soviet conditions it will rapidly die a natural death. Others understood that there must be no indulgence towards religious people, but they didn't know how to gain access to such a citadel of ignorance. Our only mitigating circumstance is the special history of Pechory. It's been a Soviet town only about half as long as other places in the Pskov region, you know. We needed time to train experienced anti-religious campaigners who are completely familiar with local conditions . . .'

'So you've been preparing to do battle?'

'We've already done so! We've recently severely criticized our lack of commitment. Experience has shown that if you leave a monastery in peace, it goes on to the attack itself. Today is an ordinary Sunday – and just look how many people there are. But if you want to see the monastery working on all cylinders (if I may use the expression), come to us at Pechory on any major festival. Then you'll see the whole "black legion" in action. Take, for example, the monastery's chief festival, the Dormition of the Virgin Mary, which falls on 28 August (new style) – it's a real dress parade of the powers of ignorance. When you see it, you'll be amazed how much darkness and ignorance are trying to creep over the threshold between the murky past and the bright communist future!'

'I'm very grateful for the invitation and I'll try to come. What's your suggestion for counteracting the "black legion"?'

'First of all, we're preparing atheist exhibits in the museum. There we'll show both the ignoble history of the Pechory Monastery at Pskov and the activities of the holy fathers . . . But we expect most success from the fact that the district committee of the party is preparing a group of public guides. Among them will be assistants at the local museum, teachers and lecturers from the Society for Spreading Political and Scientific Knowledge. We're preparing to declare war on the monks with hundreds and thousands of trippers who'll visit the Pechory Monastery.'

On a subsequent visit by the author, this plan was already in action.

'But how do you co-ordinate your work with the monks?'

'Badly, to be honest. The monks have declared a real "cold war" on us and won't let us into the churches and catacombs. Nevertheless, were not losing heart. We go around the circumference of the monastery and talk about the churches in the courtyard, without going inside. Naturally, the visitors are sorry that they can't get into the catacombs. But even like this the excursions give incomparably more than before. There's no longer a monopoly of ignorant monastic guides.'

The speaker goes on to claim that the atheist exhibition at the museum is having a great success, however.

I again visited Pechory in the summer of 1962. Since I was last there a few changes had occurred at the monastery. Firstly, rates for candles, prayer-offerings and other forms of service to believers had been brought into line with the new monetary system. Secondly, under the influence of criticism in the press, the monks had completely stopped acting as guides. Now only public ones were operating.

It is true that the holy fathers were secretly continuing to conduct people through the catacombs and were receiving money for doing so, but they no longer attracted crowds of people.[6]

ANSWER TO GENNADI GERODNIK
(A. Krasnov-Levitin)

Among the numerous works of anti-religious and anti-monastic literature, Gennadi Gerodnik's pamphlet, *The Truth about the Monastery of the Caves at Pskov*, is worthy of attention. It was published in Moscow by the State Publishing House for Political Literature in 1963 in an edition of 200,000 copies.

This pamphlet, written in an animated and literary style, stands out a little against the sombre background of grey anti-religious cant. It is worth pausing in greater detail over it, the more so because the Monastery of the Caves at Pskov has now acquired new significance. It is one of the four male monasteries which is still preserved on Soviet territory and perhaps it is the only one which has fully maintained its manual of discipline and the complete structure of the pre-revolutionary monasteries.

Levitin discusses some of Gerodnik's historical points.

Apparently Gerodnik himself found that he had gone too far, because he decided to protect himself, should the need arise, by referring to a certain Georgi Petrovich (Gerodnik intentionally does not mention a surname) who is supposed to have recounted all this to him. So 'Georgi Petrovich' (if he is not a mythical personage) and his pupil, Gerodnik, are quite sure that their readers will not take the trouble of digging into sources – any more than they themselves have done.

A long passage is devoted to countering Gerodnik's account of the oppressive role played by the monastery in the past.

From the nineteenth century Gerodnik leaps precipitously into the twentieth – in which we will follow him. . . .

After the liberation of the Pskov region by the Soviet forces, Pavel Gorshkov, the abbot, and Lin, a monk, were brought to trial for collaboration with the occupying forces. No other monk was accused. Despite repeated checks, the MGB organs found no grounds for bringing any other monks to trial (and this was in the time of Stalin and Beria, when everything was in deadly earnest).

D

But Gerodnik is a greater royalist than the king and a greater Beria-supporter than Beria's own men – he accuses all monks indiscriminately of betraying their native land.

. . . . Who now comprises the brotherhood of the monastery? Let us begin with the most important, Archimandrite Alipi, the man who has inherited the seat of St. Kornili. He is a colourful and individual character.

He is a real Russian, a native of the Moscow region, the son of a shepherd. As a layman, his name was Ivan Mikhailovich Voronov. At twenty he left the country, moved to the capital and became a labourer on the metro-building project. He worked days and nights, receiving thanks and awards. Then the war came and Ivan Mikhailovich went to the front, fighting throughout the four years and defending Moscow. He was wounded several times and awarded orders and medals.

After the war he stopped to think. He thought for long and sought the truth. He went to the Baptists and other sects, but finally entered a seminary and the monastery. For a long time, in peasant fashion, he tried it out and finally took the irrevocable step.

He works night and day at physical labour: hewing wood, carrying planks, breaking ice, painting, whitewashing, cleaning. He makes everyone else work, too. He is a talented man, a good artist. He is a brave warrior, defending the monastery resolutely and courageously. If the need arose, he would die for it.

To look at him you would think he was a thickset peasant, bearded and coarse; he is a real abbot, though – strict but just, capable of anger, but humane.

He reminisces pleasantly about his mother; he talks in a tender, sincere and good way with people and he is obviously compassionate towards them.

I have been at his services and heard his sermons. He officiates with feeling and preaches with conviction. I have talked with him several times. He looks at me and my writings with a certain amazement, I feel. I am one of the old-styled intelligentsia, apparently not comprehensible to him. He simply boggles at any sort of innovation, Christian socialism and so on. 'What sort of thing is this?' he would ask.

In concluding this sketch of his character, I would say that he is a real Russian and very close to the people. It would be impossible to imagine anyone with a greater understanding of their life.

What are the other monks like? Here is a short selected list.

Archimandrite Sergi (Ivan Ivanovich Losyakov) was born into a working family and worked eighteen years as a first-class engine-driver on the railway, then five years as a railway metal craftsman and twenty-two years in a glass factory at Chudov, Novgorod region, as an artist, an engineer in a machine department and head of a mechanical section. He has worked in all for 45 years and earned a pension. From 1943 he worked for twenty years in the domestic department of the Monastery of the Caves at Pskov. His four children are at present working in manufacturing in-dustries and all of them served in the front line during the Second World War.

Archimandrite Yermogen (Georgi Vasilievich Krylov) worked for seven years in a trading concern. He arrived at the monastery in 1945 on the instructions of His Holiness, Patriarch Alexi. . . .

Abbot Ieronim (Ivan Matveyevich Tikhomirov) worked from 1935–40 on a *kolkhoz*, was at the front throughout the war with Finland and was again called up to the front in 1941. He was wounded on the north-west front near Tikhvin and was awarded the 'Victory over Germany' medal. From 1943 he worked for four years as a shoemaker in various workshops in the Urals and was awarded the 'Medal for Outstanding Labour'.

Abbot Kiprian (Karp Rodionovich Novikov) fought for four years at the front in the Second World War and was five times decorated.

Priest-monk Antipa (Vasili Mikhailovich Mikhailov) was called up to the front in 1942 and decorated with the 'Victory over Germany' and 'Bravery' medals, before being demobilized in 1946. He is a goods manager by trade and was thrown from a train while performing his duties. He is now pensioned off from work as an invalid. He is of a peasant family. . . .

Abbot Sofroni (Igor Konstantinovich Iogel) lived in China from January 1917, because his father worked there. In 1954 the Soviet Government announced its repatriation programme. In 1952 Abbot Sofroni applied to return to his native land. In 1960 the necessary formalities were completed and he left China, arriving at the Monastery of the Caves at the end of the same year.

Fourteen monks are included here altogether.

As may be seen from this list, the absolute majority of the monks are real Russians, mentally healthy, simple people who have trodden a long and difficult path in life. They have not come here to rest, but to live in a manner pleasing to God, to pray and to work, to build the Kingdom of God on this acre of Russian soil.

There are not only monks. Believers, the Russian Orthodox people, pour in from all corners of Russia (just as Gerodnik so rightly notes in one passage).

What are they seeking here? Gerodnik's pamphlet describes several aspects of monastic life, including ironic comments on the external aspect of monastic prayer, which shocks him. The refrain of the whole work is: 'In the middle of the twentieth century it is shameful to be concerned with such things.'

Levitin then quotes two of Gerodnik's descriptions of life in the monastery, including a festival procession.

One is simply confounded to meet such animal coarseness and self-satisfied, small-minded banality as suppurates through these lines.

You, Gerodnik, pass for a cultured man, you even know the poems of Igor Severyanin; yet you are much less cultured than these old women about whom you talk with such scorn. Culture is not being correctly dressed in a jacket and trousers with braces. It is to know how to feel sensitively, to understand people's feelings and to respect them. Culture is knowing how to distinguish the most refined gradations of feeling, to know how (if you want to use dialectical terminology) to distinguish the important from the secondary, the essential from the accidental, the external from the internal. Maxim Gorki, for example, knew how to do this. One need only cite his description of the procession of the cross at the end of his story, *Confession*, where the bearers do not carry the miracle-working icon, but it flies of its own accord above the people like a golden bird; a miracle occurs in the crowd – a paralysed girl begins to walk. . . .

It is true, Gerodnik, that you also can quote one great authority, L. N. Tolstoi – his description of the liturgy in the novel, *Resurrection*. You have made him a model for your description of worship and in one place you even name him directly.

Tolstoi was a genius, Levitin continues, but with a flaw: that of over-simplification. He tried to take the mystical aspect out of religion.

But what are you capable of doing? Of mocking what you are ordered to mock and offending defenceless people?

Yet I pity you. You have been meted out a very thankless task. Just look at yourself – you advise that the icon of the Virgin Mary should be sent to a museum. But what would you give people in return? A text-book on dialectical materialism, where they would be told about 'particles – atoms and electrons'? A harvesting campaign? Severyanin's poetry? Or perhaps you would replace it by the bust of some leader and teacher? Do you really think this would satisfy the people? Would you yourself be satisfied? No, you would not be.[7]

POCHAEV

The case of two individuals, the Monks Andrei (Shchur) and Apelli (Stankevich), was presented in the previous chapter.* We now give the full account of the recent history of the Pochaev Monastery, as reported by its Spiritual Council in 1966. This document was included in the underground literary publication, *Phoenix 1966*.

* See pp. 74–84.

TO COMRADE PODGORNY, CHAIRMAN OF THE
PRESIDIUM OF THE SUPREME SOVIET OF THE USSR.
BRIEF DESCRIPTION OF RECENT OCCURRENCES
AT THE POCHAEV MONASTERY
(The Spiritual Council of the Pochaev Monastery)

Popular tradition traces the appearance of monks on Mt. Pochaev back to the times of the first missionaries to the Slavs, Cyril and Methodius (that is to the ninth century, or before the general baptism of the Russian people).

Monks began to live together permanently on Mt. Pochaev from the thirteenth century, from the time that the Virgin Mary appeared in a pillar of fire beside a miraculous spring left behind after her appearance (a trace of Her Footprint on a stone was filled with health-giving water). In the sixteenth to seventeenth centuries the great hermit, St. Iov of Pochaev, withdrew to this spot and his holy relics have been now resting in the monastery for three hundred years. Thus, the Pochaev Monastery has now been in existence for more than seven hundred years.

In our day the life of the monastery was disturbed during the period of Khrushchev's rule, when churches and monasteries were closed down in large numbers. Monks from the suppressed monasteries collected together at Pochaev, but this was not the end of the persecutions, for they became worse and worse. . . .

Officials of the Council for Russian Orthodox Church Affairs have assumed complete control over religious matters and started acting as overlords in the church.

In 1961 they set about directly interfering with the Pochaev Monastery. They hesitated to close down or liquidate it. Desirous of concealing their criminal behaviour and giving it a semblance of legality, they deprived the monastery of material resources for the monks' existence, they forbade access to it by Christian pilgrims and directed all organizations and shops not to supply the monks with provisions and other commodities, in order to make it impossible for the monastery to continue its existence.

In this way they hoped to finish it off by announcing in the Soviet press that it had disintegrated by itself.

These coercive and repressive actions have been introduced gradually, but more and more insistently. In 1959 the monastery's own plot of land (ten hectares) was taken from it and after that we lost the so-called 'bishop's' fruit garden adjoining the bishop's palace and the Cave Church of St. Iov, with its garden, hothouse, drying-room, gardener's cottage, store and other ancillary premises. Then they took away an apiary containing more than a hundred hives of bees. Next, in 1960, they banned the carrying out of repair or restoration work in the monastery and forbade it to admit new members to the brotherhood or to contract with specialists to carry out artistic and joinery work. Some attempts were made to reduce the number of brethren in the monastery and all the motor vehicles (four lorries and one car), machinery, equipment and the repair and restoration materials purchased in our time from monastery funds have been removed. Christian pilgrims arriving from other towns have been strenuously persecuted. They began removing local Christians from their jobs because they were going to the monastery to pray. They dismissed Nadezhda Klotkina (of 40 Pletenka St., Pochaev), who worked as assistant bookkeeper in the district communications office of the *zavkhoz* of the Pochaev district hospital, and several hospital nurses. The militia and KGB organs persecute Christians day and night in the monastery, trying to find some pretext or other for objections and making arrests. They register them as members of the banned anti-Soviet sect of *Leontievtsy*,[8] pass sentence on them and deport them. It is categorically forbidden to allow visitors to spend the night either in the monastery or in the town. After the war and until 1959, the Pochaev Monastery utilized the 'bishop's palace' as a hostel for visiting pilgrims. In 1959 monks from closed monasteries were accommodated there; they came, for example, from the hermitage of the Pochaev Monastery, while others came from the Monastery of the Caves at Kiev,* from that of the 'Cossack Tombs' in the Volhynia region, from

* See p. 85.

the Kreshchatin Monastery in the Chernovitsy region and else-where.

The main block still had one room where relatives and friends of the monks were sometimes allowed to stay the night. The KGB categorically forbade people to be admitted. The head of the Pochaev KGB, Captain Nikolai Vasilievich Maximov, went round every night to check how his orders were being obeyed. On one occasion he found two people there, drew up an affidavit and forced Abbot Anatoli (Korneichuk), who resided there, to sign it. He also summoned the monastery watchman, Nikolai Rabush, an aged invalid, to sign the document, but the latter, seeing how inhumanely the KGB men were behaving, was slow in appearing, whereupon Maximov, furious because his orders were not being immediately obeyed, ran up to the watchman and in a menacing tone shouted, 'Come here and sign!' The old man said nothing, so Maximov seized him and with all his strength threw him down the steps. Fortunately for the watchman, the Monk Nestor was standing below and caught him in his arms – otherwise there might have been a fatal accident.

That is how Maximov mocks at the Christians in the monastery.

When it saw the difficult situation created for visiting pilgrims, the monastery administration, at the people's earnest request, kept the church open for devotions 24 hours a day. But Maximov very soon refused to allow people to spend the night here either. For several days he went around looking out for those who were starting up the nightly prayers, reading and singing (he was trying to find the fervent Christians). When he learnt who they were he would then, when a favourable opportunity occurred, arrest them one by one, sentence some or merely clear others out of Pochaev. Even this did not satisfy Maximov, for more and more Christians kept coming along and the monks of the monastery managed to keep the prayer services going successfully.

Then Maximov adopted a different method: he accused the monks of using the church as a doss-house. Not all the Christians were able, because of their state of health, to keep awake and pray round the clock and some of them would fall asleep at their prayers from exhaustion. So Maximov drew up a document to the effect that 250 people were illegally spending the night in the Trinity Church of the Pochaev Monastery and ordered the monk on duty there, Brother Pior, to sign it – which he refused to do, as it was unjust. . . .

Maximov, following his own line, categorically forbade worshippers being allowed into the church at night and very soon had the recalcitrant monk struck off the monastery house register and driven away from Pochaev, even threatening to have him sentenced for alleged anti-Soviet agitation.

In 1961 stormy scenes began to occur in Pochaev. The 'bishop's palace' was taken from the monks and turned into a polyclinic,[9] while the monks were herded into one block. The 'holy gates' were removed, along with the adjoining buildings. A small residential building, known as the 'joiners' shop', was taken, as well as the pump-house, complete with machinery and equipment.

When all the buildings surrounding the monastery had been taken over and only the large block next to the Dormition Church was left, then the KGB and the militia turned upon the inmates. There was now nowhere else to move them to, so they began dispersing them in all directions. Every day groups of ten to fifteen monks would be called up to the Pochaev police station for questioning; there they were split up one to a room and subjected to interrogation. The conversation would proceed like this: 'Your monastery is being closed down; get out of it quietly. We've licked Germany and we've no need to bother ourselves with you. If you don't get out, we'll chase you out and still close the monastery.' Then they began the dispersal – they began worrying the life out of each of the monks in turn; for days on end they were harried in the offices of the militia and KGB; they locked them in the preliminary investigation cell[10] and jeered at them to their heart's content. Four or five KGB agents, often in an intoxicated condition, would assault a single monk, telling him to quit the monastery. The insults and the expressions which they used towards the monks cannot be described: swearing, the foulest terms of abuse, shouting, thumping on the table, ordering

them to look straight into the interrogator's eyes or in one direction, tearing about from room to room, orders to get out, come
in, to write explanations about all sides of monastic life. . . . By
the grace of God we put up with it and bore it all, but all of a
sudden they adopted another method – they began to take away
our passports.

At first a group of KGB and militia officials came along:
Major Danilov, Captain Belik,* First Lieutenants Boreiko, Lysak,
Yurchak and others. They would ask for the monk's passport,
ostensibly for checking, but when the owner handed it over for
this, he would get it back with a cancellation stamp. Captain
Belik, head of the passport section, would explain: 'Now you've
all been struck off; get out of the monastery, otherwise we'll
prosecute you under §196 of the Ukrainian Penal Code for
breach of the passport regulations.' Then Bochkarev and Maximov would immediately fix a three-day time-limit for leaving
the monastery. In response to the entreaties and tears of the monks
that this was violence . . . . the KGB officials retorted that they
had made the laws, the Constitution was written for communists
and believers were 'deprived of rights'. The officials also said that
they had been given different instructions on the party line and
they were carrying out government orders which they would
not show to anyone. . . . Then they imposed fines and set in
train criminal proceedings against 'violators of passport regulations', entailing a sentence of a year's imprisonment.

Thus excessive sentences were imposed on the monks of the
Pochaev Monastery: Abbot Vyacheslav (Pasman) had lived forty
years in the Lavra – almost all his life – yet in his old age he
was made out to be a 'violator of the passport regulations'. The
following were subjected to similar repressive treatment: Priest-
monks Amvrosi (Dovgan) and Sergi (Solomko); Priest-deacons
Antoni (Korystelev), Apelli (Stankevich) and Andrei (Shchur);
Priest-monks Vladimir (Soldatov), Valerian (Popovich) and
Dionisi (Komonyuk); Priest-deacon Gavriil (Uglitskikh); the
Monks Nestor (Onuk,) Daniil (Klyutkin) and Grigori (Unka). . . .

* See pp. 75–6.

The church is separated from the state, but in actual fact the CROCA officials grossly interfere in church matters and do what they like. Yet in order to have something to refer back to, they brought pressure to bear, through a CROCA official, on Bishop Grigori of Lvov, who now occupies the see of Trans-Carpathia, to get him to issue a decree for the dismissal of the monks. It was on this they relied, claiming that the monks had been dismissed by the bishop and so the only place for them was prison.

None of the monks listed above has, of course, committed any crime whatsoever. Before entering the monastery they worked honourably in civilian jobs; some of them fought in the Second World War of 1941–45 and immediately it was over entered the precincts of the monastery to serve God, others had from their youth pursued their occupation in the monastery. Their past history would seem to be even deserving of respect – for instance, in connection with the twentieth anniversary of the victory over Germany all who took part in the war were awarded medals and honoured. Yet believers and especially monks who had done war service – men such as Amvrosi (Dovgan), Sergi (Solomko), Antoni (Korystelev) and others – were repeatedly arrested and sent to prison for breaches of the passport regulations.

As they could not make up their minds to arrest and sentence everyone in turn (we do, after all, have freedom of confession!), all organizations set about fighting the monastery and its resident monks. The principal task was left to the public health bodies. The monks had somehow to be declared sick and sent away compulsorily for treatment. To this end the authorities organized medical inspection of them. A commission was set up under the Pochaev District Military Board which found certain monks (Golovanov, Mirchuk, Shvoruk and others) mentally ill, although they were completely healthy, and they were held for a protracted period in a mental hospital and discharged from the monastery. The 'treatment' was so strenuous that it resulted in some of them dying – Golovanov died at the age of 35. In September 1961 another commission was set up, composed of KGB agents and medical officials, the so-called 'regional medical commission' which held its meetings on the monastery's premises in the Spiritual Council's room. Monks were summoned before it and examined for infectious diseases like dysentery. These examinations were more like a farce than a commission meeting, but under this noble guise they ruled that a group of monks (Volynets, Dubrovsky, Lisitsky, Korneichuk, Galsevich and Tsentkevich) must undergo a course of hospital treatment. For these reasons the group in question were forcibly evacuated to the Kremenets District Hospital for treatment (the monks, of course, were all fit and well and had never been ill).

Next, on 13 March 1962 the commission set up a new medical board for chest examinations. The monks had already in the previous commissions noticed how things were going and the consequences that followed, so they began categorically to refuse to appear before it, on the grounds that in the USSR treatment is supposed to be voluntary and not compulsory. . . . If any monk asked for an explanation of the commission's purpose, Captain Belik forthwith struck him off the house register of the monastery. In this manner a further group of sixteen monks were struck off, having again emerged as violators of passport regulations, and they were at once handed over to the courts.

While all this was going on, a further series of medical commissions for young men was set up by the Pochaev District Military Committee to deal with younger monks who had not done military service in the Soviet Army, but had been exempted as 'white card holders'. On the orders of the KGB, the doctors pronounced them fit and conscripted them into the military construction companies of the Soviet Army, which sent them to the northern areas of the country to do forestry work. The following came into this group: Priest-deacons Pankrati Timoshchuk, Georgi Loshkarev and Alexi Baranovsky; Priest-monk Vlasi Bolotov; and Monks Anatoli Piletsky, Dimitri Petrovtsy, Ivan Pastukhov, Vladimir Klochkov, Anatoli Kapinos and Isikhi Nikitenko. Bolotov, Piletsky and Nikitenko were in extremely poor health, one had a fractured spine, another had extremely weak (0.2%)

eyesight which made him completely unsuitable for hard physical labour. Nevertheless, the doctors passed them 'fit' for military service, simply in order to get them out of the monastery. They were brought only as far as Ternopol to the assembly point, held there for some time and sent away, but during that time they had been crossed off the monastery house register and no-one would hear of reinstating them or discussing the matter. . . .

Constant supervision was established round the monastery. Not a single motor vehicle or cart with fuel or produce was allowed to enter it – it was deprived of all supplies, so as to add hunger and cold to the general pressure. . . . In the morning, as the Christians go to church, motor lorries are driven up, the Christians are bundled on to them with vulgar imprecations and beatings, then they are taken forty to fifty kilometres away from Pochaev and sternly warned that if they should so much as appear at the monastery they would be put in gaol.[11] They took from local residents of Pochaev a personal signature undertaking not to go to the monastery to pray or allow travellers to spend the night with them. Anyone who fearlessly continued to worship or go to the monastery the KGB struck off the Pochaev residents' list and deported. Every day they went round the houses in the town checking to see whether their orders were being executed, under the pretence of inspecting passports. If they found pilgrims had arrived anywhere, they arrested them and fined their hosts.

These exhibitions of mockery spilled over into fanatical behaviour: drunken policemen and their chiefs burst into houses at midnight, threw sleeping pilgrims into the street, robbed and beat them, jeered at their hosts. Under such pressure residents began to be afraid to take anyone in for the night and pilgrims arriving in Pochaev were forced to spend the night on the street in the open or huddle in a church porch. Even here the Pochaev militia left no-one in peace but, on the contrary, resorted to the coarsest form of brutality: drunken KGB agents and militiamen went around at night armed with clubs and guns and began thrashing the pilgrims who scattered helter-skelter in terror. Then they were picked up one by one, robbed, beaten and thrown into a mental hospital where they were told, 'You'll not travel to Pochaev again'.

On one occasion the monastery's yard-watchman, the novice Isidor Lishchinyuk, was unable to endure such outrageous behaviour and intervened on behalf of the suffering pilgrims. 'What are you doing?' he exclaimed, 'Why are you taunting the people? You're persecuting innocent old women.' But, quite unashamed of the monk's reproaches, one of the militiamen, Sergeant Medyany, rushed at the watchman shouting, 'I'll show you . . .' Hurling curses at him, he started to hit him in the face and all over his body, while the others mishandled the pilgrims.

The abusive behaviour did not stop and the policemen went unpunished; on the contrary, the KGB shortly afterwards took away the watchman's passport, removed him from the monastery register and deported him from Pochaev. . . .

By September 1962 out of 140 monks only 36 were left, but they continued to keep the monastery running, holding services in it and meeting the needs of the persecuted Christian population.

Here follows a description of how the KGB acquired duplicate keys for all the locks and treated the remaining monastery property as if it had been requisitioned.

During the whole period of persecution the local press also refused to leave the monks alone. Special KGB staff composed all kinds of fictitious stories about the monks, more especially about Archimandrite Sevastian, the head of the monastery. Articles were fabricated over the name of a former Pochaev novice, Iosif Baiduk, who was serving in the Soviet Army. They claimed that he had lived for ten years in the Pochaev Monastery, but he was now renouncing religion and breaking with the monastery. They went on to spatter its inmates with filth. In fact, however, he had written nothing and adhered to his religious convictions; on being demobilized he wrote an indignant protest about forgeries having been fabricated in his name. He had lived only ten days in the monastery but would like to return as one of its inmates. Baiduk was then subjected to a campaign of repression; they arrested him, handed him over in Ternopol to the KGB and from there sent him off to a mental hospital in Vinnitsa and treated him as a sick prisoner. In 1962 a brochure of the Pochaev Museum of Atheism was published by Andriyuk, its director, entitled *The Pochaev Museum of Atheism*. Here use was again made of previous materials based on slanderous assertions allegedly made by Baiduk and other anonymous authors – in addition to which Andriyuk mentions the figure of 69 monks who had voluntarily left the monastery. . . .

Abbot Iosif (Golovatyuk) was a venerable old man of seventy who had nearly all his life (more than forty years) followed an occupation in the monastery and did not want to leave it. However they might torment him, he wanted to end his days there. Sixteen militia and KGB men came to him in his cell, grabbed the old man and dragged him out of the monastery – some took his arms, others his legs; another seized his collar and squeezed his throat so hard that he nearly died. . . . An ambulance was then driven to the monastery and Iosif was bundled into it. Escorted by two KGB agents he was taken to the mental hospital at Budanov – an entirely healthy man thrown in among sick patients! That was not the end of it either: his hair and beard were shaven off and every day he was forced to have some kind of injection in very large doses. As a result his whole body, especially his legs, swelled up and became as stiff as a board; his skin nearly burst from the fluid which the doctors kept injecting every day and this continued for a protracted period. Only after petitions from relatives and widespread protests from believers was he discharged after six months to a nephew residing in the village of Malaya Ilovitsa, Shumsky district, Ternopol region. There was a condition that he would never again appear in the monastery, otherwise the same procedure as before would be repeated and he would be sent back to the mental hospital.

The document goes on to describe the efforts of the KGB to deport the rest of the monks on 1–3 September 1962. Some barricaded themselves in the church.

The doors had been rather stoutly built, being forged from iron, so that they could not be forced open with ordinary tools and the KGB men were quite unable to get inside the church. In the end they tried a different method. On the first floor of the residential block on the left there was an entrance leading to the library, which was situated beside the altar above the sacristy. From it one could hear the service and look into the church, as it was connected by three large embrasures and formed a kind of lateral choir. These embrasures were closed by plywood sheets only and it was to this point that the KGB and militia agents directed their efforts. They broke open the entrance doors to the library and, as the partitions also had doors which were secured from the inside only by latches, the KGB agents could easily look down into the church from above. The first floor of the library was rather higher than the altar, however, so the KGB agents, in order to get down to floor level, brought along ropes and began letting themselves down by them to the altar.

Archimandrite Samuil was standing at the altar and Captain Kirichenko, with Maximov and others, dropped right on top of it. Samuil took fright and stood motionless, unable to utter a word. They fell on the old man and dragged him to the exit. The remaining monks scattered in all directions over the church as best they could. Infuriated because they had had to use so much effort to get into the church, the KGB agents vented all their rage on the innocent monks. They seized them by the hair and beards, twisted their arms, beat them up and dragged them out to the inner courtyard where vehicles had again been parked.

All the monks in the church were thus caught, except that they failed to find Priest-monk Valeri Matkovsky. When he heard the KGB penetrating through the library into the church, he crept into a small cupboard where he used to sell candles. While searching the church they failed to find Valeri. But Maximov, when he got to the candle cupboard, remarked that they would need to take a good look here, as he had been selling candles, so he set about opening the cupboard himself and discovered Valeri. . . .

These monks were not conveyed to their places of birth, but taken to Dubno railway station in the Rovno region. All were ordered to buy tickets and travel to their place of birth, while the KGB agents stood relentlessly by and watched.

The Christian people did not remain indifferent to this, but directed their utmost efforts to protecting the persecuted brethren of the monastery. When the militiamen surrounded it, the assembled Christians managed to burst through the militia posts at the Holy Gates and get right up to the residential block. . . .

At the main entrance to the monastery hostel, close by under the windows, there was a heavy oak bench, which they grabbed and began battering in the panelling of the gates. Under the repeated heavy blows the lower panelling on the right side gave way, split open and burst completely, forming an opening, through which the Christians began to penetrate inside the block. Here a militiaman standing at the door took fright at what the Christians were doing. They dashed down the passage towards the yard, but were too late – the last of the monks had just been chased out. The militiamen, noticing the Christians bearing down on them, attacked them furiously, shouting: 'Beat them up!' Senior Sergeant Prokopchuk, Sergeant-Major Kotsyuba, Sergeant Medyany, First Lieutenants Boreiko, Yurchak and others began hurling the Christians against the walls and kicking them, while at the same time bringing the monks out through the yard. Under the assault of the militiamen the Christians again scattered in flight. Some of them were seized by the militiamen and placed under arrest; many of the beaten-up victims were sent to the Pochaev hospital. One who was particularly assiduous in maltreating the Christians was Sergeant-Major Kotsyuba. He nearly beat Maria Yarosh to death and attacked Agafia Savenok with shouts of 'Beat her, she's a priest's daughter!'. . . .

The only monks left in the monastery that day were those who held administrative posts: the temporary deputy superior, Abbot Varfolomei (Babyak), the rural dean, Abbot Vladislav, the book-keeper, Abbot Kalinnik, and a few of the very aged whom Maximov promised to take away on the next trip to an old people's home. . . . However the plans made by Maximov and others in the KGB went awry. To their astonishment the monks they had removed appeared again the following day in the monastery; they were again seized and removed, but the monks kept on returning again and again to their place in the monastery. . . . In spite of all these difficulties, services there never stopped. . . .

Three monks – Alipi Shinkaruk, Kasian Negodyuk and Isaia Yamkin, wrote an account of the acts of brutality perpetrated and took complaints to Moscow to Patriarch Alexi, to Kuroyedov at CROCA, and to Rudenko, the Prosecutor-General of the USSR. Their mission was not very successful, since the Patriarch had no rights. He gave no audiences himself and his office merely expressed regrets. At CROCA the monks were received by the head of department, Plekhanov, and two inspectors who refused to give their names, but furiously attacked the monks, saying: 'You're slandering the Soviet Government; we'll hold you criminally responsible!'

Plekhanov claimed that the petition was incorrectly formulated.

Plekhanov threw the monks' protest into a table drawer, led them off to an empty room, sat them down at separate tables, gave them paper and ink and told them to write. The monks unburdened themselves again of their griefs – it had now become second nature to them. A few old women came in from the country complaining that the local authorities had closed down the church and they asked for it to be opened. Kuroyedov's men laughed them to scorn, saying: 'What do you old grannies want with a church? Go to the cinema or have a dance in the club. Why do you want to say your prayers?'

The monks made a number of other equally fruitless approaches.

They were received by Taran, a senior solicitor. True, he no longer pretended that it was a slander. He did not doubt that the local authority had acted as stated, but merely remarked to another legal official that they had rather overdone it. It was best to ensure that there were no complaints. So it was explained to the monks that they were heading for communism, when there would be no monasteries and so there were no grounds for their complaint.

On their return to Pochaev they were interrogated and told to leave the monastery.

It was admitted that it had been a mistake to throw the monks completely out on the street – they should have been given some kind of place to live in. Every effort would be made now to send the monks to villages to work as parish priests. The official gave permission for those who had not been ordained to be made priests, on condition that they should leave the monastery. . . . Following the complaints and protests of world public opinion[12] and after repeated attempts to find some way of expelling the monks from the monastery, the local authorities temporarily left those who still had a Pochaev Monastery registration stamp in their passports to stay on, so that they were reinstated, as it were. The majority, though, had been struck off the register and so the situation arose that a large group of monks went on living there after their registration had been cancelled. . . . These monks were fined ten roubles each almost every month for continuing to live in the monastery. . . .

Monks who had served their terms of imprisonment also kept returning there, but one young novice, Grigori Unka, born in Moldavia in 1937, where he had previously been a member of one of the monasteries, did not return from prison. His mother received a telegram from the prison administration in Chertkov, where the Ternopol regional gaol was situated and where Grigori was under investigation, that her son had 'died suddenly' and she should come and take the body away (corpses of prisoners held for investigation are handed over to relatives). The mother collected the remains of her beloved martyr-son. Although the body was dead and silent, it still bore many visible marks – it was black and blue from bruises, the clothes were torn and pierced right through the side. He had never had any physical ailments and had been tortured to death in his prime at 25 years of age. May his soul rest in peace!

Throughout 1963 the situation changed little at Pochaev. Some monks returned from prison, but their situation remained precarious, since the local authorities refused to give them residence permits. An intervention from the Patriarch saying that the monks were within their rights to return there brought no material improvement. The monks continued to campaign for their rights, but in return the local authorities kept up their harassment of worshippers and intercepted supplies of food and fuel. The following incident can be documented from a published Soviet source.

The monks tried to get firewood, as all their stock was exhausted. Their representative, Priest-deacon Iosif Balyshev, bought several dozen cubic metres in the neighbouring region of Lvov and wanted to have it delivered to the monastery. . . . Balyshev hired lorries at the Dubno motor transport garage (Rovno region). When the two vehicles loaded with firewood drove up to the monastery, they were again held up by the police. The driver who had agreed to deliver the load had his licence taken away and they even had the effrontery to describe the episode, though in a distorted version, in an article in their press. V. Nadein wrote it for *Krokodil* (No. 6, 29 February 1964) under the title, 'Heating thieves.' . . .[13]

Here are further authentic facts: Marfa Antonovna Gzhevskaya, a young girl born in 1931, had taken vows of virginity and was living in Pochaev, carrying out various duties there. She had lived there since 1956. Latterly, in 1962, she had been struck off the Pochaev town residents' list for constantly visiting the monastery churches to pray, but she continued to pray there on religious festivals. The Pochaev militia and guards frequently picked up Marfa, took her to the police station and deported her from Pochaev. At the festival of the Ascension in 1964 Marfa came again to the monastery to pray and wanted to stay on in Pochaev until Trinity Sunday. Therefore by day she was at her prayers in the monastery and at night she would go to a woman she knew, Anastasia Religa, who lived at 10 Pletenka Street, and hide in her attic.

After Ascension Day some of the people had dispersed, but the police began applying all kinds of terrorist methods to repress those still left. . . . Belik and Gordeyev, with their squad of militiamen and guards, continued their non-stop efforts to track down worshippers and check what Christians were in Pochaev. On the evening of 12 June 1964 they came to the house of Anastasia Religa, made a search, and found Marfa in the attic. Belik gave orders that she should be maltreated in such a way that she would never again want to worship in Pochaev. The militiamen brutally grabbed Marfa and threw her down from the attic. Then they intimidated the owner of the flat and dragged Marfa outside into the garden. There they defiled her virgin body, pulled her out on to the road half-dead and left her there. The following day Marfa was seen by the residents and taken to hospital. She was already unconscious and she died there shortly afterwards. On learning of her death, Marfa's mother, who lived at Berezniki in the Perm region, arrived. She burst into tears and lamentations and tried, for the benefit of other Christians, to complain against the culprits. On the instructions of the police, however, the doctors diagnosed that Marfa had died from acute lung trouble, thus covering up the crime of the guilty parties. They made her mother give a signature that she would leave Pochaev immediately, so with tears in her eyes she left for home exclaiming: 'May God be their judge!' In Pochaev they similarly killed Lidia Tokmakova, of Lipovaya Street, who was constantly praising God and singing evening services in the monastery. . . . The police lay in wait at the communal lavatories and picked up those who needed to go out at night, dragging them along to the headquarters of the people's auxiliary police and dealing with them there as they liked: girls were raped, money confiscated and people beaten until they lost consciousness. And so they roamed around the monastery all night like wild beasts, showing no respect even for old age: they robbed and raped Maria Andreyevna Morozova, an aged nun, residing at the following address: Flat 4, 24 Nizhnaya Pervomaiskaya, Moscow K-203. The same happened to Maria Gerasimchuk and Iustina Korolenko. . . .

On 20 November 1964 the KGB, militia and auxiliary police again set about arresting and sentencing monks in the Pochaev Monastery. They broke into cells, removed the doors, seized the monks and rampaged through the churches and the living quarters of the monastery. The following were arrested and sentenced: Priest-monks Valerian Popovich and Vladimir Soldatov, Priest-deacon Gavriil Uglitskikh. Monk Mikhail Lonchakov, because of his age, was accorded the 'indulgence' of confinement in a mental hospital instead of being imprisoned. During those days it was impossible to get into the monastery; all the Christians were being picked up and sent to a mental hospital from where they were assigned to different places and investigated. Some were sent to prison, others were removed from Pochaev and released, on condition that they should not come back any more to Pochaev; others who were more fervent believers were kept for a long time in the mental hospital and forcibly given injections harmful to their health. Many were dispatched to other mental hospitals in Vinnitsa, Budanov and other places. Pochaev became quiet; the few monks who had survived the attack were barely audible. Many of them had to go into hiding in conditions of considerable difficulty, in order to evade further arrest and imprisonment. Some monks managed to choose a time to pass through the blockade and made an appearance again in Moscow with petitions. One was now drawn up by almost all the monks who had survived (with the exception of Avgustin, Gladarevsky's henchman) and it was addressed to all representatives of the Soviet Government. . . .

By the end of office hours the monks had managed to get themselves received by a certain Nefedov. He listened to their complaint and told them in reply, speaking on behalf of the Party Central Committee, that the latter approved of all methods of combating religion and that in no case would it ever extend protection, even though the method in question was unjust. Then he added: 'In my personal opinion all believers are psychologically abnormal people and it is entirely natural for them to be sent into mental hospitals'; generally speaking, 'it is our aim to liquidate religion as quickly as possible; for the time being we partially tolerate it for political reasons, but when a favourable political opportunity arises we shall not only close down your monastery but all churches and monasteries'. . . .

Many monks died prematurely and passed on to eternal life before their time. Yevlogi died after torture outside the monastery, as did Abbot Andrei and a number of others. Some who remained alive lost their good health. . . .

In the daytime they spy on the Christians and at night they terrorize them. On the night of 15–16 July 1965 the militiamen beat up the Christians who were taking overnight refuge in the cemetery.... Using specially prepared clubs, Captain Belik and his subordinates fell upon and beat up the Christians. They completely disfigured the face of Yevdokia Ivanovna Bogdanovskaya of Kommunarsk, Lugansk region, smashing her nose and the whole of her face and knocking out her teeth. She crawled along in a concussed state to the monastery, whence they transported her to the hospital. It is not known whether she survived. They also beat up Yekaterina Iosifovna Voloshinskaya (of 8 Panfilov Street, Lvov), Irina Anisimovna Semyonova, Maria Ivanovna Vorobyova and several others.

Amvrosi (Dovgan) and Sergi (Solomko) made further appeals for justice.

Amvrosi was then arrested and on 18 January 1966 sentenced to two years' imprisonment on the same charge as before – 'breach of passport regulations'. Sergi evaded arrest and is still living in hiding, but if they find him the same fate awaits him also. The same can be expected by other monks who are also living in hiding. It follows, therefore, that they are now doomed to lifelong imprisonment or the same kind of gradual death. We have already appealed to all Soviet organizations, asking for the restoration of our rights which have been infringed. This happened most recently at the 23rd Congress of the CPSU,[14] but we have no positive results whatsoever to record.[15]

To his defence of monasticism,* Levitin added fourteen appeals from individual monks and groups connected with Pochaev.[16] While these do not contain a great deal of new information not included in the long document partially quoted above, they provide massive

* See pp. 86–97.

confirmation of many of the points contained there. By 1965 the decision had obviously been taken to keep the monastery open and the Moscow Patriarchate attempted to allay the fears which had been expressed in the West by publishing several articles about Pochaev and allowing a few foreign visitors to go there. The vast majority of Russia's monasteries received no such publicity, however, and they have now ceased to function.

FESTIVAL AT THE POCHAEV MONASTERY

On the day of the festival itself, there were liturgies in all the churches of the monastery.

It was a beautiful, sunny autumn day. The late liturgy began at 10 a.m., but before it the clergy processed out of the Dormition Cathedral to the prior's lodging to meet Metropolitan Pimen and pay him a tribute of honour.[17]

CELEBRATIONS AT THE POCHAEV MONASTERY

Every year with great solemnity the Pochaev Monastery celebrates the acquiring of the relics of St. Iov (on 28 August, old style). For this day many clergy and worshippers came to the monastery.

This year two days before the festival the following came to the holy hill of Pochaev: Archbishop Filaret of Kiev and Galicia, the Exarch of the Ukraine; Archbishop Nikolai of Lvov and Ternopol, an honorary archimandrite of the Pochaev Monastery; Bishop Nikodim of Argentina and South America; Bishop Mefodi of Chernovitsy and Bukovina; and also about two hundred clergy from Lvov and other towns and villages.[18]

THE SEMINARIES

Although far less is known of the suppression of the seminaries than of the monasteries, such evidence as we have points to the employment of very similar direct police methods against them.

UNMASKED BY THE FACTS (Complete text)
(Anonymous)

Three years ago thirty-seven students entered the Leningrad Seminary, sixteen a year later and last year only eight. The number of students is diminishing in the seminary, not only because of a systematic reduction, but also because of a frequent refusal to become a servant of the cult. Not only one, but several dozens of former seminarists have broken with religion.

The heads of the theological schools have themselves been forced to admit these facts. Therefore they have declared that they will battle for 'every soul'. So as not to traumatize the students, it has been decided to refrain from . . . making known any unsatisfactory marks, so as to retain the students for longer in the bosom of the church.[19]

UNTIL THE BELL CEASED
(A. Ivashchenko)

Such attention [individual atheist work with theological students] has turned out to be a catastrophe for the Lutsk Theological Seminary. Its rector, Archimandrite Mefodi, complains: 'There's no first year at all, while only five are in the second; it's become difficult at the seminary . . .'[20]

TO THE WORLD COUNCIL OF CHURCHES, ODESSA[21]
(A Group of Believers)

It is very difficult to enter a seminary. The government authorities do their utmost to prevent young people from joining them. They examine incoming mail. There have been instances where requests for admission have been retained for two weeks at the post-office, while others have completely disappeared. That is not all. When a demand for admission arrives at the seminary at Zagorsk, the full name and address of the applicant are immediately communicated to Trushin, the CROCA official of the Moscow region, who demands them. The latter then sends on this information to the applicant's place of work or residence. Then he has to face a dreadful ordeal. If the applicant comes from a *kolkhoz*, he does not receive a passport (with us *kolkhozniki* are slaves to their *kolkhoz*; having no passport, they cannot leave it). If the applicant lives in a town, he is taken to task and has to undergo 're-education'. A month before the commencement of studies he is summoned to a military office, where his papers are taken for checking and retained for two months. They are returned to him after the entry examinations have finished. Sometimes it is the passport office which keeps back the applicant's papers, for without passport and military exemption certificate no-one can be accepted into the seminary.

If the applicant manages to find some clever way of leaving his place of residence, satisfying the military authorities, passing his examinations and being accepted for the seminary, even this does not signify that he can study there. After he is accepted, his papers are again sent to the government official, who can always refuse a residence permit, without which he can neither live nor study at the seminary. When this is done, the administration of the seminary itself is ordered to send the student home. Every year about twenty students are systematically refused residence permits. This year (1964) Trushin published in advance the names of those who would receive them, but later refused ten of these.[22]

4 Destruction of Parish Life

OFFICIAL ADMISSIONS

IN DEFENCE OF CULTURAL MONUMENTS
(Ye. Dorosh, P. Korin, K. Fedin, I. Erenburg and others)

On 2 June this year the sound of an explosion was heard at Ufa. The dumbfounded inhabitants gazed and saw how the Smolensk Cathedral, a most valuable historical and architectural monument, tottered, collapsed and turned into a pile of stones. It had been destroyed despite the protests of the Academy of Sciences and the Ministry of Culture of the USSR, despite the fact that there had been no special permission from the government, which is obligatory in every such instance. . . .[1]

THE PERM MONASTERY
(L. Khalif)

Hundreds of priests perform their rituals throughout the region. Neither frost nor the impassability of the roads deters the fathers from their work. If only the Perm propagandists had such zeal! . . .

'We've got a city of hard workers, but rituals which send us back into the middle ages', said the *Komsomol* members of Perm when they demanded that the cathedral should be turned into a youth club. They collected tens of thousands of signatures protesting against the hysteria in the city centre. Bishop Pavel went to Moscow and the demand of the young people has remained unsatisfied. . . .[2]

The Journal of the Moscow Patriarchate – no less – wrote in 1961:

THE LIFE OF THE STANISLAV DIOCESE
(Bishop Iosif of Stanislav and Kolomyya)[3]

From 1944 at Stanislav there existed a Russian Orthodox parish which used for its religious needs a former Armenian church adapted for Orthodox worship. The church was frequented mainly by believers from the eastern regions and also by local inhabitants who were convinced supporters of the Orthodox eastern rite. Services in the Church of the Veil were held strictly according to Orthodox ordinances and the church was a model, as it were, for all others in the Stanislav diocese. However, as a result of a bomb which exploded nearby, it suffered during the war and, despite temporary repairs, it now needed thorough restoration inside, which was beyond the resources of the local parishioners. It was decided to unite the congregation with that of the cathedral, to hand over all its property and to transfer the clergy and staff of the Church of the Veil to that of the cathedral parish.

On Sunday, 5 February. . . . the first united service of the two congregations took place. The cathedral was full of believers. . . .

. . . . Two congregations which hitherto existed independently and performed their worship in different ways have from today joined in one family, in order to glorify the Lord God with united hearts and voices. . . .[4]

SILENCED BELLS
(V. Repkin)

This church stands in the middle of the village of Nitsinsk,[5] its cupolas reaching up towards the clouds. Only now there are no crosses visible on it and the sound of bells is no more, which up to a few months ago enticed parishioners either to matins or to mass*. . .

When the news about the priest's hooliganism reached the parishioners, their grumbles were beyond bounds. The religious ardour even of the members of the *dvadtsatka*, the church's controlling body, was extinguished. Many of them . . . resigned from it and after this only a few individuals remained among the church zealots.

The church emptied, while there were more visitors than ever to the club and the library. It became crowded there. Then one of

* For the introduction of this prohibition, see p. 148.

the former believers expressed the thought: 'Why do we need a church? Wouldn't it be a good idea to hand it over as a *kolkhoz* club? Let the young people have an easier life.'

This sounded a good idea. A village meeting was called, at which it was unanimously* decided to turn the church into a cultural focal point.[6]

'THEY NURTURE NO EVIL IN THEIR HEARTS ...'
(V. Kondakov)

.... The church warden knew that in the towns and villages of the Volhynia region[7] 180 churches had been closed in recent years on the demand of the workers. ...[8]

GRASS IN THE CHURCH PORCH
(O. Kuprin)

Conversations went round the village: 'Will the church remain, or won't it?' What's the use for it if hardly anyone goes to it? ... The church had no business to be standing next door to the school. Moreover, in summer there was usually a pioneer camp in the school. Finally, before the war there wasn't a sacred building here at all. From 1939 there was a café there, with a snack bar in the chapel. The church at Yastrebino was opened by the Germans during the occupation. 'So it's an echo of the war,' ran the argument in the village. ... But the weightiest argument, which had an effect even on believers, was this: the children. ...

They all argued about religion, but finally arrived at the same conclusion – a club. .. You could argue about a church, but not about a club ... Everything was clear. It was needed – that's all there was to it.

Thus Father Nikolai was at the centre of stormy events, even though he took no part in them. During this time he finally realized that he must retire and go away. ... By now in surrounding villages they were already gathering signatures beneath an

* For a Christian view of such 'unanimous' decisions, see pp. 129–33.

application to the village *soviet* requesting the closure of the church.[9]

ON BOTH SIDES OF THE OCEAN
(V. Nekrasov)

I would not mention this sad fact of twenty years ago, if it were not that even now some of those upon whom the fate of various monuments of architecture depends were not of the opinion that any church or icon is primarily 'opium for the people' and only secondarily a work of art. About a year or eighteen months ago in a fairly influential Kiev newspaper there was an article in which it was stated that here or there it was necessary to remove certain churches and synagogues of the eleventh and twelfth centuries. They were apparently spoiling the countryside. . . . [10]

YEAR OF QUESTS, YEAR OF HOPES
(V. I. Kochemazov)

. . . . In many monuments the condition of the paintings is not satisfactory and in several cases it is extremely grave. For example, of the fifty monuments in the city of Yaroslavl and its region, twenty-five are used as warehouses. Loss of paintings is the result of this misuse of buildings. Many monuments in Vologda, Gorki, Kostroma, Vladimir, Moscow and other regions are still in poor condition. . . .

Now that the All-Russian Society for the Preservation of Historical and Cutlural Monuments is everywhere beginning its activities,* it is becoming more and more clear that a great deal of harm was done to the cause of protecting monuments by the groundless removal from the inventory of many valuable structures of antiquity in 1960-62. Agencies for the preservation of historical and cultural monuments had a difficult time during that period and even now it is not always easy to eradicate the practice that has grown up in the recent past. . . . To this day there remain cases of groundless removal and demolition of historical and

* For Talantov's view of this society, see pp. 136-7.

cultural monuments. Thus a fourteenth-century monument was destroyed in order to build a playing field for a pedagogical school in the city of Galich, Kostroma region, in September 1966.[11]

WITH BLESSINGS
(N. Siskevich) (Complete text)

Late on a January evening the inhabitants of the village of Svilo, Gluboksky district,[12] were awoken by the hooter of a fire-engine.

It began in this way. After a regular service in the local church, the chairman of the church auditing committee, Georgi Kuril-yonok, the churchwarden, Avksenti Litvinenko, and the treasurer, Fyodor Redko, dismissed the parishioners in peace and began counting the collection. They decided to squander part of it on drink in honour of the Christmas holidays.

In the village shop the servants of the cult found a considerable quantity of Moscow vodka and began a feast of celebration. Having become drunk, the revellers noticed too late that the church was enveloped in flames.

They had become so engrossed in their drinking bout that they had forgotten to put out the charcoal in the censer. This was the cause of the fire. By the time the firemen reached the scene, there was nothing they could do. Where the church had been, there was nothing but ruins and piles of ashes. It was possible to save the adjacent *kolkhoz* houses.

Vitebsk, 9 March (1968) – by telephone.[13]

There is something odd here. Why should events of early January be reported by telephone two months later? This article is reminiscent of several in the 1960–64 period. Here are two further reports from 1968.

ACTIVELY AND WITH CLEAR PURPOSE
(L. Anufriev)

In the Odessa region, for example, 210 religious congregations of various denominations have in the last decade ceased to operate and have been 'snuffed out' of their own volition. During the same period more than 37 servants of the cult and seminarians have given up religion. . . .[14]

ATHEIST PROPAGANDA AND ITS EFFECTIVENESS
(V. Drugov)

Here[15] before the revolution more than eight hundred churches, monasteries and prayer houses were operative. Now there are seventeen. . . .[16]

LAMENT FOR THE CHURCHES OF NOVGOROD

(Untitled)

One cannot remain silent about the oppression of believers and we all unite our voices and requests to open the churches. Just see how much new building there is round about; we have our share of labour in it. Towns are growing, our hearts rejoice – yet there is not one church. People have nowhere to go to pray. In the villages for dozens of kilometres round about there are no churches. In the whole of the area round Moscow you can see that there were churches at one time, for their walls are still standing. . . .

There is no record of how many churches have been converted into various store-rooms, repositories and offices, where until very recently the Holy Spirit of the Living God had his dwelling. What desecration of a sanctuary! We beg to have churches opened for those of our people who wish to pray to God. There is no harm in believers here nor reason to persecute them so. Take the Novgorod region, where at Borovichi they have closed and disbanded the monasteries and turned them into theatres. The monastery of St. James the Just has been closed and converted into a store. The cathedral has been closed, too. They have perpetrated other outrages: in 1964 they closed a church where there had been a cemetery and they turned it into a children's playground, with all sorts of amusements on top of human remains. They levelled out all the grass and made a sports club and a secular wedding hall out of the church. We, mainly women, have written complaints, we have travelled to Novgorod and even written to Moscow, but the authorities continued on their course. . . . The honourable and assiduous people have sufficient building material without having to rob the walls of the churches, in which the beauty of so much labour is enshrined. Their memory is very dear to us and we beg all of you who are present at the congress[17] to open our churches and restore them. In the whole town and district we have built one small wooden church, where people are packed in such numbers that at times it is impossible to breathe. A corner has been made for the choir, but the ceiling almost touches people's heads. There is no daylight, but the light of Christ reaches the people! They have no other consolation. Why are we separated from the church and so oppressed? Why are we separated from life also? When our common fascist enemy attacked us, we were not set aside from the communists, but they trusted us and we went to fight for our homeland. Our fathers, husbands, sons and even daughters failed to return to their own homes. They suffered martyrdom and perished for their homeland. But if they could see us, they would be horrified that now we are considered enemies of the people, mocked at our work and our labour is not respected. We are considered as of little worth in society. At school our children are considered to be beneath the children of non-believers. People fear the cross like fire. . . .[18]

THE STRANGULATION OF A DIOCESE

THE CALAMITOUS SITUATION OF THE ORTHODOX CHURCH IN THE KIROV REGION AND THE ROLE OF THE MOSCOW PATRIARCHATE
(Boris Talantov)

'The situation of the Russian Orthodox Church has been – and still is – entirely normal. . . . With God's gracious help, it is

E

quietly and confidently fulfilling its mission of salvation.' (Alexi, Patriarch of Moscow and of all Russia, 14 March 1966, Moscow).[19]

I. *The mass closing and destruction of churches in the Kirov region during the anti-religious campaign of 1959–64*

As is well-known, the anti-religious campaign of 1959–64 aimed above all at disbanding congregations *en masse* and destroying churches (prayer houses). This objective was brought about by the Council for Russian Orthodox Church Affairs (Council for Religious Affairs)[20] and its area officials, with the help of the local authorities.

The methods for shutting churches in the Kirov region were usually these. The regional official of CROCA would arbitrarily cancel the registration of the priest of the church due to be closed, or he would be transferred elsewhere. Then over a period of six to eleven months he would refuse to register any of the suggested candidates as priest for this church. When representatives from the church congregation asked him why he refused, his reply would be: 'I don't have to answer to you for my actions.' Sometimes he would simply say to believers: 'Don't keep on coming to me, begging and trying to persuade me. I'm not going to register anyone.' Quite often the official, with no further ado, would push the believers out of his room. In the period 1960–63 the Kirov regional officials of CROCA (Smirnov, Medvedev, Lyapin) arbitrarily removed twenty-one out of the eighty priests active in 1959 and registered no-one in their place.

While the church was without a priest, the local authorities would try, through intimidation, to force various members out of the *dvadtsatka* and this would be declared the disintegration of the church congregation. At the same time the regional executive committee would pass a resolution to close the church and it would assign the building to the local *kolkhoz* or town *soviet*. This resolution, contrary to existing legislation, would not be announced to the church congregation, but would be sent to CROCA. The latter, disregarding the protests of believers, would deprive the church congregation of its registration and would hand the building over to the local *kolkhoz* 'to be used as a club'. This method of closing a church was flagrantly illegal, because CROCA knew perfectly well from the written protests and emissaries of the believers that the church congregation had not disintegrated, but that the CROCA official was refusing to register any priest for the church which was being closed and that the *kolkhoz* had no need of the church building. That is why the resolution to withdraw the registration of the church congregation and hand over the church building to the *kolkhoz* or city *soviet* was not announced to the believers. The believers of many disbanded church congregations tried for many years to make the authorities show them this resolution, but they failed. Clearly these resolutions are kept in the most strict secrecy because they are flagrantly illegal.

When liquidating places of worship there would be a show of brute force. This would be carried out under the protection of the militia and auxiliary police, often at night. Believers would be forbidden to enter the church. The valuables would be removed without any inventory being made. In the Kirov region, when places of worship were liquidated, the interiors would always be barbarically destroyed, icons and holy vessels burned and all the valuables stolen.

After the destruction of a church, believers would usually over a long period of time send in a great many protests and petitions to CROCA, to the Moscow Patriarchate and the central press with the demand that the church be reinstated and its building returned.

In answer to these petitions, the believer activists, as organizers, would be subjected to various forms of repression: fines, denunciations, judicial and administrative action.

Up to the present, these petitions have had no effect; not one of the closed churches has been re-opened.

We will give a few typical examples, based on documented evidence.

> *Example 1: The closing and destruction of the church
> in the village of Roi, Arbazh district, Kirov region.*

Deep in the countryside, far from the railway and main road, stands the little village of Roi, containing the wooden Alexander Nevsky Church built in 1888. The church congregation of Roi was legally registered in 1956, having the necessary number of members and a church council. The activity of the congregation was conducted within the limits of the Soviet law. The congregation was able to finance the clergy and the upkeep of the church.

However, in 1960 the leaders of the local *kolkhoz* and village *soviet* decided to shut the church at Roi. With this in view, they first began putting pressure on the local priest, N. Shchelchkov.

Thus, on the night of 12 September 1960 (the evening before the church's festival) they called him before the village *soviet*. Those present were: the chairman of the village *soviet*, Zhuravlev, the chairman of the *kolkhoz*, P. P. Suslov, and the secretary of the party organization, I. N. Zlobin. They threatened the priest with violence if he remained in Roi. Then they went to the church porch, where some old women were spending the night because of the festival. The officials pushed all these old women out into the street at night, not even giving them time to put their shoes on. One old woman, who had lost her husband and son in the war, had to spend that cold autumn night in the street.

The CROCA official for the Kirov region, on his part, did everything he could to shut the church. Fr. Shchelchkov requested him to permit the repair of the church stove. Smirnov's answer to this was: 'To the secretary of the district committee. Do not allow the stove to be repaired.'

(It should be noted that from the beginning of 1960 church councils were forbidden to deal with any routine repairs of church buildings without the permission of the CROCA official. Some churches in the Kirov region were shut merely because the church councils had refloored the church porch. Thus it is that the congregation is unable to use its money for necessary religious purposes. This is the extent to which freedom of conscience was curtailed in 1960!)

It was at once clear from Smirnov's resolution that he had decided to shut the church at Roi.

Soon afterwards Fr. Shchelchkov received an anonymous letter threatening him with lynching if he did not leave the village. Under the pressure of these threats he did leave. . . .

After this, the *kolkhoz* leaders sent agitators into three villages to take charge of meetings. The agitators proposed that the church be shut and, although the majority present protested, it was recorded in the minutes that the believers had unanimously given it up.* The minutes were approved by Zhuravlev, chairman of the village *soviet*, in spite of the believers' protests.

On the basis of these false minutes, CROCA received a petition from the Kirov Region Executive Committee and decreed that the church should be shut and given to the *kolkhoz* as a club (although there was a new one in Roi).

On 21 December 1960 Babintsev, the secretary of the district executive committee, unexpectedly arrived in Roi with some other workers. They called up the warden, an eighty-year-old woman, announced (orally) that the church was to be closed and demanded the keys. At this point they threatened to confiscate her house if she refused to hand them over. Having seized them, they entered the church, locked themselves in and began by drinking ten bottles of sacramental wine and eating the offering (*kutya*) brought there for a requiem.

The church was destroyed by drunken machine-operators from the *kolkhoz*. Suslov ordered dumplings and alcohol and paid them five roubles an hour from *kolkhoz* funds.

When the crosses were removed from the church, Suslov did all he could to insult the believers who were standing at a distance and weeping. All the icons, holy vessels, bells and other valuables were removed without a record being made and subsequently disappeared without trace.

Five days later (26 December 1960) the believers sent protests signed by 380 of their number to L. I. Brezhnev and N. S. Khrushchev. In reply to these protests, the district prosecutor began to call in the activist believers and threaten them with various forms of repression. Thus Natalia Yakovlevna Tokareva,

* A similar resolution was reported in the Soviet press (see p. 121).

a member of the *dvadtsatka*, was summoned by him to Arbazh, eighteen kilometres away, five times in a fortnight and was threatened with imprisonment. 'If it were 1936,' he said to her, 'you'd be taken away in a black Maria.'

Indignant at these taunts, she herself handed in a complaint to the Procurator-General of the USSR on 23 January 1961. 380 believers signed a further protest and sent it to Khrushchev on 29 January 1961.

In answer to these complaints the believers received the following communication at the beginning of March from D. L. Medvedev:

'To O. S. Meteleva, Roi, Arbazh district.

'We would inform you that the statements sent by you to N. S. Khrushchev and the Procurator-General of the USSR have been received.

'We wish to explain that the Council for Russian Orthodox Church Affairs under the Council of Ministers of the USSR sees no ground for reconsidering its decision on your case.

D. Medvedev, CROCA official for the Kirov region.'

In order to gain restitution of their rights on the spot, five hundred believers from Roi walked in an orderly manner to Arbazh, the district centre, on 7 March 1961. Here they asked Babintsev to hold an official general meeting which would come to a decision over the restoration of the church congregation at Roí. Babintsev sent them first to the secretary of the district committee, Comrade Vidyakin. The latter promised to call such a meeting in Roi on 9 March and to send along Babintsev and Semyonovykh, instructor of the district committee.

On 9 March the believers met again in Roi. Instead of Semyonovykh and Babintsev from Arbazh, the chief of police, Comrade Zaitsev, came to the meeting. The believers proved to Zaitsev that the minutes, on the basis of which the church had been closed, were false and they demanded that it should be re-opened. Zaitsev agreed with their arguments about the falsity of the minutes, but about the re-opening of the church he said: 'I didn't shut it and so I won't open it, either.'

Therefore on 14 March 1961 the believers submitted a third protest to Khrushchev and also sent a letter to *Izvestia*, asking the paper to send out a correspondent to discover for himself the blatantly illegal way in which the church had been closed.

Soon after this, the district court sentenced N. Ya. Tokareva to six months' hard labour as the organizer of the believers.

Horrified at this systematic administrative repression, about four hundred believers met in Roi on 25 April 1961 and demanded that the *kolkhoz* leaders give them back their church, icons and holy vessels. The local authorities called out the militia and auxiliary police from Arbazh and towards evening managed forcibly to disperse them. The following received injuries as a result:

1. Petelin, who had lost his legs in the Second World War;
2. a woman from the village of Chekushi, whose leg was hurt;
3. Ye. K. Posazhennikova, who was dragged along the ground by her arms;
4. M. Sharova, who was pregnant at the time and was kicked in the stomach;
5. N. G. Makhina;
6. Ye. M. Khalyavina from Kirov, who happened to be in Roi; she was beaten, arrested and sentenced to a year's imprisonment. Many believers were fined.

The following took an active part in this assault:

1. Zhdanov, the district investigator;
2. Smerdov, a district militiaman;
3. Zhuravlev, chairman of the village *soviet*;
4. Kraev, a brigade-leader;
5. Starodubtsev, a storekeeper;
6. N. M. Zlobin, vice-chairman of the *kolkhoz*;
7. a cattle-breeder from the *kolkhoz*;
8. S. F. Makhnov, a repair mechanic.

Soon afterwards, the *kolkhoz* leaders destroyed the wooden church of Alexander Nevsky to its foundations, thus showing that their demand for it as a *kolkhoz* club was merely a fine-sounding excuse for shutting the church.

V. A. Kuroyedov in an interview (*Izvestia*, 30 August 1966) maintained that 'If the activity of an organization confines itself within the framework of law, it can continue to exist until such time as the believers themselves leave it.'

From the facts presented above, it is clear that the activity of the Roi church congregation did confine itself within the framework of Soviet law and that the believers did not leave it. Yet on Kuroyedov's decision, the congregation was liquidated and then forcibly dispersed by the local authorities. It should be noted that the popular unrest caused by the forcible closure of churches in the Kirov region was not confined to Roi alone. There was great dismay in Pishchalie, Orichi district, on 22 October 1961. The organizer of the believers in this village, A. G. Dolgikh, was sentenced by a people's court to two years' imprisonment (see the local newspaper, *Put k Kommunizmu* ['The Road to Communism'] 14 January 1962).

Juridical administrative repression was applied to activist believers in all the disbanded church congregations of the Kirov region.

Frequently the 'heroes' behind the closing and barbaric destruction of the churches in the Kirov region were ignorant, irresponsible and morally degenerate people. Characteristic of this was the closure and destruction of the church at Vasilkovo, Soviet district, a neighbouring village to Roi. There on the high bank of the river Vyatka stood the beautiful stone church of the Kazan Virgin built in 1798.

The 'Red October' *kolkhoz*, on the land of which Vasilkovo is situated, was then run by Arkadi Vasilievich Grebnev. During his short period of control over the *kolkhoz* he built himself a luxurious private residence with many outhouses in Vasilkovo. He ran the *kolkhoz* like a wilful petty tyrant; he was drunk without restraint for days on end and all the year round he led an immoral life.

The following fact is an example of his pig-headedness. He once entered a shop and saw pensioner-members of the *kolkhoz* queuing for bread. He looked wildly at them and then ordered the shop assistant: 'Don't sell any bread to these parasites.'

Wishing to win the approval of the regional authorities then waging their campaign to shut churches, Grebnev began to attempt to close down the church of the Kazan Virgin and hand it over to the *kolkhoz* as a cultural centre.

Kuroyedov, in spite of the protests of the congregation, handed the church over to the *kolkhoz*. Taking advantage of this, Grebnev brutally destroyed it in August 1962 and appropriated some of the church valuables.

Of course, no cultural centre was ever created out of it. Now it is only a disfigured skeleton.

Example 2: The closure and destruction of the church in the village of Korshik, Orichi district, Kirov region.

The large stone church of St. Zosima and St. Sava, built in 1777, stands on a highway far from any town.

In the Kirov region (its area is three times the size of Holland, but its population density is twenty times lower) before the revolution there were more than five hundred churches, of which more than a hundred were built in the eighteenth century. As a result of extensive destruction during the 'thirties, only seven of all these latter remained intact, one of which was the church of St. Zosima and St. Sava at Korshik. It was not shut under Stalin. Because of its beauty, grandeur, paintings and the high quality of workmanship apparent in its carved iconostases, this church was the greatest remaining example of eighteenth-century church architecture in the Kirov region.

The *dvadtsatka* and church council of the religious congregation at Korshik were registered and they were composed of the correct number of members. The congregation kept the church of St. Zosima and St. Sava in model condition; it was a jewel of the local landscape. The church council met the compulsory and voluntary expenses promptly. They gave contributions to the peace fund and to the Patriarchate. The church's income was good. The church council also acquitted itself precisely and

E 2

irreproachably of all the duties demanded from it by the ecclesiastical and civil authorities. In short, the church council's activity confined itself within the framework of Soviet law. But all this did not prevent the congregation from being disbanded and the church of St. Zosima and St. Sava from being closed.

From the beginning of 1960 the local authorities in Orichi began energetically to shut and destroy churches situated in their district. Using brute force, they quickly shut the churches in the villages of Monastyrshchina, Pishchalie, Ilgan and Adyshevo. When the churches were being closed, their interiors were brutally destroyed, the icons, iconostases, ancient liturgical books, holy vessels were burnt and other valuables stolen. This wave of vandalism did not spare even the church of St. Zosima and St. Sava at Korshik.

On 9 October 1961 Medvedev for no reason deprived D. L. Lozhkin, priest of the church, of his registration and on the following day Sergei Stepanovich Ponomaryov, chairman of the village *soviet*, one of the heroes of this story, stole 5,800 roubles (in present reckoning) of church funds and put his own lock on the church, in spite of a protest lodged by the church council of the officially existing congregation.

Following this, members of the church council repeatedly, over a period of four months, travelled the 55 kilometres to Kirov to see Medvedev and asked him to register a priest for their church. Many candidates were put forward for registration. In particular, the church council proposed that an old priest, V. K. Sergiev, who lived at Korshik, should be registered. But Medvedev, without explanation, refused to register any of those put forward and behaved most offensively towards the representatives of the believers. It was clear that, having acted arbitrarily, Medvedev was playing for time in order illegally to close and destroy the church.

He closed more churches in the Kirov region than any other CROCA official. He began behaving like a hooligan in the discharge of his duties. He thumbed his nose at elderly believers, called them idiots, insulted them in obscene language and in the end simply threw them out of his office without giving them an opportunity to speak. It was said of him: 'Medvedev roars at believers in his office like a bear in its den.'[21]

Convinced that Medvedev's actions were of an unbearably arbitrary nature, the Korshik church congregation between January and September 1962 five times sent their representatives to the CROCA headquarters in Moscow with complaints about this and with the request that a priest should be registered. At the end of September 1962 the following visited CROCA: Agafia Mikhailovna Korchemkina, a member of the *dvadtsatka*, and a believer, Tatiana Ivanovna Petukhova. An employee of CROCA said to them: 'Don't worry, your church is not shut and won't be shut, as it's an architectural monument. Wait a few months and a priest will be registered, the padlock removed and the money returned.'

After such an assurance the church council and believers of Korshik hopefully awaited the registration of a priest. Again at the beginning of March 1963 the new CROCA official, I. D. Lyapin, promised to register a priest in the near future.

It was soon discovered, however, that these assurances and promises were pure deception.

On 21 March 1963 a workers' brigade, headed by a representative of the Orichi District Executive Committee and Ponomaryov, visited Korshik. They began by drinking up the church wine. Fortified by it, they began to tear down the icons, hack the highly artistic carved iconostases with axes and they used mallets to smash the precious chandeliers and other holy vessels. All the icons, the iconostases of the two side-chapels of the winter church, the gonfalons and all the ancient liturgical books were burnt. The carved iconostasis of the winter church was pulled down and lay on the floor until 1966. Vestments, linen, flour, candles, holy oil and other valuables were simply stolen. In particular, Ponomaryov appropriated the green paint and drying oil which had been laid in by the church council for painting the roof of the church. Feeling beyond retribution, Ponomaryov painted his own house outside and in so that the act of theft is irrefutably visible to all even now. He also obtained the church flour and much else. On

27 September 1963 he and the director of the oil factory sawed off the crosses from the top of the domes.

Later, under the pretext of turning the church into a club, the destruction of this architectural monument was carried further forward. The stoves were broken, the window bars were sawn off and holes were knocked through the outside. No club was created, but a disfigured hooligans' lair. To adapt a church building into a modern club would cost at least twice as much as to build a new club. The destruction of the church of St. Zosima and St. Sava is an act of wild vandalism.

In *Izvestia* during April and August 1962 articles were printed calling for the preservation of monuments of church architecture and for the punishment of those who were needlessly destroying them. In answer to these I sent to this newspaper in February 1963 a long letter entitled, 'On the mass destruction of monuments of church architecture in the Kirov region'. In it I first of all briefly enumerated the main cultural monuments in the Kirov region which had been needlessly destroyed in the 'thirties; then I informed them of the monuments barbarically destroyed in 1960–63. Basing myself on irrefutable facts, I described the criminally negligent attitude of the local authorities to ancient and culturally valuable monuments. I asked the government newspaper to intervene without delay to put an end to this wave of destruction and to save the little that remained in the Kirov region. For the preservation and restoration of monuments of church architecture I suggested they employ Christians, who alone and without any government grant could excellently restore all the churches, ancient icons and other artistic objects of the past.

Two years after my letter had been written, an article was published in *Komsomolskaya Pravda* on 4 June 1965[22] by V. Peskov, entitled 'The Fatherland', in which the author called for the creation of volunatry societies to preserve historical and cultural monuments. These were quickly organized. But in forming these societies the following fact was intentionally ignored, as did Peskov in his article: without the co-operation of Christians it is impossible to preserve, let alone to restore, monuments of church architecture. It is naïve to think that those who up till now have been teaching that the 'hotbeds of obscurantism' must be destroyed should now start restoring church buildings in good faith. As the facts reveal, the Kirov Society for the Preservation of Historical and Cultural Monuments is inclined to obstruct the function suggested by its name. For this reason, my letter is still relevant at the present time.

It was received by the editors on 21 March 1963 and the church of St. Zosima and St. Sava was destroyed on 20 November of that year. In the summer and autumn of 1963 many other outstanding examples of eighteenth- and nineteenth-century church architecture were barbarically destroyed.

The ruination of the stone St. Basil's Church at Baisa, Urzhum district, built in 1865, deserves special attention. Stylistically this church is an exceptional example of nineteenth-century architecture. On 5 January 1963 Lyapin visited this church with unpleasant intentions. The service register was kept by N. N. Kamenskikh, an acolyte, who had twice prevented the church from being shut. In the autumn of 1962 he was summoned to the military recruiting office at Kotelnich. During his absence this register was kept by the only priest at this church, P. I. Maramzin, because the members of the church council were not very literate. Lyapin seized upon this as a 'crime'. The priest was deprived of his registration for five months, as a result of which no services could be held between 5 January and 5 June.

The church council sent a complaint about Lyapin's arbitrary action to Khrushchev on 20 January 1963, but it received no answer.

At the end of June Fr. Maramzin asked Lyapin to re-register him and allow him to take services, but the latter, with no explanation, refused. Nevertheless, the believers continued to hope that Lyapin would register their priest and that services would be resumed again soon.

On 25 July 1963 the warden and watchman were sitting in the church porch and quietly drinking tea. Suddenly some represenatatives of the Urzhum District Executive Committee entered

with militiamen. They knocked over the table, throwing all the
tea things on to the floor, and rudely pushed the warden and
watchman out of the porch. They then drank up the sacramental
wine and began to destroy the interior of the church. Books and
icons were burned and all valuables were taken away.

Altogether in 1963 nine churches were destroyed in the Kirov
region. Thus the appeal to *Izvestia* to intervene and stop this wave
of destruction unfortunately had no effect.

The Orthodox Christians of Korshik sent four complaints to
Khrushchev in 1963, as a result of which the organizers were severely
threatened.

The facts described demonstrated even to uneducated believers
that this organized administrative pressure against them was being
organized with the knowledge of Khrushchev himself, who was
using these means to 'root out' the Christian religion from the
USSR.

Therefore the believers of Korshik and of other places where
churches had been closed greeted the news of Khrushchev's
removal from power with joy and in great hope they submitted
to A. N. Kosygin a request for the re-establishment of the congregation's rights. It was signed by 111 believers and was received
in Moscow on 4 December 1964.

On 19 December 1964 Lyapin read to A. M. Korchemkina
what purported to be a reply to this: 'Convince Korchemkina
that however much fuss she makes the church will not be opened.'

The Korshik believers were not satisfied with this answer and
sent a new complaint to Kosygin signed by 477 of their number.
It was received in Moscow on 21 March 1965.

In May S. S. Ponomaryov gave a verbal answer to Ye. I.
Shchennikova, a member of the *dvadtsatka*: 'If you sign any more
petitions for the opening of the church, you'll be given according
to your deserts – either a couple of years in prison or exile for
good.'. . .

*   *   *

From 1960 to 1964 in the Kirov region 40 churches out of 75 which had been functioning in 1959 (53%) were forcibly and arbitrarily shut. Seven wooden prayer houses were completely destroyed, one stone church (St. Theodore's in Kirov) was blown up, while in other closed churches the interiors were broken up, icons, books and sacred vessels were burned and the buildings themselves disfigured. Now, for the most part, the desecrated remains of these closed churches are used for nothing and as they stand with gaping windows they are gradually being destroyed by the elements. The Society for the Preservation of Ancient Cultural and Historical Monuments has no funds even to prevent further deterioration. . . .

The mass closure of churches occurred in other regions, too. Over this same period in the whole Soviet Union more than ten thousand churches were shut – half of all those open after the war.* The examples selected show that the churches did not close of their own accord because people had abandoned the Christian faith, but they were illegally closed under organized administrative pressure. . . .

A young man, Ivan Pavlovich Sergeyev, from Malmyzhka, Kirov region, wanted to enter the Zagorsk Theological Seminary in 1961 and submitted the necessary documents to it. At the end of July he received a call from Moscow to go for an examination, so he resigned from his work and began to prepare for the journey. Although he was preparing secretly, this still became known somehow to the local authorities. He was summoned to the town *soviet* and warned that unless he abandoned his intention he would be exiled as a parasite. He dissented from this warning, as it was illegal. On the evening of the same day he was arrested. The next morning, after a three-minute summary hearing, he was given an illegal sentence – three years' exile under the parasite laws to do lumbering work in the north of the Kirov region. Complaints were of no avail, for the local authorities had had him for a long time on their list as an activist believer. . . .

In August of that very year the same happened to another

* Cf. pp. 199–200.

young man, Pyotr Yegdarov, from Potniki, Yaron district, Kirov region. . . . The local CROCA official shut the church at Potniki and removed the priest's registration for having prepared Yegdarov for his entry into the theological seminary.

The headmistress of the primary school at Tryokhrechie lost her job for defending the wife of the local priest who was being evicted from her house.

II *The role of the Moscow Patriarchate in the mass closure of churches*

In order to understand correctly the anti-religious campaign of 1959–64 as a whole, it is essential to clarify the part played in it by the bishops and the Moscow Patriarchate.

Many priests from churches which had been shut supported the legal rights of the church communities. But there were also some who, in league with the CROCA officials, clearly aided the shutting of churches and the decline of church life. The majority of priests, however, took a neutral line during this campaign. But the activity of all priests is completely dependent on the leadership of the bishops and the Moscow Patriarchate.

From the beginning of 1960 a leading part in the Moscow Patriarchate was played by the young Archimandrite Nikodim, who over three years rose step by step up the hierarchical ladder until in 1963 he became a metropolitan. He represented the entire Russian Orthodox Church abroad. The rapid promotion of this young man is causing justifiable astonishment.

Apart from Patriarch Alexi, another influential figure in the Patriarchate from the beginning of the anti-religious campaign was Metropolitan Pimen. In recent years the young Archbishop Alexi, who is in charge of the business administration of the Moscow Patriarchate, has also been playing a role of importance. These supreme princes of the church have been directing all the Patriarchate's activities. Therefore it is possible to judge the part played by the Patriarchate in the anti-religious campaign of 1959–64 from the actions and pronouncements of these men.

The role of the Moscow Patriarchate and of the diocesan

bishops in it was correctly described in the letter of Frs. N. Eshliman and G. Yakunin to the Patriarch in December 1965.*

The church councils and believers whose churches had been shut began first of all to turn to the bishops for advice and help. It is important to note that in most country congregations the believers are uneducated and need legal help, obtainable either from CROCA officials or from diocesan bishops. But from the beginning of 1960 the officials took a hostile stand towards church organizations and became the main instigators of the closing of churches and the persecution of believers. Therefore the latter turned to the bishops for help and advice. As has been shown, the officials secured the closing of churches by first dismissing the priest and then refusing to register another. According to Soviet law this is an arbitrary act. Thus the bishops – and even more the Moscow Patriarchate – could, on legal grounds, have opposed these arbitrary acts and then there is no doubt that many of the churches would not have been shut. Yet right from the start of the anti-religious campaign, the bishops (with a few exceptions) completely dissociated themselves from any struggle for believers' legal rights.

When the believers of a church from which the priest had been illegally dismissed approached the bishop with the request that a new priest be appointed, the bishop would send them to the regional CROCA official for his permission to register one of the suggested candidates. The official, without any explanation, would refuse to register any of them. The bishop then would tell the believers: 'I've no more candidates and if the official won't register them, then I can do nothing more. Look for a priest yourselves.' When the astonished believers said that they would submit a complaint to CROCA or the Patriarchate, the bishop would answer: 'Only don't involve me, please. I didn't give you any advice and won't do so.' When the believers from closed churches addressed the Patriarchate by letter or by sending representatives to complain of the official's arbitrary act, the Patriarchate would give the following short answer: 'On the question

* See pp. 204–21.

of appointing a priest, apply to the bishop.' When, however, the believers addressed the Patriarchate with a carefully-argued complaint about the illegal closing and destruction of the church and asked for support in restituting their legal rights, then the Patriarchate remained silent.

Soon the bishops completely stopped seeing believers in person and communicated with them only through secretaries. When believers asked that a priest be appointed, the bishop, through a secretary, would send them on to the official. The latter would say: 'I'm not going to appoint any old priest. Let the bishop give the order and I'll do the registering.' So the believers would return to the bishop, whose secretary would pass on the message: 'You find a priest yourselves, I haven't any. If the official will register him, then I'll give the order.'

Thus on any normal reasoning the responsibility for all this red-tape over the appointment of priests lies with the bishops and the Moscow Patriarchate – so also does the Moscow Patriarchate bear responsibility along with CROCA for the mass closure of churches.

Soon reliable rumours were circulated that some bishops were themselves actively involved in the closing of churches.

Of great advantage to the campaign was the circular produced by the Moscow Patriarchate on the need to shut churches with small incomes and to amalgamate them with other parishes. The bishops abused this circular and closed many churches where the congregations were quite able to maintain their place of worship and clergy. Thus in the autumn of 1962 the congregation of St. Theodore's Church in Kirov was, with the agreement of the clergy, merged with that of St. Seraphim's Church. The building itself was then destroyed and thrown into the river Vyatka. At the beginning of 1964 Bishop Ioann of Kirov shut the prayer house in the settlement of Rudnichnoye, which had been built by believers themselves in 1947. Officially this was described as merging one church with another situated forty kilometres away! The Patriarchate never answered the many complaints about the bishop's illegal action sent by the believers of Rudnichnoye.

Believers soon observed that the Patriarchate and bishops not only entirely avoided protecting believers' legal rights, but actively supported every measure taken by the civil authorities against the church.

In the spring of 1964 Metropolitans Nikodim and Pimen made official statements when abroad, denying the existence of religious persecution in the USSR and confirming that the churches were being shut because of the numbers of people who were voluntarily abandoning their faith. These statements became known to believers in the USSR through the BBC.

It follows that the leaders of the Patriarchate did not dare come out with such statements before Russian believers – a clear indication of their falsity. It is now clear to many believers why Metropolitan Nikodim reached the top of the hierarchical ladder so quickly.

The complicity of the bishops in the closing of churches and in the disruption of church life became clear to believers in the Kirov region as a result of the activity of Bishop Ioann, a protégé of Pimen and Nikodim. From his first day in Kirov at the end of 1962 he became actively involved in shutting churches and destroying church life. From the end of 1963 only the malicious intent of Bishop Ioann kept the closure of the churches going. In many churches he replaced strong Christian priests by drunkards. Often in churches he himself behaved outrageously and like a hooligan. He threatened to dismiss any priest who dared disobey the oral directives of the CROCA official. It is extraordinary that he should always have played the ludicrous part of some state functionary. For example, in February 1965 he launched a two-hour tirade against a church warden, shaking his fists, and shouting: 'I'll send you off to the NKVD.' He not only closes churches, but destroys the faith in the hearts of many. The Kirov believers sent a great many letters to the Moscow Patriarchate demanding that Bishop Ioann be immediately dismissed. None received an answer.

In February 1966 a representative of the Kirov believers visited the Patriarchate with another complaint about Bishop Ioann. In

his presence representatives of the Tula believers strongly protested against the appointment of Metropolitan Antoni to the see
of Tula.[23] His interest aroused, the man from Kirov asked one of
the Patriarchate employees: 'Who's this Metropolitan Antoni?'
He answered: 'Your Bishop Ioann is chicken-feed compared to
Metropolitan Antoni – he's sent many people to prison.' But the
Patriarchate leaders do not remove either Bishop Ioann or
Metropolitan Antoni. The Patriarchate employee told the Kirov
emissary: 'Bishops are appointed and dismissed by the civil
authorities and not by the Patriarchate. Therefore the Patriarchate
cannot of its own accord dismiss Bishop Ioann from the Kirov
diocese.'

All this reveals the close connection between the Patriarchate
and CROCA and the open disregard for the law on the separation
of church and state. The leaders of the Moscow Patriarchate aim
at turning all bishops and priests into obedient tools of CROCA.

On 8 and 9 October 1966 the BBC broadcast an interview of
Metropolitan Nikodim with a Catholic newspaper on the subject
of the letters of Frs. Eshliman and Yakunin. In it Metropolitan
Nikodim categorically stated that, with a few exceptions, ten
thousand churches in the USSR had shut of their own accord
through lack of funds. Clearly one is expected to interpret it thus:
influenced by atheist propaganda, people have become non-
believers, church congregations have broken up and the few
remaining believers could not keep up the churches.

If Metropolitan Nikodim had made such a statement before
Russian believers, they would have called him a bare-faced liar.
Even the well-known Soviet jurist, G. Z. Anashkin, wrote:
'Educational work among believers has in some areas been replaced
by crude administrative measures, which arouse only discontent
and anger in them. Reactionary groups abroad are making use of
this situation in their anti-Soviet propaganda. . .'(*Sovetskoye
Gosudarstvo i Pravo* ['The Soviet State and Law'] No. 1, 1965).*

Why then did V. A. Kuroyedov, in an interview,[24] make no
bones about praising Patriarch Alexi and the leadership of the

* See pp. 41–3 for fuller text.

Patriarchate? Because by what they have done they have concretely aided the closing of churches and the undermining of church life within our country. Before the face of the whole world they have borne false witness about the state of the church.

III *Illegal restrictions imposed on the activity of existing church congregations*

The anti-religious campaign of 1959–64 was aimed primarily at the mass closure of churches and secondarily at limiting the activity of open churches in various ways, so as to undermine religious life. These restrictions were made possible because the church leadership and its councils became unconditional instruments for carrying out the oral dictates of regional and district CROCA officials*. But it took time and much violent effort. The officials obtained unrestricted power over the church congregations, firstly thanks to misuse of the law on registration† and secondly thanks to the complicity of the Moscow Patriarchate and the bishops' refusal to become involved in the struggle for believers' rights. Moreover, some bishops – for example Bishop Ioann of Kirov – obliged their priests unconditionally to accept all the officials' dictates. Bishop Ioann announced to the priests in his diocese that anyone who disobeyed the officials' orders would be dismissed.

Misusing the law on registration, the officials began off their own bat to dismiss (cancel the registration of) priests, to transfer and appoint them. Thus in the Kirov region over the stated period CROCA officials cancelled the registration of 21 priests (25%) and did not register one in their place. What is more, they cancelled the registrations of strong priests, but left those who were weak or immoral. . . .

Further, the regional and district CROCA officials, misusing the law on registration, have categorically been refusing to register new members of the *dvadtsatka*, which prevents believers being able to take a positive part in the activities of the church congregations.

* Cf. p. 196. † Cf. pp. 190–1.

Thanks to this, the majority of believers are now no more than disarrayed visitors at services who have been deprived of their parish organization.

Moreover the regional and district CROCA officials have been arbitrarily cancelling the registration of churchwardens, members of the church councils and even members of the *dvadtsatki*. Often they themselves have been appointing the wardens and church council members whom they want.[25] By these arbitrary means they have managed to obtain wardens and church council members who unconditionally obey all the oral dictates and who are sometimes immoral. There are even drunkards, thieves and traitors among them. Let us illustrate the above with two examples.

In 1963 at Kotelnich, Kirov region, the CROCA official removed the respected warden of the local church, a man chosen by the faithful, and in his place he appointed a drunkard and thief who by his actions soon caused the church to be temporarily shut. . . .

On 10 August 1966 the vice-president of the Vladimir[26] City Executive Committee, T. D. Nikolaev, demanded to see the president of the auditing commission at the Dormition Cathedral in Vladimir, A. I. Sokolova, and announced: 'You are no longer a member of the *dvadtsatka*.'

A list of others excluded is appended.

The church congregations are now represented by the church councils, most of which have been appointed by CROCA officials. These manage the affairs of the congregations without the knowledge of the believers and under the complete control of CROCA. And so from 1960 onwards the power of the Russian Orthodox Church, contrary to the law on the separation of church and state, gradually fell into the hands of CROCA (now the Council for Religious Affairs) and its local officials. CROCA made use of this power firstly to close an enormous number of churches and secondly to restrict in various ways the activity of open churches.

1. *Restrictions on church sermons*

The Christian sermon should be closely linked with contemporary life. It should not only teach the basic doctrines but unmask present-day sins, teach people the Christian life and protect the faith from the attacks of atheists. However, many priests in the Kirov diocese, afraid of losing their registration, began from 1960 turning sermons into scholastic moral treatises, divorced from contemporary life and the ideological struggle between atheism and the Christian religion. Of course such sermons can have no effect on a congregation. They are harmless even to the ignorant and coarse propaganda which we have today.

The situation now is that over the last few years priests in the Kirov diocese, on Bishop Ioann's orders, have had to submit their sermons in written form to a CROCA official.

2. *Beggars driven from church and the ringing of bells forbidden*

From 1950 CROCA officials have forced priests and church councils to chase beggars out of church buildings and precincts. Afraid of losing their registration, priests would often call from the pulpit to have beggars thrown out, so they have broken one of the most important teachings of the Christian faith. The church councils and other doubtful people heard these orders and often with astounding harshness pushed beggars and poorly-dressed people right off church premises. Sometimes they even struck them. The Kirov believers addressed a letter to Patriarch Alexi on 20 November 1963, in which they asked him to stop these harsh acts by issuing a special missive, but he maintained a deathly silence and the evictions of beggars from places of worship were repeated many times.

After 1963 the militia and auxiliary police organized several round-ups of beggars while a service was being held in St. Seraphim's Church, the only one in Kirov. Before the eyes of a crowd of believers, auxiliary policemen shoved these unfortunate people out of the church, shaking the kopecks from their pockets, and instead of a receipt gave them a good punch. Even the young women auxiliaries rummaged through their pockets. Among the beggars who collect alms by St. Seraphim's Church there is Ivan Ilich Bronnikov, a sick old man of 73. He receives no pension and has no relations. Therefore for him alms are his only means of livelihood. The district militiaman, Ananin, twice took away his money with no receipt.

From the beginning of 1961 bells were not allowed to be rung anywhere. This restriction aimed at weakening the influence which religious traditions and customs have over people. But bell-ringing is an essential part of worship. Therefore this ban contradicts §124 of the Soviet Constitution.* There are only small bells left in churches now and these cannot be heard beyond the immediate vicinity. Consequently there is nothing to justify this ban.

3. *Believers banned from spending the night in church porches*

All churches have porches where believers who have come long distances can rest and spend the night. There is a particular need for them in villages where there are only a few houses.

From 1960 CROCA officials, trying to make church-attendance more difficult, ordered all church councils to forbid believers resting and especially spending the night in church porches. The councils obeyed, in fear that their church would be shut. . . . As a result many elderly believers were deprived of the possibility of visiting a church, especially in the autumn and winter. . . .

4. *Restrictions on service times in country churches*

From 1960 CROCA officials (the secretaries of the district executive committees) banned day-time services in open churches of the Kirov region (Kirov itself excepted) between 1 May and 1 November (in some places 15 May – 15 November). They allowed them only between 10 p.m. and 5 a.m. They threatened to close

* See p. 16.

down any churches where this was disobeyed. In the majority of districts this restriction was imposed orally, but in some a written order was sent, of which this is an example:

'. . . . To the priest of the Belokholunitsky Cemetery Church, A. A. Tashevsky.

'Now that work in the fields has begun in the district, the executive committee of the *soviet* allows services to be held from 10 p.m. to 5 a.m. from 15 May to 15 November 1961.

A. Yedigarev, secretary of the executive committee of the the district *soviet.*'

Talantov claims that the excuse about agricultural needs is a feeble one, since clubs and cinemas were not subject to similar restrictions.

5. *Services at home banned without special permission*

In the country areas of the Kirov region from 1959 and in the towns from 1960, CROCA officials orally forbade priests, under threat of losing their registration, to hear confessions, give communion or anoint the seriously ill at home or to take any other services in private houses without special permission from the local authorities (the chairman of the village *soviet* or secretary of the town *soviet*). This restriction is still in force.

Then follows a quotation from Frs. Eshliman and Yakunin* and an account of objections made to this rule in the Kirov diocese.

There is obviously a purpose behind this restriction: the alienation of the priest from his flock. The local authorities, when deciding on permission for a sick communion at home, ask to see the sick person's passport, find out whether any children live there and often refuse permission. Moreover, the relatives of the sick person have to spend much time and trouble in the process. Therefore to obtain permission in time is impossible in practice and the sick die without having their wishes fulfilled. This has constantly been grieving believers deeply.

To take away a dying man's last comfort is a heartless cruelty.

* See p. 34.

To forbid the sacraments in the home without special permission is an intolerable restriction on freedom of conscience which arouses anger and protest from believers.

6. Children and young people banned from services

On 9, 10 and 11 August 1963 large groups of auxiliary police surrounded the only existing church in Kirov from 6 a.m. to 4 p.m. and prevented women with children and also teenagers from entering the church. But this use of force had the opposite effect. The women bravely struggled hand to hand with the auxiliary police and easily broke through this cordon. The latter realized that to fight openly with women and children was shameful, so on 11 August at 10 a.m. they all left the battlefield. The believers rejoiced at this victory, but their joy was short-lived.

The CROCA official for the Kirov region only had to tell the priest of St. Seraphim's Church not to hear confessions from school children or to give them communion and this was immediately acted upon without any explanation being given to believers. Completely under the control of the official and Bishop Ioann, the priest was either forced silently to obey any oral directive from the official or to abandon his ministry at the church. . . . This restriction is still in force today in the Kirov region. . . .

7. Pilgrimages to holy places banned

From 1960 the local authorities banned believers from putting up memorials to those whom they revere as saints or visiting or tending their graves. After this decree of the local authorities, many such graves were destroyed to prevent believers visiting them.

Thus in the city of Kirov the *soviet* destroyed the graves of Priest-monk Stefan Fileisky and Mother-Superior Fevronia, who are revered by local believers. In Yaransk, Kirov region, the town *soviet* destroyed the grave of Priest-monk Matvei and with the aid of the militia prevented groups of believers at festivals visiting the cemetery where he is buried.

These are intolerable acts of force. Are people in our country forbidden to visit, either alone or in groups, the graves of Pushkin, Lermontov, Tolstoi and other writers? Why should believers not be allowed to visit the graves of those whom they consider great men? What would the atheists say if the London municipality decided to destroy Karl Marx's grave?

Similarly, from the beginning of 1960 a general ban was imposed on group pilgrimages to places where there had previously been chapels, churches, monasteries or springs regarded by believers in particular areas or throughout the country as sacred places. Before the Revolution pilgrimages were a general phenomenon. Thousands of believers from the most distant parts of the country set off on foot or using any available transport to the Solovki Monastery, the Monastery of the Caves at Kiev, the Sarov Monastery, Mount Athos and the Holy Land (Palestine).

Apart from this, each region had its own holy places where, according to historical tradition, on certain dates thousands of pilgrims would arrive. In the Vyatka land (now the Kirov region), every year from 1460 onwards Christians would leave Khlynov (later Vyatka and from 1934 known as Kirov) with the icon of St. Nicholas of Velikoretskoye (1383) and go to the village of that name on the Velikaya river. . . .

Every year from 1961, between 3 and 10 June members of the militia and auxiliary police would be placed along all the roads leading from St. Seraphim's Church in Kirov to Velikoretskoye. They would terrorize the people, brazenly chase after old men and women, take them in and fine them simply for quietly and peaceably walking along the road to Velikoretskoye. The official reason behind this fight against pilgrimages was that they were hindering work in the village collective. Meanwhile no less than a thousand healthy auxiliary police are unemployed for a whole week while chasing after old men and women.

In the local paper, *Kirovskaya Pravda*, an article has usually been published before the beginning of the pilgrimage, in which honourable believers are called rogues, deceivers and charlatans. Thus on 1 June 1961 there was an article in this paper by P.

Smirnov, 'Pilgrimage Business'. This is what the author said about a number of those taking part: 'I will just say this – they are all not at all respectable and are morally degenerate'. . . .

Using the militia to fight against pilgrimages is not only stupid but an intolerable restriction on a citizen's freedom. . . .

What was the Moscow Patriarchate's reaction to this ban? Patriarch Alexi issued a proclamation in which he directly forbade pilgrimages to holy places.

Bishop Ioann in his servility outdid even the atheists here. In his notice to the believers of the Kirov region on 20 May 1964 he stated that pilgrims moving along the road from Kirov to Velikoretskoye 'were destroying all the crops on their way like locusts'. For the sake of justice, it should be stated that even the most fanatical atheists never slandered believers so stupidly.

Note

In November 1966 a group of Kirov believers addressed a complaint to the administrator of the Moscow Patriarchate about the anti-church activity of Bishop Ioann and making an urgent request for this unworthy prelate's removal from his see.

In reply, a representative of the Patriarchate stated that Bishop Ioann would remain in his diocese, since CROCA was categorically opposed to his replacement.

A few days later, on 17 November 1966, Bishop Ioann suddenly died.

10th November 1966[27]

The surprising sequel to the initiative of Boris Talantov and other Kirov Christians in making their case known is found in the Epilogue.*

ANONYMOUS LETTERS

The above letter by Talantov had been shortly preceded by a very similar one which he had written and which was signed by twelve

* See pp. 332–4.

laymen from the Kirov diocese. We quoted an extract from it on pp. 60–1. Soon after the publication of the first in Paris, Metropolitan Nikodim travelled to London and made the following statement at a press-conference:

I am prepared to swear to you here that this letter does not exist in the original. At the Patriarchate we have a type-written copy of it, but there isn't a single signature. It's quite clear, then, that it's unsigned – it's an anonymous letter. Therefore I would like to take this opportunity of requesting you gentlemen of the press not to place too much trust in anonymous letters.[28]

TO HIS HOLINESS PATRIARCH ALEXI OF MOSCOW AND ALL RUSSIA
(Boris Talantov)

On 25 February 1967 the BBC transmitted a tape-recorded interview with Metropolitan Nikodim, in which he answered questions put to him abroad. He stated that the open letter sent to you by twelve Christians of the Kirov diocese, received by the Patriarch in August 1966 and which had become known abroad, was anonymous, since it was type-written and not signed – although at the end the names and addresses of the twelve were given. Metropolitan Nikodim claimed that this letter did not deserve credence and that nothing happened in the Kirov diocese corresponding to what was described in the letter. He even said he was ready to give his oath in support of the truth of these words.

. . . . Metropolitan Nikodim's assertion that this letter was anonymous and did not deserve credence is a shameless lie calculated to prevent those who signed the letter from having the opportunity of exposing this falsehood abroad. But Metropolitan Nikodim, like all the atheists, disregards the words of the Saviour: 'For there is nothing hid, which shall not be manifested.' Therefore no lie of Metropolitan Nikodim can conceal for long the truth about the mass closure of churches and the persecution of believers in 1960–64 which was set out in that letter and with even greater detail and thoroughness in a letter to *Izvestia*.

While Metropolitan Nikodim was assuring credulous people abroad that the open letter from the Kirov diocese was anonymous and that the people who signed it did not exist, the Kirov region KGB office was summoning me on 14 February about the same letter and that written to *Izvestia*. There I gave written confirmation that I was the author of both and consequently I am answerable before society and the state for the truth of their contents. Instead of defending the truth, the faith and his fellow Christians, Metropolitan Nikodim is lying and slandering his brothers.

St. John the Divine says: 'In this the children of God are manifest, and the children of the devil: whosoever doeth not righteousness is not of God, neither he that loveth not his brother' (1 John 3:10).

Metropolitan Nikodim is not worthy to bear the high office of Metropolitan of the Orthodox Church.*

19 March 1967.[29]

SOLZHENITSYN

ALONG THE OKA
(Alexander Solzhenitsyn) (Complete text)

When you travel the by-roads of Central Russia you begin to understand the secret of the pacifying Russian countryside.

It is in the churches. They trip up the slopes, ascend the high hills, come down to the broad rivers, like princesses in white and red, they lift their bell-towers – graceful, shapely, all different – high over mundane timber and thatch, they nod to each other from afar, from villages that are cut off and invisible to each other they soar to the same heaven. And wherever you wander in the fields or meadows, however far from habitation, you are never alone: from over the hayricks, the wall of trees, and even the curve of the earth's surface the head of some bell-tower will

* Cf. pp. 331–4.

beckon to you from Gorki Lovetskiye, or from Lyubichi, or from Gavrilovskoye.

But when you get into the village you find that not the living but the dead greeted you from afar. The crosses were knocked off the roof or twisted out of place long ago. The dome has been stripped, and there are gaping holes between its rusty ribs. Weeds grow on the roofs and in the cracks in the walls. Usually the graveyard has not been kept up, the crosses have been flattened and the graves churned. The murals over the altar have been washed by the rains of decades and obscene inscriptions scrawled over them.

On the porch there are barrels of lubricating oil and a tractor is turning towards them. Or else a lorry has backed into the church doorway to pick up some sacks. In one church there is the shudder of lathes. Another is locked up and silent. In another and another there are groups and clubs. 'Let Us Aim at High Milk Yields!' 'A Poem About Peace.' 'A Heroic Deed.'

People were always selfish and often unkind. But the evening chimes used to ring out, floating over villages, fields and woods. Reminding men that they must abandon the trivial concerns of this world and give time and thought to eternity. These chimes, which only one old tune keeps alive for us, raised people up and prevented them from sinking down on all fours.

Our forefathers put all that was finest in themselves, all their understanding of life into these stones, into these bell-towers.

Ram it in, Vitka, give it a bash, don't be afraid!

Film-show at six, dancing at eight o'clock . . .[30]

5 The Ordinary Believer

KOMSOMOL WEDDINGS
(L. Zinchenko)

The system of new rituals needs one capable organizer – otherwise several bodies become involved, but to be honest none of them achieves very much. Sensible stage managers, technical equipment, proper decorations and, of course, appropriate songs and music are some of the essential elements.

For example, in the Vinnitsa region, when a marriage is solemnly registered, the official of the town or village *soviet* wears a red satin band on his shoulder. On this is embroidered the emblem of the Ukrainian SSR. In some villages the couple's hands are bound with a stole, on the borders of which are ornamentally embroidered quotations about the family from the moral codex. This is very effective. . . .[1]

THE ISTRA HOLY WELL
(V. Zharov)

The local people have nicknamed them the 'bathers'.

'The bathers have dragged themselves off to be healed!. .'

Old women – and amongst them some withered-looking young people – creep along in single file without looking to left or right. All of them have an empty can hidden in their bag, case or knapsack.

The party creeps along with the lids and handles of their empty cans rattling.

Near the mighty walls, newly restored, of the former New-Jerusalem Monastery they kneel for the first time; they clutch at their little crosses, hidden beneath their clothes; oblivious of self, they mumble prayers.

They then move along beside the walls above the steep precipice on the hillside and are hidden by the impenetrable cold screen of the elms.[2]

CAPITULATION TO IGNORANCE
(V. Varavka)

Once upon a time all was apparently normal in the Zolotov family. But then a new little citizen appeared. With whom could he be left during working hours? They had to ask a nanny along.

'I'm a believer,' she said, 'and I want your little boy to be baptized, too. If you don't agree, then we'll have to go our separate ways. I won't look after the child.'

Tamara, who had never admitted to the existence of God or the devil, was rather put out by the nanny's announcement. She tried to persuade her that those days were over, but the old woman remained adamant.

So Tamara decided to let the old lady do as she wished, but she, the young mother, would have no part in it.

The neutrality of the parents suited the pious old woman very well. She took the passports belonging to the boy's father and mother, found a godmother and carried the child off to church.[3]

DEFEAT WITHOUT A BATTLE
(O. Mamontova)

. . . . Rocking the baby, Varvara Petrovna said unusually solemnly: 'It's up to you, Nikolai, but you ought to have the boy baptized, you know – out of the respect you have for me. Let everything be done properly'. . . .

Trying to seem indifferent, he answered: 'I don't mind. Have him baptized if you want to . . .'

The next day Nikolai's mother warned: 'We'll go today . . .'

'Go on then, it's your affair. I'm off to work,' growled Nikolai.

Later there was a *Komsomol* meeting at Motor Depot No. 3. The secretary of the *Komsomol* organization, the driver Nikolai

F

Voronkov, asked that he be recommended as a candidate for party membership.

As is customary, they asked that he should give them some biographical details. They pleased everyone: he had completed seven years at school and done a course at an institute to learn a trade, he had worked on a *kolkhoz*, served in the army and had been a member of the *Komsomol* since 1950, from which he had earned a certificate of merit.

They asked him no more. Nikolai himself said nothing else, either. Why? 'Well, they didn't ask me a thing about my son, you know . . .'

But at a meeting of the Kuibyshev district committee of the *Komsomol*, where the decision of the local *Komsomol* organization had to be approved, someone suddenly became interested: 'You say you have a son? He's not by any chance baptized?'

'Yes he is . . .'

His questioner gave a snap of displeasure. A girl, a member of the bureau, said reproachfully:

'There'll soon be a man on the moon and yet you . . .'

They decided not to recommend him 'in view of a lack of ideological preparation'.[4]

TREATMENT OF BELIEVERS

ATHEISM INSIDE OUT
(S. Yurchik)

. . . . Yes, it is a fact that V. L. Zhirova, headmistress of the school, and A. A. Odushkina, Lyalya Golod's form mistress, had been constantly reproaching this *Komsomol* member for being the daughter of a priest. They did it tactlessly, coarsely and for no reason whatsoever. It is also true that the headmistress and staff member did not stop to think even when Lyalya decided to leave the school – even at this stage they did not realize their mistake. . . .

The girl, after great difficulties, was accepted at another school.

I. I. Mokritsky, chairman of the Ilich *kolkhoz*, stated: 'She's a good girl. What's been done to her at our school and at Stry can be called one thing only: anti-education'. . . .

It is tragic that such people are to be found in the calling of teachers. . . .

Lyalya has a young brother, fourteen-year-old Yurka. He has also been subject to gibes and stupid reproaches from Zhirova. He knows about all the misfortunes which his sister had to live through. He frowns with mistrust on an 'adult' world where all this is possible. He still goes to church. And . . . he has an inclination to join the *Komsomol* with the lads. Whom will he follow? We would like him to follow his sister and come on to our side.[5]

ALONE IN THE CROWD
(A. Veshkin)

Dmitri Sokhranyaev is a convinced fanatic, but at one time he was an activist. He was the *kolkhoz* accountant and was known to be an atheist. His wife, Anna, had been a member of the *Komsomol* in her youth and one of the first in her district to drive a tractor. But one day Sokhranyaev was laid low by a serious physical malady . . . From then on gloom settled over his family and later they began praying. Who knows, but this sad development might never have occurred in the Sokhranyaev family if in this time of trouble his friends and workmates had come to Dmitri, instead of a religious quack.

However, no-one in Shalokhov thought of that.

'We've no churches' is the usual answer given by the party bureau, 'so there's no need to be on one's guard against the influence of priests.'

They began to think only when the Sokhranyaev children removed their Pioneer neckerchiefs and put on crosses, refused to eat in the school dining-room and began to frequent the church. As a result of repeated failure to eat and fear before some unknown power, the little girls became physically weak, began doing badly at school and were threatened with a mental breakdown.

Now a court of law has had to intervene and save Lyuba, Masha and Dusya. The court ruled that 'Dmitri Ivanovich and Anna Sevostianovna Sokhranyaev are to have their parental rights removed'.

Case No. 2/41 is now closed. Soon it will be part of the archives. But our party conscience must not be stored away there, too. The Dmitri Sokhranyaev affair taught the Shalokhov communists a good lesson. But did it concern only them? Never must anyone forget about humanity and the morals of people building communism. One must not leave a man alone in society.[6]

TO THE WORLD COUNCIL OF CHURCHES, ODESSA[7]
(A Group of Believers)

Government officials, under threat of dismissing the priest, forbid that children between six and eighteen be given communion. This ban has been giving rise to continual heart-rending scenes. The mother and child approach the chalice and ask for communion.[8] The priest would like to give the child communion, but knows that he is being watched by the churchwarden, who has been appointed by a government official; he knows that the churchwarden will report him and that he will lose his registration. The mother has no idea what it is all about. With tears in her eyes, she begs that the child be given communion, but the priest pushes her away. Usually such scenes are accompanied by the mother's bitter sobs, the child's crying and murmurs of discontent from the parishioners. This is exactly what the government official wants. His aim is to undermine the priest's authority and to alienate the younger generation from the church and the sacraments. . . .

Believers who occupy posts of responsibility and authority can never think of going to church. Even elderly people, such as pensioners, cannot do so without danger: they are threatened with the withdrawal of their pension if they continue going to church. If you were to look carefully at the congregation in a church, you would notice that it consists, for the most part, of old women with scarves round their heads: intellectuals, afraid that they might lose their job or pension, do not go to church.[9]

TO THE EASTERN PATRIARCHS OF JERUSALEM, ANTIOCH, CONSTANTINOPLE AND OTHERS
From the parishioners and pilgrims of the Orthodox Churches and of all Russia

APPEAL

The early part of this document is very similar to the one by Varavva and Pronina.*

Let us give a further example of barbaric ill-treatment of an Orthodox priest and his parishioners. On a religious festival this summer[10] the priest at Gorny, Mogilev region, was officiating at the liturgy, when in the middle of it atheists yelled out 'Fire!' The terrified people stampeded in confusion. Five were crushed to death, fifteen seriously injured and are still in hospital, while the innocent priest is now to be brought to court.[11]

The next two documents demonstrate the situation after the fall of Khrushchev.

TO THE 23rd CONGRESS OF THE CPSU
From the faithful Orthodox people

APPEAL

There are many churches which need major repairs, but government officials have forbidden them to be carried out. There have even been instances where a priest has repaired or finished building church premises, for which he has been deprived of his licence to officiate. On 6 February 1966 our dear, unforgettable mother Valentina died, after having lain for thirty years incurably ill. She lived in the village of Koski, Dzerzhinsky district, Minsk region. On the day when our dear late mother should have been buried, Afanasiev, chairman of the Stankov village *soviet*, came

* See pp. 170–7.

and said: 'When you bring the body to the cemetery, don't sing any hymns at the grave – that's a government order.' The believers replied: 'The government can't do this – it's only come from the local officials, Kovalev and Logvinenko.'* They went on: 'Why do you go to a demonstration and sing, while we can't sing at a grave? You're interfering in church affairs, when the church is separated from the state'. . . .

There are state laws for Orthodox Christians, but we gain no advantage from them. For example, every shop, kiosk and street corner is full of atheist literature, while our religious literature is banned – Bibles, Gospels, psalters, lives of the saints and the teachings of the holy fathers. Yet it is written in the laws: freedom of conscience, freedom of the press, freedom of the word. . . .

The political conscience of many party members has gone to sleep, while you reject spiritual things.[12]

LETTER TO THE METROPOLITAN FILARET AND ARCHBISHOP ANTONI OF GENEVA[13]
(Anonymous)

Spiritually we are united. Our divisions are external and therefore temporary. We Russian Orthodox people remain at one with you in our hearts, we pray for you and beg your holy prayers and blessings.

With great joy we have heard your words of brotherly love and compassion broadcast to us. We were glad to hear that our fellow-countrymen of the dispersion are zealously preserving our true Orthodox faith. . . .

One can find people very well disposed towards Orthodoxy among those with party cards, while there are bishops, priests and monks who are serving as secret police informers. Here lies our difficulty in combating evil.

We are few in number and small in influence on those around us. The great majority of us, though not all, are old people who have been buffeted by life.

* Cf. p. 169.

There are still children – Christian children – who undergo great ordeals for their belief in the Lord at school and they are accomplishing heroic deeds of faith.

The Christian education of children is becoming more difficult than ever. One of the authors of this letter was a witness of the following event. In an official setting, with many staff and students of the Theological Academy present, a representative of the municipal authorities of Zagorsk was asked: 'In present-day Soviet conditions, in what circumstances is the Christian up-bringing of children possible in a religious family?' He replied categorically: 'In no circumstances! In the USSR we can have no Christian upbringing of children in families where the parents are believers.' This occurred last spring.

People who, despite this, try to bring up their children as Christians are subject to pressure at work from party groups and are even threatened with deprivation of parental rights. In fact, this occurs most often when there is a conflict between parents – the one of them who is a Christian is thus deprived.

Despite all this, in recent years an interest in Orthodoxy, Christian literature and art is developing among young people. A movement of young people into the church has become notice-able, but in our opinion it would be premature to talk in terms of a big influx. Vital thought is now being openly expressed among the creative intelligentsia, too – among writers and some artists ... Perhaps, if it should be God's will, it will be possible to organize a new missionary campaign in the conditions of modern paganism. One could hope for this only if we unite in ardent prayer to the Lord Jesus and to His Immaculate Mother, who has always pro-tected our country, and to all the saints who have shone out on Russian soil ...

We would like to summon our fellow-countrymen of the dis-persion, who have resolved to help their native land in any way possible, not to squander their energies anywhere outside our Holy Church, which has been and will remain united, not to yield to political passions, which only create spiritual bank-ruptcy, but completely to consecrate their strength to Orthodoxy and its affairs, for the salvation of Russia is in this alone . . .

Most revered Fathers! the help for which we wish to turn to you consists, we feel, of the following. Together we should do all in our power:

1. to print, send to Russia and distribute as large an edition as possible of the New Testament, short prayer books in small format, literature of the following content: manuals for new devotees of the faith, setting out the religious experience of the Holy Fathers and the ascetics; apologetics adapted to twentieth-century needs (positive and negative – we have materialism and Marxism principally in mind);

2. to support the movement of Orthodoxy among the creative ntelligentsia and questing youth;

3. to work for the purification of the clergy from those people who have been infiltrated into the church from outside in order to discredit it . . .[14]

All this is possible only through sufficiently frequent contact with you. . . .[15]

FEODOSIA VARAVVA

TO THE EASTERN PATRIARCHS OF JERUSALEM, ANTIOCH, CONSTANTINOPLE AND OTHERS AND TO THE UNITED NATIONS ORGANIZATION

From an Orthodox believer in Russia, F. K. Varavva, Flat 4, 1a Lemkovskaya St., Lvov 9

PETITION

Meekly kneeling before your saintly feet, I, humble Feodosia, venture to bring to your attention the facts about the awful mockery and persecution of us faithful Orthodox believers, monks and true pastors, at the hands of atheist communist teachers in the schools of our Orthodox Russia. . . .

I wish to say a few words about myself. I am the mother of

two children – my son is fourteen and my daughter twelve. When danger threatened Russia I, as a young girl, voluntarily joined the army on 30 June 1941 and was assigned to one of the mobile front-line hospitals. I worked there throughout the war, honourably fulfilling my duty to my country. It was my responsibility to take care of the most seriously injured: gas gangrene (Anton's fire, as they popularly call it), fracture of the pelvis, rupture of the spine, tetanus cases and so on. When labour was scarce, I had to serve as stretcher-bearer, hospital attendant and nurse, although my only course had been as a doctor's assistant. Yet, because I am a believer, because I go to an Orthodox church and take my children with me, because I bring them up as Christians, I have had to experience awful persecution and brutality against myself and my family and to suffer severe humiliation from the atheist communists.

Here follows a lengthy description of Varavva's attempts to secure for herself and her family an adequate flat. The four were living in a single room at Minsk. Each parent, in bad health, had to share a bed with one of the children.

I wondered why we were not given a flat – after all, my husband was a party member. But we happened to have a neighbour who was a good communist. She had submitted a report to the district party committee against my husband because I was a churchgoer, took my children to worship and had icons in my flat. They decided to expel my husband from the party, but first of all they requested that he should divorce me, with the condition that the children should stay with him so that the authorities could help him to deprive me of my parental rights. But my husband refused to remove the children from their mother, so they devised another stratagem. A woman from the district party committee, a communist, approached me and tried to persuade me to renounce God, saying they would give us a splendid flat, place the children in a kindergarten and provide me with a good job. But I replied to this communist woman: 'I will not renounce God and I don't want your flat!'. . . .

F 2

Now let me describe all the harassment which came my way
from the school for taking my children to church and bringing
them up as Christians. I began to be persecuted in 1959. We then
still lived in Minsk. My son was only six when he asked me to let
him serve as an altar-boy for the archbishop in Minsk Cathedral –
which I did. Then my son began to attend School No. 18 in
Minsk.

When he was in the second form, the children were on their
way to church when the headmistress saw them. Immediately she
summoned me to her office to reprimand me for taking my son to
church. According to her, attendance at church was crippling the
souls of my children. She spent about two hours arguing that I
should stop taking my son to church and corrupting him. She
went on to tell me that I should permit him to join the Pioneers.
I answered that I would not allow him to do this because it was a
godless organization and I, as a religious mother, could not let my
child join an atheistic organization. I take my children to church
because this is our balm which heals our souls and bodies.

. . . . The headmistress began to exert a secret pressure on my
son in order to induce him to join the Pioneers. The leader of the
Pioneer group suggested to my son that he should join it secretly
without my permission, that he should wear the neckerchief and
take a place in the back row in the class, but remove the neckerchief before going home. With God's help I was able to frustrate
this secret pressure on my son. I told the Pioneer leader: 'I teach
my child to tell the truth, but you teach him to lie and incite him
against me. Your education isn't worth a brass farthing.' But the
secret pressure on my son continued and, finally, from being a
fine obedient boy he turned into a lout.

Because I taught my children to pray and observe the fasts,
impressing on them the necessity of following the commandments
of the church, my husband and my neighbours rose against me.
They fabricated all sorts of ridiculous accusations that I was
allegedly starving my children and they invented all sorts of
fantastic tales.

One day, in connection with petitions from my neighbours, I

was again summoned by Orlova, the headmistress of School No. 18. She again repeated her warning that I should stop taking the children to church, because she had been receiving calls from the City Health Administration suggesting that a commission should be set up to investigate me and that I should be sent to a psychiatric establishment, for I must be mad if I bring my children up as Christians. Again I replied to Orlova that I had been taking my children to church and would continue to do so. When Orlova realized that I was adamant, she summoned a meeting of the parents' committee and they all visited my home together. I happened to be out at the time, but my husband was there. She told him that I would be tried by a public court and that the children would be sent to a boarding school.

The family moved to Lvov before Varavva could be brought to court.

. . . . The teachers of School No. 58 in Lvov, which my children attend, had taken advantage of my absence and wanted secretly to entice my children into the Pioneer organization. Here is how all this came to light. I happened quite accidentally to approach my daughter just as I had returned from a trip to Pochaev.* She began to scream and then she said she had to go to the toilet. Immediately I sensed that she was hiding something from me and I told her: 'I won't let you go until you explain to me exactly why you were screaming.' Then my daughter pulled a red neckerchief out of her underpants and handed it over to me. Then she told me everything. Apparently in my absence two fourth-year teachers beckoned to her, one of whom was Yelizaveta Balyandina. They said to her (I repeat their words), 'Don't listen to your mother, join the Pioneers. If your mother takes you to church, tell her you won't go. Say there's no God. If your mother beats you, report it to the school.'

Next morning I kept my daughter home from school. The teachers of School No. 58 sent the whole class to our place, allegedly to find out why Zina was absent. But one could hear

* Cf. pp. 98-116.

from those fourth-year pupils all sorts of gibes and derisive remarks about me, an elderly woman (I was over fifty). They asked
why I forbade Zina to join the Pioneers. These very Pioneers
laughed and sneered for a long time, so that I was finally forced
to come out and chase them away from our entrance. They moved
away, but stood for a long time gazing through our window.

After all these incidents I had to see the teacher Balyandina,
who is in charge of my daughter's class, to ask her for an explanation of why they were inciting my children against me. When I
came to the school and went to the staff-room, I found that the
teachers were there, as well as the chairman of the parents' committee, Comrade Antipova. In the staff-room I said: 'What's
happening? I teach my children to obey their teachers, not to be
naughty, to learn their lessons well, to serve as an example in
school – and it transpires that you teach them to disobey me and
to be rude to me.' Antipova retorted: 'A mother like you
shouldn't be obeyed. We'll take your children away from you
and put them into a boarding school!'

Finally Varavva was visited by a newspaper reporter and again
threatened with a trial. Then she goes back to describe earlier events
at Minsk. She repeatedly went to Kovalev, the official responsible for
church affairs in Belorussia, to demand that her children should be
admitted to communion.

. . . . So I went for the third time and it happened that the
secretary of our diocese, Fr. Viktor Bekarevich, was with Kovalev.
I began to beg and entreat him to help me with my problem, but
he ran away from me as if I was the plague.

After my third visit to Kovalev, he rang the cathedral and
ordered that communion should be administered to my children.
My children then received the sacraments secretly in the sacristy
for six months.

. . . . We wrote a complaint to Moscow, saying that state
officials had taken full power over the church and that in eighteen
months three churches in Minsk had been closed, two of which
were immediately demolished and razed to the ground: that of
the archbishop at Senitsa and the church at Kozyrevo. Only two

churches remained in Minsk – the cathedral and the little church at the Military Cemetery, both of which were overcrowded. . . . It has gone so far that the government official, Logvinenko himself, has been standing guard at the doors of the cathedral, noticing whose children went in and scolding Velichko Sila, warden of the cathedral. The latter – a servant of anti-Christ – mercilessly chased the children out of the church building. Those children who refused to obey him he seized by the collar and knocked their heads against the wall. The dean of Minsk Cathedral, Fr. Mikhail Chupris, helped to drive the children from the church.

. . . . When the officials Kovalev and Logvinenko had finally succeeded, by dint of various repressions, in banning the children from the churches and prohibiting the administration of communion to them, Kuroyedov* issued an order forbidding the administration of the sacraments to children of school age and their admission to the churches everywhere. Children now receive communion only in Zagorsk and in the places which are visited by foreigners. This is calculated to convince the latter that religion is totally triumphant in Russia. . . .

Since children have for two years now been barred from the church and from communion, last May I went to see a government official in Lvov, whose name is Vinnichenko. I showed him the Soviet laws and, on the basis of these, I demanded that children should be permitted to receive communion. He showed me some brochure, but did not allow me to read it, since it was a secret instruction. Then I understood why he refused to let me read it. In January 1964 a secret meeting was held by the communist atheists, at which they decided to take away children from those parents who were bringing them up as Christians; they would prosecute the parents, because the communist atheists had entrusted all education to the schools, in contravention of Soviet law.

. . . . Let the communist atheists go about bringing up their children as they please – that is their business. But let them not touch my children, nor apply violence to me and them. I bring

* See p. 24.

my children up in piety and purity. Let them not incite my children secretly against me, since children are like dough and they can be moulded into accepting anything; they cannot yet distinguish well what is good and what is bad. . . .

I do not know what awaits me, now that I have exposed the whole truth in this letter. It could be prison or banishment to the far north, or perhaps martyrdom for the truth. I beg and entreat everyone who will read this letter, or listen to it, everyone who believes in the triune God – raise your humble prayers to the Holy Trinity and our great Protectress of Christendom, the Mother of God, who is our intercessor before the throne of the Most High. Ask Her to fortify me, a humble sinner, to withstand to the end all the torments and sufferings visited on me for my sins, so that no tortures, no sufferings, no persecution for the truth can ever shatter my faith, nor that of my beloved children. May our faith be built on the corner-stone of Christ.[16]

TO THE EASTERN PATRIARCHS OF JERUSALEM, ANTIOCH, CONSTANTINOPLE AND OTHERS AND TO THE UNITED NATIONS ORGANIZATION

From the Orthodox Christians of all Russia
(signed 'Varavva, Pronina' – and two illegible signatures)

. . . . The Orthodox faith has increased and is being strengthened in the crucible of bitter suffering.

On the radio, in the newspapers, throughout the entire Soviet Union there is much talk about peace; representatives of the communist government travel abroad, allegedly fighting for peace in order to prevent a nuclear war and thereby save all mankind from death. But the godless communists are paying only lip-service to peace, while launching a horrible war against the believing Orthodox people. They are using violence with great success, closing down the monasteries and churches, destroying holy, health-giving springs – all against the will of us believers. . . . They pay lip-service to the precepts of Lenin, while in fact they continue the work of Stalin, whom they themselves have condemned for having destroyed many innocent people. Now they simply act a little more quietly. . . .

The authorities have forbidden children above one-and-a-half or two years of age to be baptized. . . . In order to have a child baptized, it is necessary for its mother, father, godmother and godfather to write an application to the church council with a request for this and they all must present their passports. Without an application and a passport it is not possible to have a child baptized. At the end of the month, the addresses and registration must be submitted to a government official. If the parents come from another district or region, the baptism may not be carried out and the child is sent home without it. On the occasion of baptism, everybody's documents and passports are inspected. It is forbidden to bring children to church and they cannot be admitted to communion, with the exception of babies in arms. The godless communists have decreed that the children should be simply driven away from the churches. Babies in arms may be brought only by their parents.

A priest may proceed to a funeral only with written authorization from the regional executive committee or the town *soviet*, but the latter refuse to grant such permits. A funeral service for the deceased may be held only with a permit from the regional executive committee or the town *soviet* – and only in the cemetery at the grave (winter and summer alike). Priests are not allowed to hold funeral services in the home of the deceased.

Collection of money in the churches has been prohibited in Belorussia and in other regions, since, according to the godless communists, this is considered as extortion. Instead, an alms-box must be placed in the middle of the church and conscientious believers are expected to put money in it. No collections for the needs of the church are permitted – people should put their money into the box. No money is to be contributed to the choir – amateurs should sing. More money must be donated to the peace fund – but they use it to build cinemas for themselves. Churches and monasteries are forbidden to carry out repairs. After each service all the money must be put into the bank – it belongs to the people and may not be kept in the church. Priests' salaries must be reduced – and if they are discontented, they should change their profession.

The priest has no right to interfere with church business; according to their opinion, he is a hireling.[17] For infringement of these regulations, priests' licences are revoked, registration of parishes is removed and even court proceedings are instituted. District and village committees have been organized by the godless communists to keep an eye on the churches, priests and believers. In summer the priest must finish the liturgy before 10 a.m., in winter before 12 noon, including all personal services for individuals. It is therefore necessary to begin the liturgy at five or six o'clock in the morning in an empty church in order to finish in time. There have been cases where for running over by a mere fifteen or twenty minutes churches have been shut down for three months. . . .

At Easter this year auxiliary police were posted near the churches in all towns and villages to prevent young people from attending the Easter Mass. . . .

We recently read in the newspaper *Izvestia* an article entitled 'The Twilight of the Gods' (28 April 1964).[18] This article, written by godless communists, refutes the statements of foreign clergy and journalists who, allegedly, slander Russia in claiming that the Orthodox faith is being persecuted here and that churches are being rapidly closed. If foreign clergy and journalists have come to the defence of the Orthodox faith and its churches and are s ruggling against our godless communists for freedom of conscience, then we pay our deepest respects and express our heartfelt thanks to them, for having shown to us sinners the Christian love which was vouchsafed to us by our Lord Jesus Christ himself. By this, they sustain our spiritual strength, which is being exhausted by the battle. In this article the godless communists brand these foreign clergy and the journalists as slanderers. On the contrary, it is our own red-cassocked metropolitans who are slanderers. Pimen and Nikodim, members of the Holy Synod, are wolves in sheep's clothing and they deny the existence of dreadful persecution and the rapid closing of churches and monasteries. They have no fear of God, they do not remember that for their own calumny and lying and for the closing of the churches and monasteries eternal fire awaits them. From all this, foreign clergy and journalists should be able to see what kind of pastors we have.

In a short period at the beginning of this year, two thousand churches were closed, excluding those in Belorussia and the Ukraine. Hundreds of Orthodox believers daily come to the Patriarchate and the government, staying for as long as two months in Moscow in the hope of persuading these bodies to forbid the local authorities to shut churches and monasteries. But all complaints have gone unheeded and no satisfaction whatever has been given to our requests.

. . . . Most of our true pastors have had their licences revoked, because they have defended apostolic traditions and the enactments of the ecumenical councils. They have been thrown out of the church and compelled to live as vagrants. Some have small children, others are very old; none can find shelter, since they have been expelled from the church.

Moreover, in *Izvestia* (28 April 1964) our red-cassocked metropolitans and members of the Holy Synod, Nikodim and Pimen, say that no arrests are being made among the clergy. Why, then, do they say nothing about the Pochaev monks who have now been imprisoned for the third time? . . .

Here follows an account of some of the Pochaev arrests (cf. Chapters 2–3).

Let us now describe the proceedings at the trial of Sub-Deacon Andrei. The judge who handled his case displayed in court a contempt and hatred of Orthodox people and of monks. The trial took place in Ternopol, at 35 Kotlyarevsky Street. . . . The judge simply refused to let the defendant speak whenever he referred to attacks on monks and pilgrims by the militia and the auxiliary police, the seizure of holy books, crosses, money and the icons belonging to the pilgrims, their expulsion from Pochaev and the extraction of pledges from them that they would never reappear there. The complaint addressed to the UN[19] was read only in short fragments, which were amplified by the court, so as to prove the defendant's guilt. The basic facts outlined in Sub-Deacon Andrei's complaint . . . . were not read at all and, in the words of the judge, everything that the former had written in his complaint was slander.

. . . . Every one of the believers present at the trial was photographed, both from the front and from the back. Some of them wanted to speak in the defence of the accused, but the judge refused to let them do so. A pilgrim, Grigori Petrovich Veremeichuk, an invalid of the second group living at Baku (57a, 17th Zavokzalnaya Street) wanted to appear in the court as a witness and to tell how he had been beaten in the Pochaev Monastery of the Holy Assumption. He was registered as a witness, but when he was summoned to the court he came in with a wooden cross in his hands, so the judge immediately refused to let him speak and ordered him to be thrown out.

Here follows an account of the evidence Veremeichuk would have presented.

. . . . The judge was so angry with the believers that he ordered Natalia Zaboborina out of the courtroom for making the sign of the cross. Feodosia Varavva, living at Lvov (Flat 4, 1a Lemkovskaya Street) was also attending the trial and took notes from time to time. When the judge noticed this, he ordered that they should be taken away from her, for note-taking was not to be done. After the confiscation the judge recessed the court for five minutes. Varavva slipped out to a shop and on her return a KGB car was standing at the courthouse. She was whisked into it and driven to the KGB headquarters. There she was told: 'What has happened to Father Andrei also awaits you, because you make trips to Moscow to complain and make slanderous statements'. After checking her documents, they released her, but not until the trial was already over.

Sub-Deacon Andrei was tried for the simple reason that a complaint addressed to the UN had been found on his person. All this became apparent at the trial. He was fearfully tortured: they put a rubber shirt on him and he was given the electric hammer treatment in an attempt to extract from him the name of the person who had typed the complaint and who had written it.

Archbishop Andrei of Chernigov has been sentenced to eight or ten years' imprisonment because he refused to yield – in other words, close down a convent. We beg and entreat the Eastern Patriarchs and the UN to obtain the release from jail of Sub-Deacon Apelli, Priest-monk Dionisi and Sub-Deacon Andrei, who have been illegally sentenced, and to have them returned to the Pochaev Monastery and given residence permits. We also solicit the release from jail of Archbishop Andrei of Chernigov, since he has been illegally sentenced, requesting that he be returned to the Chernigov diocese and given a residence permit.

Let us describe the conditions under which the Chernigov Convent was closed down. The nuns were told to go wherever they pleased. Some old women without passports were thrown into prison and those who had no place to live were sent to camps. Moreover, beyond Karaganda there is a camp for imprisoned monks and priests. It is located in the steppes near the Sea of Aral and is surrounded by barbed wire. This camp was transferred there from the Solovki Isles. About thirty thousand monks, nuns and clergy are confined there. . . .[20]

At the end of March 1964 we were received by one of our red-cassocked metropolitans, Pimen, a member of the Holy Synod. It was he who sent four Pochaev monks to become parish priests, while the churches in these parishes were being closed down, so that the monks would find themselves ousted from the monastery. The Pochaev monks refused to submit to the metropolitan's order, so as to retain their residence at the cloister. Then the metropolitan defrocked them.

Here follows a similar account of the murder of Marfa and of various other atrocities to that contained in the Pochaev document quoted earlier.*

The Zhirovitsy Monastery has also now become a target of violent persecution. The godless communists have taken the nuns from two convents and brought them all to the Zhirovitsy

* Pp. 112–13.

Monastery, which is a cloister for men. The Grodno and Polotsk
Convents have been closed and merged with the Zhirovitsy
Monastery. Now every effort is being made to close down this
monastery as well and let the monks and nuns scatter over the
wide world. Through all kinds of tricks the godless local authorities have succeeded in closing down the Zhirovitsy Seminary. But
these barbarians were not satisfied at that. They began to covet
the big three-storey building previously occupied by the seminary
and wanted to appropriate it as a school. But, by the grace of God,
they failed in their efforts, because the building was assigned to
the nuns, who had been living under the same roof as the monks,
although this is against monastic rules. When the chairman of the
regional executive committee, S. T. Kobyak, failed to lay his
hands on the building, he tried to grab the Zhirovitsy Monastery's
orchard and kitchen-garden, but again the grace of God prevented
him. Now, this summer (at the beginning of July 1964) Sergei
Terentievich Kobyak began to have designs on the other buildings of the monastery: the brothers' dormitory, the bell tower with
its inhabitable annexes, the teaching block and sixteen acres of
kitchen-garden. He requested Bishop Sergi of Minsk and Belorussia to sign a document transferring these buildings to the committee and he did so. . . . Kuroyedov, the government official
concerned with all the churches of Russia, ordered the expulsion
of all the monks from these buildings by 15 August. We, the
pilgrims and parishioners of the Zhirovitsy Monastery, requested
the local authorities not to destroy the belfry cupola and not to
remove the cross from it. We begged them to preserve these
buildings as historical monuments, but the local authorities
answered: 'We're communists – we'll do whatever we like.' We
beg and entreat you to stand up in the defence also of the Zhirovitsy Monastery and not to permit the confiscation of the above-
mentioned buildings from the monastery.*

Satan's nets are so stretched out over Russia that it is very difficult for us believers to save ourselves. Now the Orthodox

---

* Through Archbishop Yermogen's confinement there, we know that this
monastery has not been closed down (see p. 239).

faithful who are employed in industry must go to work on such big holidays as the Annunciation, Easter and Christmas.

. . . . We are spiritual orphans who have no pastors. Most of our pastors have bowed to the godless communists and serve their will, not apostolic traditions and the decrees of the ecumenical councils. The true pastors, of whom there remain so few, are themselves harassed by state officials and by those pastors who have submitted to the godless communists. We hope and trust that these letters of ours will soon bring us great joy through you, the divinely appointed Patriarchs of the East, and that by providence our Lord Jesus Christ Himself will, in your persons, stand up in the defence of us sinners and of our children, who are perishing in a terrible morass of sin. . . .

1 August 1964.[21]

THE DANGEROUS MISTAKE OF FEODOSIA KUZMINICHNA
(K. Ustimenko and A. Grigorovich)

. . . The last conversation ended with Feodosia Kuzminichna's thumping on the headmistress's table with her fist and, furious, announcing for all to hear:

'Yes I am a believer and bring up my children according to God's commandments. I don't want my children to become anti-Christian atheists! That's why I refuse to let my children join the *Komsomol* or Pioneers' . . .

. . . The following events preceded our difficult conversation. In April last year, two young comrades joined School No. 58 at Lvov: Pavlik Varavva went into the sixth class and his little sister, Zinochka, into the third. Their parents had moved permanently from Minsk to Lvov.

Time passed and then after getting to know her new pupil V. M. Daletskaya, the form mistress, turned her attention to the report written by her colleague in Minsk. It contained such lines as: 'The boy's mother is strict, religious, and tries to inculcate religious sentiments upon her son. The child is confused and has divided loyalties . . .'

The perceptive teacher, Comrade Daletskaya, immediately turned a particularly observant eye on the boy. Tact and wise approach had their effect: during various heart-to-heart talks with his teacher, Pavlik let out how difficult it was at home. His mother, Feodosia Kuzminichna, considers it her duty to bring her children up in 'the fear of God'; prayers, fasting and severe punishment in her opinion impose high moral principles and Christian ethical standards upon children.

Very soon the teaching staff of School No. 58 were certain that Feodosia Kuzminichna not only spoke of her 'credo' publicly but also, with great persistence, applied it to life and prevented the school from educating her children. She followed the school time-table hour by hour and if Pavlik was kept in school after lessons, she would set off to the school to 'obtain an explanation and remove the cause'. These visits were accompanied by rude sallies at the teachers who were, she said, 'encouraging the boy to dis-obey his parents'. Through such actions, their mother is preventing Pavlik and Zina from experiencing the full and varied life of Soviet children.

All the efforts of the teachers to show this 'strict mother' the error of her ways were fruitless. Attempts to influence Feodosia Kuzminichna through the head of the family met with no more success: Pyotr Vlasovich Varavva prefers to 'remain neutral'.

The first meeting with Pavlik took place at school. To be honest, the authors of these lines were worried by the following question: what were the fruits of a 'strict religious upbringing', what precisely had Feodosia Kuzminichna achieved by prayer and the belt? . . .

And so here is Pavlik in front of us. Let's get to know him and have a chat.

Yes, his fanatical mother has done her work well. Religious vigils, fasts and various forms of punishment (even including beating) have retarded the boy's physical development. In front of us stood not a life-loving fourteen-year-old adolescent, but a sickly-looking, pale child. But in this feeble body there was the fighting spirit of someone who thought like us. Pavlik persistently opposes the religion forced on him by his mother.

To the question of what was his favourite occupation and particular interest, the boy answered:

'I love sport, particularly boxing, and I enjoy radio mechanics . . .'

'What success do you have?'

The boy sighed, 'None. I'm not allowed to play sport or make radios'.

'They say that you go to church?'

'How can I help going if I'm made to?'. . .

'Would you like to go to a boarding school?'

Pavlik thought for a moment: 'I'm sorry for Daddy. We love each other . . . Look, you talk to him. He'll tell Mummy to give us some peace from her God and church.'

'How about your little sister, Zina?'

'Well, she's still a coward. But even Zina understands everything . . .'

Such were Feodosia Kuzminichna's 'fruits of a religious upbringing'. Family opposition against the mother is growing and she is losing all that is most precious: the respect and love of her children.

We were invited to Pavlik's house. In the children's room we saw an enormous iconostasis: from floor to ceiling were all kinds of different icons, some standing, some hung on the wall. Before them lamps and candles were smoking.

Feodosia Kuzminichna tried to get a discussion going. Brandishing the text of the Constitution and various pamphlets, she endeavoured to prove that to bring up her children as Christians was not only her duty, but even a right guaranteed by Soviet law.

We then talked to Pyotr Vlasovich Varavva. We have to admit that there are no grounds for sharing Pavlik's childish belief in the strength of his father.

'I have lost heart. What can I do? I'd be ashamed to get a divorce at my age, but she won't hand over the children to me of her own free will. The daily scenes and the fanatical persistence of my wife have broken me in the end . . .'

Yes, it's hard to believe that this man before us was once an officer in the Soviet Army and a member of the Communist Party of the Soviet Union. We note that he was only recently excluded from the party 'for complicity in the spiritual corruption of his children'. That is what lack of will-power and character reduces a man to . . .

But Pyotr Vlasovich is 62 and he bears the responsibility for his own behaviour and actions. What about the children, though, of whom the elder is only fourteen? . . .

Here we must give a completely clear and exact explanation of Feodosia Kuzminichna's attempt to prove her 'right' to bring up her 'own children' as Christians.

She has no such right.

Soviet children are brought up by the whole of socialist society, including the school and family; it educates them as communists. As for freedom of conscience, to which Feodosia Kuzminichna so likes to refer, it is a freedom enjoyed by adults in our country. Once Pavlik and Zina are grown up, they will then begin to enjoy all the rights of Soviet citizens, including freedom of conscience.

As regards Feodosia Kuzminichna herself, her behaviour should concern the whole public of Lvov.[22]

THE DANGEROUS MISTAKE OF
FEODOSIA KUZMINICHNA
(N. Bryusova)

Feodosia Kuzminichna Varavva also spoke at the parents' meeting of School No. 58. Her verbose speech showed that the mother of Pavlik and Zina had understood and learned nothing. Even today the spiritual coercion of her children persists.

'On the day of the Last Judgment I do not want to have to answer before God for the lost souls of my children. Therefore I shall defend them from your ungodly organizations, from your ungodly teaching with all my rights as a mother' – announced Feodosia Kuzminichna at the parents' meeting.

. . . . When parents and those replacing them do not honestly fulfil their parental duty, we have applied, are applying and will apply social and administrative measures, as well as, in certain cases, undertaking legal proceedings. It seems to me that the situation in the Varavva family should concern the district social organizations and most of all the court of parental honour.

I wish to take this opportunity of indicating that recently such courts have been created in all towns and districts of our region. Guided in their work by the Statute on Comrades' Courts, they study data on the incorrect upbringing of children, bad behaviour in the family and dishonourable behaviour towards women.

The removal of parental rights is the most extreme measure and is taken in cases when the court comes to the conclusion that the parents are crippling their children both morally and physically. In such cases as when parents or other persons aid children to commit a crime, the former are liable to be held criminally responsible, according to §208 of the Penal Code of the Ukrainian Republic, which stipulates a sentence of five years' imprisonment. I note that recently there have been a number of people convicted in Lvov under this article.

Measures to influence parents who do not fulfil their parental duty are undertaken by the party and trade-union organizations, according to the correct social practice.[23]

It is noteworthy how Varavva has completely resisted all pressures of the long campaign against her. This article was published in *Nauka i Religia* seven months later than the last of the above attacks in the Lvov press.

BROTHER AND SISTER
(V. Shkolny)

. . . . In my hands I have the blue school exercise book which so worried the Russian-language teacher. On its cover is written 'Zina Varava,[24] Class 5'. Here is another sheet written in the same childish hand, a letter to the editor of the regional newspaper, *Lvovskaya Pravda*. It says: 'If I go to church once or twice a week it's not a crime and I'm not ashamed. I don't want to join the Pioneers – I have so many lessons and I would have to stay on at the meetings. I've no time and don't wish to'. . . . .

'Is it true you wear a cross?'

'Yes ... Mummy makes me. I do go to church. The singing is beautiful there'. . . .

I am at 1a Lemkovaskaya Street. There is no bell, so I knock. A tall, middle-aged woman opens the door. We introduce our-selves: she is Feodosia Kuzminichna Varavva. Her face is sickly and furrowed. Silence reigns in the rooms. There is a huge icon-stasis in the corner of the children's room. . . .

'My son has slipped away from me', said Feodosia Kuzminichna. 'He's an atheist, but I won't let my daughter go. My son will come back, too. You don't know the souls of my children – it's God's secret. I've been taking them to church and will continue to do so. It's my maternal right to bring them up as Christians. I'll never let them join the Pioneers, the *Komsomol* or any atheist organization – they shan't go to hell.'

It is difficult to believe that this woman was formerly in the front line, a military doctor's assistant,* because now instead of thinking of Pavlik's and Zinochka's future she is maiming them. . . .

These children, boy and girl – they are two young lives, two destinies. Even now, as I write these lines, I see their big sad eyes. Brother and sister are both small for their age and have pale faces. Like all children, they study at school and laugh, but as soon as the bell goes for the end of the last lesson their fanatical mother carries them off into 'God's world'.

More church, prayers, fasting and the terrifying silence.[25]

VADIM SHAVROV

SPRING THOUGHTS AND REMINISCENCES
(The confession of a man who believes in God)

I was born in Moscow in September 1924 into the family of a prominent military man, an old Bolshevik. In World War I my

* Cf. p. 165.

father, Mikhail Yurievich Shavrov, who came from simple peasant stock, proved himself a brave and courageous soldier. . . . He took an active part in the October Revolution and was one of the organizers of the Red Guard – one of those who were present at the birth of our glorious army. . . .

My brother Alexei, who was later killed in action at the front, and I were brought up by our father in a spirit of devotion to our homeland and the ideas of the Communist Party.

Our father tried especially to instil in us the precepts of materialism and atheism. Being a militant atheist, he treated with revulsion anything that even vaguely smacked of 'priestliness'. All I gleaned from my father about priests was that they were, to a man, drunkards, gluttons, thieves and 'agents of the tsar's secret police', and about religion – that it was 'the opium of the people' and 'the grave of reason'.

I remember how I rejoiced when St. Yermolai's Church, next door to us on Bolshaya Sadovaya Street, was blown up and destroyed. We had a good view of the church from the windows of our flat. As a mischievous boy of twelve, I took pleasure in throwing lumps of mud at the bowed backs of the priests, as they were being evicted from their wretched wooden houses which stood near our gates. I also remember how I and my schoolfriends from the Pioneers chanted almost unprintable ditties when the Convent of the Passion, on Moscow's Pushkin Square, was destroyed. . . .

Shavrov and his brother fought in the Second World War. Shavrov became a sailor and took an active part in both the Battle of Stalingrad and the Siege of Leningrad, suffering severe wounds. He says there were aspects of his life then that he would prefer to forget, however.

. . . . I developed quite a thoroughgoing passion for vodka. The crude smut of a seaman never left my tongue. What is more, I was always spoiling for a fight. I was very proud of the fact that, if I chose, I could floor the strongest fellow with a single blow. Sometimes it was worse and we came to using knives. In the autumn of 1944 at the age of twenty, I first formed a liaison with a woman, while on sick leave in Pyatigorsk on account of my wounds; from that moment women became part of my life. . .

So it was that my youth passed by – amid the haze of gunpowder smoke, the thunder of weapons, the drunken fumes of day-to-day life in the army. . . . .

In spring 1943, just before I left for the Baltic, news reached us that my elder brother, Alexei, had been killed in an aerial battle near Rostov. Grief-stricken, my mother decided to hold a funeral service for him, even though she did not have his body.

At her request I went along to the service. On 2 May 1943, with a lighted candle in my hand, I stood in the church of the Prophet Elijah in Obydensky Lane, Moscow, wearing naval dress uniform. Mournful sobbing sounds drifted up from the choir: they were mourning my only brother, whom I loved dearly, and promising him – as one of those who had fought and died for us – rest, peace, and a serene eternal life. For the first time in my whole conscious life I was standing in a church. That mournful simple melody cut deep into my heart. Although I still did not believe, at that moment I already felt a presentiment of some great eternal Truth, as yet unknown to me. Then, as I left the church, the mood vanished and I again plunged, alas, into the thoughtless round of my daily life. . . . .

After the war Shavrov began a course at the Moscow Law Institute, but, though he had a thirst for knowledge, he spent most of his time in restaurants with young women.

. . . . In spring 1948, since I had a set of excellent references and testimonials, I applied to become a candidate member of the party. The *Komsomol* willingly supported my application. . . . .

I was undoubtedly sincere when I applied for admission to the party. I saw it, first and foremost, as the guiding spirit which had inspired our motherland's heroic defenders to fight frenzied German fascism. By nature I am neither doctrinaire nor a theoretician. As the war showed, my patriotism is neither abstract nor rationalised, but inward and heartfelt. . . . .

Meanwhile, I felt that the question of life's meaning was not secondary, not incidental, but the main one, the most important of all. Till an answer to this question is given, all other questions and answers (about the five signs of imperialism and commodity production) simply have no meaning. At the same time I grew more and more convinced that I should find no answer to this most vital question among the materialist philosophers. In this way the seeds of doubt ripened in my soul. . . .

One day in June 1948 my father was arrested.* Since he was a convinced Bolshevik, completely honest and sincere, his arrest literally stunned me. Within a few days I, too, had to share his fate. . . .

After an enquiry lasting six months, in which the investigators showed unparalleled insolence and cruelty because I refused to give false evidence against my innocent father, I was sentenced to ten years. . . .

The imprisonment was a decisive factor in my inner development. Only in prison did I get to know life properly – life without the trimmings.

'Life Proved Stronger' is the title of an article about the former priest, Darmansky, once a sectarian pedant who has since given up his office. I can say 'Life proved stronger' with even greater justification. After all my experiences, I have come to realize that life's practical wisdom lies in religion and I have turned to God. . . .

I have already mentioned that I am no theoretician – and, indeed, the theological doctrines of those priests whom I met in prison bored me to tears. . . .

There, in prison, in the midst of a vast and varied collection of people brought together by kaleidoscopic caprice, I was in the thick of life and I came to the unshakeable conclusion that the one force which can transform, refresh and spiritualize even such a body of people as this is love – the love of God, brought to earth by Jesus Christ, God's only Son. I accepted His Gospel into my heart without hesitation or doubt and at once felt such an inexpressible happiness and joy as I had never known before.

* In 1955, having been completely exonerated, he was reinstated in the party and restored to his military rank (Shavrov's note).

. . . . 1954 – the sixth year of my life in a prison camp – a wonderful, unforgettable year!

A great and decisive revolution occurred in my inner life. After I had turned to Christ, I confessed my sins and took the sacraments, the holy and life-giving mysteries of Christ. And in my outward conduct a striking change took place. I completely abandoned the wicked ways I had developed in thirty years of life. . . .

I became a religious man and joined the Orthodox Church. Perhaps someone will ask why I chose this faith rather than another.

I have no desire to engage in polemics with anyone here: all believers are one in the fight against atheism. . . .

I must just say that the Orthodox Church seems to me the purest expression of Christ's Gospel message. In its prayers and canticles I have found the fullest statement of my own religious and devotional experiences. For me, the mysteries of the church have become the source of an inexplicable spiritual lucidity and bliss. The eucharist – the living, direct contact with the Living God – has become the basis of my whole spiritual life. The saints of the Orthodox Church are living stones from which is built the living temple of the Living God. And the Orthodox Church itself is an oasis of living water in a dead and desert-like world. . . .

September 1954 – another sharp turning-point in my life. On 21 September, the festival of the Nativity of the Holy Virgin, there came a resolution from the Public Prosecutor's Office releasing me from custody. My rehabilitation came later, just after my father's release. . . .

In spring 1955 I entered the Odessa Theological Seminary. I did an accelerated course and left the seminary within a year. I read many books which proved the truth of religion and still more which refuted it – but, as before, life was my main teacher. Alas, I must disappoint our anti-religious fanatics – the more I learned from life, the more it brought me to God. I became still more convinced that faith in God is the main source of all joy, vital energy and spiritual nobility. . . .

Of course, mixing in ecclesiastical circles I had even more opportunity than in the prison camp to take stock of the Orthodox clergy. I saw among them quite a few hangers-on – greedy, unconscientious, shallow people, unworthy of their high calling. Even in the upper ranks of the clergy, I met some who were weak in spirit, evasive and insincere. Fortunately, though, on the whole the clergy is without a doubt made up of honest, good, Christian folk, who entered the church with a sense of vocation. Many of them are thinking people with great experience of life.

Seminary friends were of this type. The vast majority of them were honest, untiring workers. It is no coincidence that, among the friends who graduated with me in 1956, there occur such names as Rasnyansky, at one time quite a famous railway engineer, now known as Priest-monk German; a coal-cutter, Mikhail Lukin, now a deacon; a regular army captain, F. Abramov, now a priest; A. Alekhin, once an ordinary metal-worker and now a deacon; I. Silakov, formerly a philologist and art-critic, now a priest; a petty officer first class, Nikolai Zolotukhin, once a sailor in the Black Sea Fleet and now a venerable priest, and many others. . . .

True, side by side with these deeply religious people, all straightforward and sincere, the Odessa Seminary has had other types of graduates: I am thinking in particular of the notorious Duluman* and his henchman Darmansky. . . .

After graduating from the theological seminary, I did not enter the priesthood, mainly because I did not yet consider myself worthy of the office. At present I live in Moscow and am preparing to sit the examinations of the theological academy as an external student. I am reading and thinking a great deal and taking as active a part I can in the life of the church. The deeper I delve into life, the stronger my faith becomes, the more calm and contented I feel. . . .

What, then, are the results of my becoming a Christian?

Vodka, which in the past often played a disastrous part in my

* See p. 64.

life and considerably reduced my value both as a citizen and as a man, has now entirely disappeared.

I have ceased to be a shallow person and have overcome my frivolous, coarse and animal attitude to women.

I have stopped smoking tobacco, that stupefying and intoxicating agent which had such a pernicious effect on my health.

Whereas at one time I used to frequent the servicemen's clubs in Moscow and many of the seaports of the USSR, I have now forsaken my life of debauch and rowdyism.

Only now have I really begun to participate in intellectual life. I have begun to take an interest in reading and now feel the need to write.

Although I am quite a sick man, being to this day a second-category invalid of World War II, I have greater energy and capacity for work now than in the early post-war days, when I was an out-and-out atheist.

By becoming a true son of the Russian Orthodox Church, I have become an even greater patriot.[26]

6 The Legal Dimension

ESHLIMAN AND YAKUNIN

TO THE CHAIRMAN OF THE PRESIDIUM OF THE SUPREME SOVIET OF THE UNION OF SOVIET SOCIALIST REPUBLICS

To Comrade N. V. Podgorny
From Citizens of the USSR:
N. I. Eshliman (priest)
Flat 10, 4/2 Pushkin St.,
Moscow, K-25;
G. P. Yakunin (priest)
Flat 13, 7 Zhukovsky St.,
Moscow, K-62.

DECLARATION

We, as citizens of the Soviet Union, address you with a protest against illegal actions of the leaders and representatives of the Council for Russian Orthodox Church Affairs under the Council of Ministers of the USSR. These actions have flagrantly violated the principle of socialist law and the basic legislative requirements of the Soviet Government determining the relations of the Soviet State to the church. . . .

In order to control the observance of the laws determining the relations of the state to the church and for mediation between the church and state in civil matters, CROCA was established as a department of the Soviet Government.

Nevertheless, during the period 1957–64, under personal pressure from Khrushchev, who permitted 'subjectivism and bureaucracy in the leadership', which were finally condemned by the Communist Party of the USSR, by the Soviet Government and by all of Soviet society, CROCA radically changed its function. From being an official department for arbitration, it became an

G

organ of unofficial and illegal control over the Moscow Patriarchate.

Moreover, the intrusion of CROCA leaders and officials into the internal life of the church took on forms which must be regarded as a flagrant violation of the very principles of socialist justice and Soviet legislation on religion and the church.

The very method of using unofficial oral decrees, which CROCA leaders and officials chose as a means of systematic interference in the internal life of the Orthodox Church, is a violation of the principles of law. . . .

1. *Illegal registration of the clergy as a means of interference in their placement.*

. . . . Thus, while it grants the right to remove individuals from membership of the executive body of religious societies,* Soviet law in no case grants civil authorities the right of removing clergymen when being assigned or transferred. . . .

Nevertheless, contrary to the law, CROCA officials have acquired for themselves the right to remove clergy, thereby transforming the registration of clergy from a formal into a sanctioning act.

Using this unfair juggling, the leaders and representatives of CROCA have established a practice in the Russian Church whereby it has become impossible to ordain, assign or transfer clergy without first obtaining oral approval from leaders or representatives of CROCA so as to gain official registration. . . .

Moreover, the interference of CROCA leaders and representatives in the assigning and transferring of clergy is a flagrant violation of the principle of socialist justice, for it is brought about by unofficial oral decrees.

2. *The illegal campaign of the mass closing of churches and monasteries and the illegal liquidation of religious societies.†*

. . . . The liquidation of a prayer building in no way signifies the dispersion of the religious congregation, for, according to law,

* See p. 17.   † Cf. Chapters 3 and 4.

after such an event the religious congregation has the right to keep the objects of the cult ('icons, vestments, banners, covers etc.') and transferable property ('money, as well as incense, candles, oil, wine, wax, firewood and coal') ('*On Religious Associations*, §40, Pars. c and e)[1]. . . .

Nevertheless, contrary to the law, these rights have been flagrantly violated.

It is well known that during the period 1961–64, under the personal initiative of Khrushchev,* an active campaign was conducted in our country for the widespread closing of Orthodox churches.

Within the time of this campaign no less than ten thousand churches and dozens of monasteries were closed, among which should be specially mentioned the Monastery of the Caves at Kiev, the most ancient sacred place of the Russian people. ∴ . .†

Moreover, we consider it our right as citizens to call your attention to the undeniable fact that the actively inflated campaign of mass closure of churches created an atmosphere of anti-religious fanaticism which led to the barbaric destruction of a large number of superb and unique works of art. . . .‡

6. *Violation of the principle of separation of church from state by means of administrative interference in the financial life of a church congregation.*

. . . . In violation of Soviet law, in 1961–62 CROCA officials obliged the executive organs of church congregations systematically to present a financial report to the local authorities (district executive committees) and to allow the representatives of the local authorities to inspect the financial life of the congregation without interference.

In practice this has led to the point where representatives of the local authorities have put themselves in the position of managers

---

* Cf. p. 38.   † Cf. p. 85.

‡ The material in sections 3–5 closely corresponds to what is reproduced in the next document (pp. 196–8, 201–2). Cf. Talantov's account (pp. 147–52).

of the church congregations, flagrantly interfering in all aspects of the administrative and economic life of the church. . . .

7. *Illegal limitation of the number of members of a religious society to the* DVADTSATKA *and the denial in practice to the large majority of believers of their legal rights to participate in managing the administrative and economic life of the Russian Orthodox Church.*

According to Soviet law, a religious society is recognized as a community of believers which is made up of no less than twenty adult citizens of the USSR. The numerical growth of a religious society is not limited by law. All local residents of a corresponding faith have the right to become members of a religious society at any time after its founding and to sign the contract for receiving use of the building and the property of the cult, 'thus obtaining the right of managing the property equally with those persons who first signed the contract' (*On Religious Associations*, §3 and §31).[2]

Such are the provisions of the law. Nevertheless, CROCA leaders do not abide by these provisions. Its representatives, by means of administrative pressure on the executive organs of the congregations, systematically limit the size of religious societies to twenty or thirty members. In some instances they even prevent the number of members of a religious society from reaching the minimum norm envisaged by the law. . . .

8. *The illegal limiting of the staff of clergy, inhibiting the performance of religious rites.*

Here, too, CROCA officials flagrantly violate Soviet law: taking advantage of the 'right' to remove clergy that they have illegally acquired . . . . CROCA officials systematically diminish the active numbers of Russian Orthodox Church clergy.

. . . . Here it is appropriate to note that at a time when parishes of the Russian Orthodox Church severely need priests, many hundreds of priests, through the fault of CROCA officials, are in retirement. . . .*

*   *   *

. . . . Thus the leaders and officials of CROCA, radically distorting the lawful purpose of the organization, have transformed it into a clearly discriminatory body, whose entire activities are directed at a systematic violation of the laws concerning the separation of church from state and of school from church, and a systematic hindering of the performance of religious rites. This is a criminally punishable act, as formulated by §§142 and 143 of the Penal Code of the RSFSR.[3]

It is not suprising that, in order to implement their illegal activities, CROCA officials have selected a method of unofficial oral dictates, in contradiction to the principles of socialist justice and the law on secret instructions. In this way they tried to conceal their illegal acts to avoid accountability.* CROCA leaders have gone so far in attempting to keep out of the public eye (which is characteristic of every illegal group) that the building occupied by the council has no name on it. This is an insignificant detail, but it is very characteristic!

In connection with this the following fact is remarkable: in 1959 and 1965 two collections of party and state documents on religion and the church were published.[4] In neither one is any mention made of CROCA, the authoritative body in this field.

A convincing proof that CROCA hinders the enforcement of Soviet legislation on religion and the church is found in the following fact. Through the efforts of its leaders, the teaching of this legislation . . . . has not been introduced into the theological schools of the Moscow Patriarchate. . . .

The principle of further strengthening socialist justice demands that the scandalous policies of the leaders and officials of CROCA, being a persistent legacy of the period of arbitrariness which has been condemned by Soviet society, be finally brought to light. They should be carefully and completely examined and legally

* For concrete examples, see pp. 73, 239.

condemned, so that all the activities of the council may be brought into complete compliance with the state's legislation on religion and the church. . . . Moreover, all the churches, monasteries and theological schools illegally closed in the period 1961–64 should be rightfully returned to the Russian Orthodox Church.

Finally, in view of the fact that the relations of the church and state, in principle, contain nothing secretive, it is necessary to place all activities of CROCA under the conditions of legal publicity and to submit it to systematic public control, with the right of the Russian Orthodox Church to be represented.

15 December 1965.[5]

TO HIS HOLINESS, THE MOST HOLY PATRIARCH OF MOSCOW AND ALL RUSSIA, ALEXI

from the priests:
Nikolai Eshliman,
serving in the Church of the Veil of the
Blessed Virgin, Lyshchikov Lane, Moscow;
Gleb Yakunin,
serving in the Church of the Kazan Icon
of the Mother of God,
Dmitrov, Moscow Diocese.

AN OPEN LETTER

. . . Your Holiness!

This letter is the fruit of earnest prayers, of spiritual struggle and severe doubts. But, forced by Christian conscience and pastoral duty, we considered it necessary to turn to you and in your person to the mother of us all – the Russian Orthodox Church.

On 21 November 1944 you pronounced the following words of spiritual wisdom which unfortunately turned out to be prophetic: 'The administration of the church is secure so long as we take care not to trespass beyond the limits of canon law; as soon as we do, for some arbitrary reason, it will be hard to define the limit beyond which one must not go. One step outside the boundaries of canon law creates a great danger and gives to zealots excuses for serious and well-founded accusations.'[6]

Today the bitter truth is obvious to everyone who loves Christ and His church. It is clear that the Russian Church is seriously and dangerously ill, and that her sickness has come about entirely because the ecclesiastical authorities have shirked from fulfilling their duties; they have overstepped the limit 'beyond which one must not go'. . . .

Recognizing our human unworthiness and our spiritual weakness, we have waited for a long time for a champion more worthy than ourselves to break the bonds of sinful silence and turn to you (and in your person to the catholic self-awareness of the Russian Church, seeking therein healing for the sickness of the church).

The radiant image of the wounded Christ powerfully commands us to delay no longer and to shoulder the burden of such a heavy duty. . . .

I

. . . . The Orthodox Church has always recognized the absolute right of the state to leadership in the civil life of society and for this reason has always instilled in her members the obligation to submit themselves, according to their conscience, to the state.

The unconditional non-intervention of the state in the internal life of the church, on the one hand, and the free co-operation of the church with the state in civil affairs, if the state so desires, on the other hand – such is the principle of the free relationship between church and state. . . .

However, during the period 1957–64 . . . CROCA radically changed its function, becoming instead of a department of arbitration an organ of unofficial and illegal control over the Moscow Patriarchate. . . .

We stand with respect before the mystery and grandeur of the episcopal rank, we have the fear of God in our hearts, we recognize our own human unworthiness. Nevertheless, moved by the intractable demands of Christian conscience, we feel that it is our duty to say that such a situation in the church could occur only with the connivance of the supreme ecclesiastical authorities, who have deviated from their sacred duty before Christ and the church and have clearly violated the apostolic command by 'compromising with this world'.

The serious guilt of the church administration consists in having chosen to obey the unofficial oral instructions of CROCA, which, in violation of the clearly-stated Soviet law, have been used as a means of systematic and destructive intervention in ecclesiastical life. Instructions issued by telephone, oral demands, undocumented and unofficial agreements – such is the unhealthy, mysterious atmosphere which has swathed in a heavy mist the relations between the Moscow Patriarchate and CROCA.*

If the *Spiritual Regulation* of Peter I, which placed a believing lay official at the head of the Holy Synod, aroused a justifiable protest from the Christian conscience, how much more shocking is the situation in which the activity of the Moscow Patriarchate is silently directed by atheist officials.

Your Holiness!

We are perfectly well aware of the exclusive responsibility we bear for the accusations we make, but we are positive that they are true and are prepared to answer for every one of them before the judgment of God. . . .

A long list of facts confirms every one of our accusations.

1. *Illegal registration of baptisms and other ceremonies.*†

Is it imaginable that in the apostolic age, when many thousands were baptized upon hearing the words of Christ's apostles, certain selected members of the church community, following the requirements of the apostles, should have taken the names of those who wished to be baptized before the celebration of the sacrament and then submitted these lists to the Roman or Jewish authorities?

It is sinful even to consider it! But however sad it is to say this,

* Cf. p. 241.   † Cf. pp. 309–10.

precisely such a situation exists today in the Russian Church and her priests are forced, in obedience to episcopal authority, actively to participate in this sin as a result of Circular No. 1917 issued by Your Holiness on 22 December 1964.*

Unconditional submission to existing illegality, which this circular demands, places the pastor in the situation of an informer against those who have entrusted themselves to the care of our Mother Church.

The fact is that during recent years in the vast majority of parishes a 'system' has been introduced under which the sacrament of baptism is performed only after prior and obligatory registration. Everyone who wishes to be baptized himself or to secure it for his children is bound first of all to submit his passport to a representative of the church council, who registers it (or his birth certificate) on a special form. Moreover, for the baptism of children the presence of both parents is required. Similarly, illegal registration is necessary for other ceremonies: matrimony, unction, communion at home and funerals.

It is well known to the administration of the Moscow Patriarchate that the registration papers for baptism and other rites are thoroughly scrutinized by local governmental departments and have until recently been used by atheist activists for coarse persecution of those who have been baptized, of parents who have had their children baptized, of those married in church, and so on. They have been 'worked over' in their jobs and at school, submitted to 'administrative pressure', caricatured alongside drunks, debauchees and parasites and their names appeared in the press with unflattering commentaries.

At the present time, anti-religious zealots continue to use the registration of church ceremonies, which the local authorities receive directly from the church councils, for the ideological struggle with the church and for administrative intervention into the private religious lives of citizens.†

* This does not introduce the regulations, but merely obliges priests to conform to the already-existing legislation (note by Eshliman and Yakunin).

† Cf. pp. 149–50.

The administration of the Moscow Patriarchate is well aware of all this, and it is also aware that the present 'system' of registering baptism and other church ceremonies is contrary to Christian conscience, to canon law and to pastoral duty; it is a blatant illegality and arbitrariness, which flouts the principle of freedom of confession.

How did this practice come about? Where is the law, or even written instructions, ecclesiastical or civil, by means of which it was introduced into parish life?* They do not exist! . . .

Moreover, it will not be beside the point to add that the illegal registration of church ceremonies is undermining the trust of the people in their Mother Church and is a serious stumbling block for those who wish baptism for themselves or for their children. In this way, by actively permitting this illegal practice, the Moscow Patriarchate is taking upon itself a most serious sin, by giving rise to spiritual temptation and by turning human souls away from salutary grace.

Can a Christian conscience remain impartial to such blatant illegality?

2. *The mass closing of churches, monasteries and theological schools†*

Orthodox people from the earliest times have loved God's temples. They have put into the construction of His churches all the depth and beauty of their Christian vision, the wisdom of the gospel and their spiritual strength, the enlightened sense of harmony and their rich talents. The building and treasuring of Christian churches was always considered a matter of prime importance and of religious expression. 'I have loved the beauty of Thy house and the place of Thy habitation,' for the Orthodox church is indeed the house of God, the focal point of church life, the spiritual table which feeds the faithful with the incorruptible gifts of divine grace, the place of encounter between the divine and the human, the heart of the Christian community (*ecclesia*). . . .

* See note on p. 197.   † Cf. Chapters 3 and 4.

The rights of a community to use a church are protected by law. . . .*

During the last forty years the Russian Church has undergone two periods of mass closure of churches. The first time was during the period of Stalin's personality cult, the second was during the rule of Khrushchev. Over the short period 1961–64 thousands of Orthodox churches were closed. They were closed contrary to the wishes of the believers, in violation of the stated law and not in accordance with the envisaged legal procedure.

A great disaster struck the Russian Church. One loss followed another: Glinskaya Pustyn, a very ancient shrine of Russia, the Monastery of the Caves at Kiev, St. Andrew's Cathedral which housed the holy relics of the great martyr Barbara, the cathedral of Novgorod, the 'Holy Hermitage' of the Pochaev Monastery,[7] thousands of churches in the Ukraine and Belorussia, monasteries in the Carpathian Mountains and in Moldavia, the holy churches of Russia! Calamity also struck the seats of Christian learning. The seminaries of Kiev, Stavropol, Saratov, Volhynia and Zhirovitsy were shut down one after the other.† A cry of woe shook the Russian Church! At this time the profound suffering of the faithful turned their hearts to their pastors, hoping for assistance. For who else, if not the pastor, must lay down his life for the sheep, protecting the flock from destruction? A flood of complaints and protests, signed by thousands of Orthodox, swamped the diocesan bishops and the administration of the Moscow Patriarchate. Hundreds of plaintiffs filled the chancelleries of the ruling bishops during those days. Messengers from suffering parishes and monasteries came thousands of kilometres to Moscow, in search of protection and support from the Holy Patriarch.‡

Alas, these hopes were in vain!

It was with polite indifference, with cold callousness, as though these were annoying complainers, that the diocesan chancelleries met the supplicants of the church's agony.

Although capable of giving effective assistance, the majority

* See pp. 19–20.   † Cf. pp. 116–18.   ‡ Cf. pp. 143–4.

of the bishops of the Russian Church did not find enough courage to rise to the defence of their flocks. We are not speaking of those few who were consciously serving the cause of lawlessness, personally helping the atheists to close churches; of these it is written, 'Let his habitation be desolate, and let no man dwell therein: and his bishopric let another take' (Acts 1:20). But even those bishops who in their hearts grieved for the suffering of the church helplessly raised their hands, as if to say, 'The Lord hath forsaken the earth, and the Lord seeth not.' (Ezek. 9:9). Is this so?

Does not the sacred duty of a bishop command him to lay down his life for the sake of the sheep of Christ's flock? The bishops had full opportunity not only to direct the protest of the faithful along legal channels, but themselves to plead before the civil authorities for the cessation of this lawlessness.

The example of such a bishop, the Most Reverend Yermogen, Archbishop of Kaluga, who does not have a single closed church on his conscience, reveals that where the bishop has shown enough courage and effort in the defence of his flock, the lawlessness has retreated.*

Ten thousand closed churches and dozens of closed monasteries are the undeniable evidence of the fact that the Moscow Patriarchate did not fulfil its duty before Christ and the Russian Church, for only with the assurance that the highest church administration would remain silent could the atheists close the churches of God!

If the enemies of the church had not been certain that the Moscow Patriarchate would turn away from the lawful defence of its flock, they would never have dared to deprive Orthodox communities of the lawful rights of their legal existence. Thus, the mass closure of churches, monasteries and theological schools bears undeniable witness to the unconditional submission of the Moscow Patriarchate to the secret dictates of atheist officials. Hundreds of thousands of Christian souls in vast areas of our country who are deprived of the nourishment of the church will witness to this lawlessness before the Lord.

* See pp. 250–1.

3. *The almost complete discontinuation of services in private homes and of requiems at cemeteries.**

.... According to the civil law effective today in our country, the celebration of church services outside the building is permitted under the following conditions: in order to celebrate a service in the open, unless it is an essential part of a service in a church, it is necessary to have the authorization of the local governmental departments. In order to have funeral services and particularly for services in private homes, no special authorization is required (*On Religious Associations*, §§58–61).

Under such legislative conditions, the pastors of the Russian Church had, until recently, the possibility of celebrating un-hindered funerals at cemeteries and services in homes: prayer services, blessing of houses, prayers for the dead and requiems.

About five years ago the celebration of services at home and of requiems at cemeteries was virtually stopped. However, we would search the legal codes in vain to find any basis for this discontinuation. There is no foundation for it in the laws. As always in such cases, this cessation was the result of an unofficial instruction by CROCA officials, illegally interfering in the internal affairs of the church and grossly sweeping aside the civil law in force. Thus, in the diocese of Moscow, for example, during the re-registration of the clergy in 1961–62, all the priests were invited to sign an unofficial directive from CROCA which permitted the celebration of services in homes and of requiems at cemeteries only after authorization from local authorities (which in practice is almost never granted); moreover, Trushin, the CROCA official for Moscow and its region, issued priests with registration documents only after they had signed that they would comply with this directive. It is important to note, also, that the 'directive' remained in the hands of Trushin, while the priests who had signed it did not receive even a copy.

.... The immediate implication of this 'directive' is that no citizen of the Soviet Union can invite a priest into his home, to conduct a prayer for the health of his sick child or a requiem for

* Cf. p. 339.

his deceased parents, without a risk that the priest – his pastor and guest – will be threatened with the withdrawal of his registration!

The administration of the Moscow Patriarchate is well aware of all this, but in this instance, too, the supreme ecclesiastical authorities, through their unprincipled silence, conceal the illegal activity which is aimed at the general asphyxiation of church life.

4. *The compulsory estrangement of children from the church.* *

. . . . There is not one point in Soviet legislation which either forbids or limits in any way the participation of children in the life of the church. Moreover, the decree, *On the Separation of Church and State*†. . . . gives the right to all citizens to teach and to study religion in private.

During recent years, CROCA officials have, by means of oral instructions to bishops, parish priests and church wardens, forbidden any participation of children and adolescents up to eighteen years of age in church services. Moreover, during great church festivals the militia and auxiliary police often simply stop young people from entering the churches. Last of all, the 'struggle against children' which has been imposed on the Russian Church, has reached such a point that in certain dioceses, under pressure from CROCA officials, priests refuse to give holy communion to children.‡

. . . . Until 1961–62 many parishes legally possessed, together with the church building, a special building for baptisms. This enabled infants to be baptized under the most favourable conditions. Now this possibility has been taken away on secret instructions from CROCA, which, without any legal basis, forbade the holding of baptisms outside the church building.

5. *The intervention of 'secular leaders' in the appointment of clergy.*

Eshliman and Yakunin establish the canonical position of the church's essential independence in appointing its own leaders.§ They quote several authoritative texts including:

* Cf. pp. 166–70.   † See p. 16.   ‡ Cf. p. 160.
§ This is the starting point for much of Archbishop Yermogen's thought. Cf. pp. 240–7.

'Any election of a bishop, priest or deacon which is made by civil authorities shall be invalid' (Third Canon of the Seventh Ecumenical Council). . . .

In this way, the canons of the church categorically proscribe the intervention in any form of the civil authorities in the appointment of the clergy.

The laws in effect in our country which regulate the relationship of the state to the church make no claims whatsoever on the inalienable right of the bishops to ordain clergy as they see fit. The Soviet laws do not envisage any prior sanction on the part of the civil authorities in the ordination of clergy, nor in their appointment or their transfer.

However, in recent years a practice has developed in the Russian Church, in which not one consecration of a bishop or ordination of a priest or deacon is possible without prior sanction from CROCA officials. Making use of the well-tried method of secret instructions, CROCA officials use all possible means to prevent the ordination of those people in whom they see a potential strength, capable of taking a future stand against the illegal activity of the atheists, which is directed at the destruction of the church. Guided by this principle, CROCA officials make a tendentious selection from among the graduates of the theological schools, hypocritically covering up their action with a concern for the good of the church; they obstruct the ordination of worthy candidates, who may not have a theological education, and do not allow those who have received a higher secular education to devote their talents to the service of the church.

Moreover, CROCA assists in infiltrating the clergy and promoting the progress of morally unstable people, of those lacking in faith and at times of totally unprincipled characters, capable of furthering the cause of destroying the holy church and of renouncing Christ altogether at some convenient moment.*

There can be no doubt that such an intrusion by CROCA officials into the realm of the sacred has been made possible only through the acquiescence of the supreme ecclesiastical authorities,

* Cf. pp. 50–5.

who for the sake of pleasing the 'secular leaders' have permitted
a mockery of religious freedom.

In an attempt to justify the existing situation, certain people
refer to a passage in the Epistle of St. Paul to Timothy, in which
the apostle lists the qualities which are essential for a candidate for
ordination and writes:

'Moreover he must have a good report of them which are
without; lest he fall into reproach and the snare of the devil'
(I Tim. 3 :7).

This passage cannot serve as the slightest justification for the
intervention of CROCA officials in the appointment of clergy,
since it is certain that St. Paul is speaking of the witness of outsiders concerning the good life of the candidate, not a formal
'attestation'. Moreover, the apostle does not identify the term
'those which are without' in any way with the authorities, but
means 'those believers who do not belong to the Church of Christ,
Jews and Greeks'. To be well thought of does not imply the
possession of formal written evidence from outsiders which must
be presented to one's own people, but that the candidate for the
episcopate must have a good reputation even among those who
are not believers. In what sense? Not, of course, because of his
external position, but 'on account of his generally-recognized
moral integrity and good deeds'[8]. . . .

II

Eshliman and Yakunin quote at length from the 1945 and 1961
statutes of the Russian Orthodox Church.*

It will be seen that the Statute of the 1945 Council and the
Synodal Decree of 1961 directly contradict one another, defining
the position of the priest in the parish and the scope of his pastoral
service completely differently.

The Council of 1945 sees the pastor as the father and head of
the parish, who is concerned not only with the liturgical aspects

* See pp. 43–6.

of church life and the behaviour of the clergy, but who also exercises spiritual control over the administrative and economic life of the flock entrusted to him.

In contradistinction to this, the decree of the Synod, which takes away from the priest the administrative and economic management of the parish, in actual fact lowers the priest to the level of an employee who celebrates the liturgy and holds services on a contractual basis, making him entirely dependent on the executive body.

In practice, this brings about a situation in which the council of laymen is freed from the supervision of the pastor; it is not only able to apply material and administrative pressure on the priest, but at the same time acquires the right, unthinkable for the Church of Christ, arbitrarily to dismiss its spiritual father.

It is clear that such a situation fundamentally contradicts the teaching of the church concerning the priesthood. Christ's pastor is the foundation of the church. Our Lord established his church on him, in the person of St. Peter, and entrusted him with its care.

'And I say also unto thee, that thou art Peter, and upon this rock I will build my church; and the gates of hell shall not prevail against it'. . . . (Mat. 16:18).

The Lord alone, who gave pastoral authority to his apostle, and in his person to the bishop and presbyter, is the pastor of the flock, and none other!

Any attempt to limit the hierarchical authority of the church, to put it into the hands of the flock, is anti-ecclesiastical and anti-religious. The responsibility of the pastor for his flock is all-embracing and includes not only the liturgical aspects of church life, but also the administrative and economic aspects. For unless the pastor has active control over these matters, he cannot be sure that the purity of the flock entrusted to him is truly preserved, nor prevent discord and protect his flock from 'wolves and thieves'.

Our supreme Pastor gave an example of such concern for his flock and for the purity of the church when he threw the merchants out of the temple with a scourge (John 2:13-16). The imitation of

Christ in all things has always been considered by the church as
the greatest of virtues. If, however, today a pastor of the Russian
Church attempted – not to drive out with a scourge – but merely
by his pastoral admonitions to stop the wolves from scattering
the flock and from turning the temple into a house of merchan-
dise, he would inevitably bring upon himself the accusation of
intervening in matters which – according to the present situation –
are forbidden to him. If, moreover, 'wolves' are to be found
among the members of the *dvadtsatka* and even among the members of the church council, then inevitably, by administrative
means, the pastor is taken out of the centre of his flock and may
be deprived of his 'registration', which, as is well known, prevents
the pastor from continuing to serve. . . .

As is made clear in these examples and canons, the holy church
never conceived of a spiritual authority which would be limited
in its functions to 'the service of the word', in the same way as it
does not conceive of a body which is not subordinate to the soul.

The existing split between the 'body' and 'soul' within the
organism of the church – the separation and insubordination of
the material and economic to the spiritual – is an obvious sickness,
nurturing dangerous consequences.

The Synodal Decree was a serious assault against the canonical
defences of the church, leaving an easy breach for the intrusion
of powers hostile to it. Their actions were soon revealed in a most
direct way. Thus the executive organs of the church councils,
which were elected and functioned without pastoral blessing and
were therefore free from the proper canonical authority of the
bishop and the priest, have come under the control of the local
civil authorities and CROCA officials.

Today, four years after the introduction of the Synodal Decree,
its sorrowful consequences are obvious; in the great majority of
parishes spiritual life has to a large extent broken down. The unity
of the flock has been destroyed, for the executive organ has become
a means of access for persons not belonging to the church and
often for influences hostile to it, which seek to submit the altar to
their rule, openly tempting and enticing, giving rise to strife and

all kinds of disorders which have become so characteristic of parochial life today.

Following the Synodal Decree, the parishes of the Russian Church have become victims of a destructive principle: 'divide and rule'. Profound anger in the hearts of the faithful is aroused by the fact that this principle, which is so destructive for any unity, has become rooted in the life of the church and has been legalized by the supreme ecclesiastical authorities who are called upon to preserve the unity of the flock!

The question naturally arises: on what basis did the Synod of Bishops in 1961 confirm the curial decree of the Holy Synod, which was to be so harmful for the life of the church?

Anyone who is familiar with the acts of the 1961 Synod* is struck by the lack of correct canonical argumentation. Superficial references to unnamed canonists, unsubstantiated and completely unproven ecclesiastical and historical arguments, the unfounded introduction of principles of 'wholesale democratization' into the area of ecclesiastical and hierarchical relations – these are the shaky 'arguments' which the fathers of the synod opposed to the canons of the apostles and of the ecumenical councils.

Your Holiness!

In your introductory address at the 1961 Synod, you said that the freeing of pastors from involvement in 'economic and financial activity of the community . . . finds justification in the decision of the holy apostles, described in the book of Acts, for the ministers of the church to give themselves to "prayer and to the ministry of the world" and to entrust the concern for the "tables" (economic supervision) to persons elected from the community of the church (Acts 6: 2-8)'.

We do not understand how it is possible to exclude from the ranks of the ministers of the church the holy archdeacon Stephen, the first martyr, Philip, Prochorus, Nicanor, Timon, Parmenas and Nicholas of Antioch!

Every Christian knows perfectly well that these seven men chosen from among the people, 'men of honest report, full of the

* See partial text, pp. 44–6. Complete text in JMP 8, August 1961, pp. 3–29.

Holy Ghost and wisdom', were 'set before the apostles: and when they had prayed, they laid their hands on them' (Acts 6:3-6). Thus, only after the ordination to the diaconate did these men acquire the authority to manage the economy of the church!

The example of the election and appointment of the seven deacons not only provides no argument for the 'freeing' of the pastor from the management of the administrative and economic activity of the community, but, on the contrary, demonstrates quite clearly that in the true apostolic tradition all aspects of church life are subject to the hierarchical principle.

The Decree passed by the Synod of Bishops in 1961 is thus a blatant violation of apostolic tradition and of canon law. To use your own words, it has trespassed beyond the limits of canon law, created great danger and given cause for serious and well-founded accusations.

Eshliman and Yakunin continue with an account of how the administration of church finances has illegally passed into the hands of the secular authorities.

After this description of the tragic state of the Russian Church, the question that naturally arises is: how could this situation come about? Why did the supreme ecclesiastical authorities become a submissive tool in the hands of atheist officials? Why do the pastors and bishops, for the most part sincere and honest people, incomprehensibly cover up this blatant illegality with their silence?

In answering these questions, we must point out first of all that there are in the Russian Church today several bishops and priests who are consciously serving this illegality.* These are the ones who have acquired infamy in the closure of Orthodox churches, who value any instruction of local authorities higher than the word of the Gospel and the canons of the church, these are the ones who deprive children of the holy communion, who abuse the sanctity of the church,† who have sold their brothers, who

* For a concrete example, see pp. 143-4.

† A blatant example of this was the blasphemous burial of the holy and glorified relics of St. Feodosi of Chernigov, which Bishop Ignati carried out on the instructions of local officials (note by Eshliman and Yakunin).

have lost the fear of God and assist militant atheists in their attempts to destroy the holy church.

All these people are well known, but the matter does not end with them. We consider it our special duty to turn the attention of Your Holiness to the following undeniable fact: that at this time in the Russian Church there is a whole group of bishops and priests who, under a guise of piety, are consciously and actively perverting the spirit of Russian Orthodoxy. These men have conceived the evil idea of corrupting the Russian Church and of implanting in it a spirit of indifference, servility and pharisaism, the corrupting leaven of 'this world'. They would like to turn the supreme ecclesiastical authorities into a bureaucratic office, a sort of 'Ministry for the Affairs of the Orthodox Faith', empowered to restrain and regulate the religious feelings of believing citizens.

A spirit of self-confident prosperity against the background of general anxiety, rapid success on the official front, a 'one hundred per cent' readiness to serve 'this age', a submissive and pliable conscience – such are the distinguishing characteristics of these men. They almost repeat the words of the representatives of the Church of Laodicea:

'I am rich and increased with goods, and have need of nothing' (Rev. 3:17). 'They have a form of godliness, but deny the power thereof' (II Tim. 3:5).

This active and growing group of 'evil pastors' is now becoming the most dangerous threat to the Russian Church.

Another great danger is that the overwhelming majority even of those bishops and priests who are extremely dissatisfied with the present situation in the Russian Church remain silent and by their painful silence contribute to its deterioration. We are not speaking of those who keep silent out of fear or despair – these motives alone are so reprehensible that they demand no special refutation – no, we have in mind those bishops and priests who attempt to justify their silence by 'higher considerations'. Some bishops seriously consider that by their silence they can save the Russian Church. 'If we start protesting against the illegal actions of CROCA we will be deprived of our registration and then our vacated bishoprics will be seized by the most successful opponents of church freedom, which will be worse than the first', they say.

Indeed, if, in order to preserve their bishoprics from 'malicious pastors', the bishops who have taken upon themselves the 'mission' of saving the church remain silent, and by their silence close their eyes to the evil mockery of church freedom by CROCA officials, permitting the 'wolves' to scatter and plunder the flock, then what is the purpose of it? Whom, apart from themselves alone, do these bishops save? Do they not invoke on themselves the terrible words of the prophet:

'Thus saith the Lord God unto the shepherds; Woe be to the shepherds of Israel that do feed themselves! should not the shepherds feed the flocks?' (Ezek. 34:2)?

The evil 'tactics of silence' contradict what we learned from the fundamental example set by the holy apostles and by great confessors of the church. St. Paul knew well and stated clearly that after him 'wolves, who will not spare the flock' would enter the church; nevertheless, not only did he not seek to spare himself, but, contrary to the insistent pleas of his beloved children courageously undertook his task as a confessor (Acts 20:17-38). It is useful to remind those pastors who think that they are saving the church of the fact that it is not we, her weak children – bishops, priests and laymen – who save the Church of Christ, but that it is the church, our devoted Mother, who saves us and the church is saved by Christ!*

Christ did not found His church on the weak and fluctuating will of man, but on His almighty and unchanging grace; for this reason none of us needs flatter himself with vain thoughts about his role as saviour, but should humbly and courageously fulfil his duty to the Mother Church, constantly asking Christ our God for help and firmly believing that He alone, who according to His word is with us until the end of the world, is the ruler of our destinies.

Besides these false concepts of 'saving' the church, there exists among Russian pastors another temptation to which parish priests

* Cf. 330-1.

in particular are prone. Many good and active priests sincerely lament the tragic situation of the Russian Church and the grievous silence of the bishops; yet they, too, remain silent, salving their consciences with the excuse that they are trying to do a great deal towards the propagation and maintenance of a true Christian life within their own parishes. Unfortunately, these priests forget that the church is a single organism – the Body of Christ – and if, in the words of St. Paul, the sickness of one member is the sickness of the whole church (I Cor. 12:26), then, even more so, the sickness of the whole church is of necessity the sickness of every one of its members. Let there be no mistake – there cannot be a single healthy parish in a church that is sick.

Those parish priests who are aware of this general sickness, but nevertheless remain silent, should know that by their sinful silence they conceal illegality and in this way are assisting all the enemies of the holy church. Can the right to priesthood be bought at such a price? Does this not contradict the words of our Lord: 'Neither can a corrupt tree bring forth good fruit' (Mat. 7:18)?

The expression, 'We must keep quiet, or else they will take away our registration', which is widespread in the Russian Church, is an evil self-justification, not worthy of a Christian pastor. The priest should not be thinking of preserving his registration, but of remaining true to Christ and to the church. But ecclesiastical narrowmindedness and a limited parochial outlook is a spiritual sickness; it is the loss of a vision of the church as a whole. The universal concern of the Christian economy has been forgotten. The development of this sickness leads inevitably to sectarianism.

The Russian Church is heavily afflicted! Her grief is profound, her sorrow is bitter, but we are seriously convinced that this sickness is not unto death, but is for the glory of God! Not for this did our most Holy Lady take the Russian Church under her merciful protection; not for this did the first apostles of the Slavs preach the Word of God; not for this the glorious army of Russian saints stand in the church, 'invisibly praying to God for us'; not for this did St. Sergius – the great servant of God – shine forth in the heart of Russia; not for this did the holy blood of Russian martyrs flow abundantly; not for this have the Easter bells rung out over Russia for a thousand years with such triumph as has never been heard elsewhere in the world. Are all these riches, this sacred treasury, this beauty and glory to be terminated by a pitiful bureaucracy, by a submissive agent of powers which are against the church?

May this never come about!

Your Holiness! We do not wish to bear witness only of the tragic plight of the Russian Church in our letter to you; the time has now come to bring evidence that by the grace of God there are also in the Russian Church thousands of men 'who have not bowed the knee to the image of Baal' (Romans 11:4) and who are now protecting the church from within by spiritually opposing all lawlessness. . . .

III

. . . . The twentieth century is a tragic one of world wars and of great social upheavals, a century of rapid scientific development and of an ever-increasing technological strength, a century of great discoveries as well as of great aberrations. This has confronted the church with the spiritual obligation of transforming Christian teaching in a new and creative way. In our age the necessity for such a transformation is keenly felt by all Christians. The clearest evidence of this is the Second Vatican Council of the Catholic Church and the active preparations of world-wide Orthodoxy for an ecumenical council. There can be no doubt that the Russian Church has a special role to play in the great universal task of a new Christian renaissance. There is much to convince us of this.

Despite its tragic situation, of which we have already spoken, the Russian Church still remains the largest of all autocephalous Orthodox Churches and the most influential representative of catholic Orthodoxy among other Christian confessions. The historical fate of the Russian Church is inseparably linked with the fate of the Russian people, whose role in world history has been steadily increasing for the past five hundred years.

From the first days of its existence the Russian Church was always under the special protection of the Mother of God. Under her blessed protection over the course of its millennial history the Russian Church has gathered together great and rich treasures: the spiritual experience of the saints, an amazingly profound and powerful religious art, a strong and penetrating theological system.

Besides this, the Russian Church has made a unique contribution to the secular history of its country and as a result has acquired a great practical experience in the teaching of Christianity – and of moral leadership in the life of the people. It is well known that the Orthodox Church brought to Russia not only a religious but also a general cultural enlightenment. Under the spiritual guidance of the Kievan Metropolitanate the brilliant culture of pre-Mongol Russia flourished. The Russian Church supported the awareness of national unity among the people during the hard times of the Tartar occupation, fostering courage and instilling faith in a future liberation.

The religious zeal of St. Sergius and of his disciples ideologically paved the way for the uniting of national territories around the principality of Muscovy, brought about a great renaissance of Russian culture in Moscow and inspired the people to a decisive struggle with the Tartars.

It would not be an exaggeration to say that the State of Muscovy was literally nurtured by the Russian Church and that monastic colonization brought culture and economy to large uninhabited regions of northern Russia.

Eshliman and Yakunin give a brief résumé at this point of the contribution of the Russian Church to the country's cultural development.

In this last period the immediate beneficial effect of the elders of Optina was experienced by great representatives of Russian culture, such as Khomyakov, I. Kireyevsky, Gogol, Dostoyevsky,

K. Leontiev and Vladimir Solovyov. It was to the monastery of Optina that Lev. Tolstoi, tortured by doubts, came shortly before his death.

To balance the primitive utilitarianism of secular civilization which swamped Russia after the reforms of Peter the Great, the grace of God established in our country a glorious army of Christian thinkers, artists and scholars.

It is well known that Mikhail Vasilievich Lomonosov, the father of modern Russian culture, was not only a faithful son of the Orthodox Church, but a brilliant defender of Christianity. When the men of the French 'enlightenment' turned their senseless anger against the church, making crafty use of reason and science, the ingenious Lomonosov took up arms against this temptation. Following in the steps of St. Paul (Romans 1:19-25), he insisted on the close relationship between faith and science.

The authors continue with a roll-call of the great names of Russian culture which have been associated with Orthodoxy.

But however glorious the riches of the teaching of the Russian Church, however excellent its fruits, however radiant the aspirations which it implanted in the hearts of Christians, even in the past it could not consider itself above reproach and was not always ready to accomplish its Christian mission in the exceptional conditions of the new age, for in the history of the Russian Church there were also certain elements which tarnished its radiant image.

For two hundred years it suffered under a heavy burden, which to a large extent paralysed its spiritual activity. This was revealed essentially in two ways: the unfortunate tendency of Russian bishops to submit to the illegal demands of lay officials and the comparatively weak authority of the parish priest.

It is instructive to remember that the first significant manifestation of this was the acquiescence of the bishops in the arbitrary ruling of Peter I, who by an imperial decree illegally abolished the Patriarchate and imposed the *Spiritual Regulation* on the Russian Church, submitting the ecclesiastical powers to the Tsarist regime.

Contrary to the commandment of the Gospel, 'Render to Caesar the things that are Caesar's and to God the things that are God's' (Mark 12:17), and to the canons of the church, the Russian Tsar was recognized as the official head of the supreme ecclesiastical authority – the Holy Synod of the Russian Orthodox Church. The acceptance by the bishops of the illegal intrusion of the Tsar into the internal affairs of the church created a dangerous precedent and significantly undermined the church's self-awareness.

Eshliman and Yakunin then trace the development of the church's opposition to this state of affairs.

The continuous protest of the church's conscience against Peter I's *Spiritual Regulation* finally led to the active preparation at the beginning of the twentieth century for an All-Russian General Church Council, which was finally called in August 1917.

The restoration of the Patriarchate at the General Council, which had been prepared by the Orthodox renaissance of the nineteenth and the beginning of the twentieth century, was a great and blessed event in the history of the Russian Church. This council was a sign that the Russian Church had emerged from a critical situation and it laid the foundations for the rebirth of the church's independence. It is important to note here that on 23 January 1918 this was followed by the decree of the Soviet authorities on the separation of church and state.

The restoration of the Patriarchate, by God's grace, freed the Russian Church from its long sickness – the degradation of the supreme ecclesiastical authority to the level of a government office. At the same time the legalized separation of church and state created the conditions necessary for the holy church to realize its work of salvation under an atheist government. . . .

The entire activity of His Holiness Tikhon, elected as the eleventh Patriarch of all Russia at the council, was aimed at the realization of this principle. Calling upon the faithful children of the Russian Church to submit themselves to the authority of the Soviets not out of fear, but from their consciences ('There is no power but of God: the powers that be are ordained of God'

(Romans 13:1)) the holy Patriarch Tikhon at the same time consistently and unwaveringly insisted on the internal independence of church life: 'For there can be no power on earth which could bind our reverend conscience and our patriarchal word.'

Forty years ago on 7 April 1925, the feast of the Annunciation of the Blessed Virgin, the holy Patriarch Tikhon died a righteous death after seven years in office. Before this, addressing his whole Russian flock, His Holiness wrote: 'The all-conquering power of God is found only in faithfulness and firm obedience to the truth. "This is the victory that overcometh the world, even our faith."' (I John 5:4).

The fundamental truth of the church's existence in a secular society is the prevention of the intervention of 'civil leaders' in the internal life of the church, and at the same time the strict observance of civil legislation by the powers of the church. This was the principle which the holy Patriarch Tikhon, who faithfully exemplified the collective mind of the Russian Church, bequeathed to his successors.

However, the history of the Russian Church over the last forty years undeniably shows that, beginning with the lengthy rule of Metropolitan Sergi (Stragorodsky) as *locum tenens*, the supreme ecclesiastical authorities flouted the Patriarch's will and arbitrarily changed his course, which led directly to the liquidation of church freedom.

Rejecting the grace of God, which had healed the Russian Church of its long sickness, the leaders of the church during the 'Sergi' period,[9] under the cover of the Patriarchate, in actual fact restored a 'synodal' system, this time in a much more serious form, because, instead of a Christian official at the head of the Holy Synod, the helmsmen of the church's administration turned out to be atheist functionaries.

The angry words of St. Peter can justly be applied to the church leaders of that period: 'For it had been better for them not to have known the way of righteousness, than, after they have known it, to turn from the holy commandment delivered to them' (II Peter 2:21).

Unfortunately, this rebuke applies also to the present church administration, for, having inherited a clear historical opportunity of furthering the great renaissance of the church, the Moscow Patriarchate did not utilize this possibility in its most important spiritual and canonical aspect. Instead of rejecting the fruitless and pernicious methods of the 'Sergi' period, which threatened the Russian Church with the complete dissolution of all its legal forms of existence in a secular state, and instead of returning to the way of salvation entrusted to it by Patriarch Tikhon, the present church administration made the practices of the 'Sergi' period the guiding policy of its own activity. The present administration of the Russian Orthodox Church has wasted many of the spiritual treasures which had been bequeathed to us by our ancestors, while the Moscow Patriarchate has not only brought back the spiritual sickness of our forefathers, but considerably worsened it.

In this sense, the submission of the Moscow Patriarchate to the secret oral dictates of atheist officials and the affirmation of the decree by the Synod of Bishops in 1961, which placed the pastor in a position of a hireling, was an assault on the life of the Russian Church which cannot be compared even with the activity of such antagonists of church freedom and assailants of the holy church as Peter I and Catherine II.

Your Holiness!

We have written all of this to you '. . . not because ye know not the truth, but because ye know it, and that no lie is of the truth' (I John 2:21).

We do not doubt that there will be some evil people who will bring false witness against us, denying the veracity of our accusations.

Foreseeing this, we refer the entire matter to the judgment of God: we are prepared, before the entire church, to affirm our accusations with an ecclesiastical oath on the cross and the Gospel!

At the same time we demand a similar oath before the whole church from anyone who should accuse us of lying. . . .

Who are we to give you advice? . . . . He who infinitely surpasses any distinction, He, before whose face we are all small children, commands us as a father unashamedly to speak the truth. . . .

The suffering church turns to you with hope. You have been invested with the staff of primatial authority. You have the power as Patriarch to put an end to this lawlessness with one word! Do this!

Put an end to the intrusion of 'Caesar' into the internal life of the church which can be borne no longer. Restore the canonical norms of church life.

Summon a new General Church Council with the widest representation, allow the voice of the church to be heard freely, for its soul is worn out from remaining silent; the church is longing for an occasion to demonstrate its love – give it your blessing, for it no longer has the strength to refrain from obeying God's will.

Give the church your blessing, for we do not doubt that the collective wisdom of the Russian Orthodox Church, inspired by the Holy Spirit, will find a means of curing its ailments and also that the way to a great new renaissance will open before it.

'Let it be so!'

Render unto God the things that are God's and Caesar will be amply rewarded, for in truth the interests of the church in the civil sphere coincide with the interests of a free and just government.

But it is only by putting an end to the intervention of 'civil authorities' into the sphere of the sacred, however, that 'God's' Russian Church will be able to serve our country without hypocrisy and with effectiveness. By the very fact of its free existence, the church will witness to the whole world that in our country the sacred right of man to religious freedom is actually realized. Only a witness of this kind will bear any weight in the eyes of millions of people of good will in all countries of the world and such a witness cannot be supplanted by a lie. Neither the cunning of the Foreign Relations Department of the Moscow Patriarchate, nor any interviews and 'authoritative' statements, nor any participation of Russian church leaders in international movements, are capable of proving something that does not exist – the freedom of the Russian Church. . . .

Your Holiness! The time has come to listen to the voice of God!

'For lo, the winter is past, the rain is over and gone; the flowers appear on the earth, the time of the singing of birds is come, and the voice of the turtle is heard in our land' (Song of Solomon 2:11-12). . . .

There is daily an ever-increasing awareness of the impossibility of suffering such submission to lawlessness; there is a growing desire in the Russian Church for purification from the disease which has been growing in it through the fault of the church authorities; there is an ever-increasing desire in the church for true conciliar communion; and finally, there is an ever-increasing feeling of responsibility for those souls who, through the fault of the pastors of the church, have not been enlightened by the light of the Gospel and who, despite their awakened religious thirst, remain outside the frontiers of the church. . . .

The supreme ecclesiastical authorities are now confronted with an unavoidable choice: they must either redeem their serious guilt before the Russian Church by definite actions or else completely join the enemy camp, for 'no man can serve two masters . . .' (Mat. 6:24).

If the supreme authorities of the Russian Church decide to follow the path of life, they will be obliged to carry out the following measures:

1. It would be most proper at the present time, when, in all areas of civil life in our country, those faults which were permitted in the past are being corrected, that Your Holiness, as head of the Holy Synod, should request from the Government of the USSR:

    the eradication of the consequences of 'subjectivism and bureaucracy in leadership' which have been allowed to affect the church;

    the precise legal definition of the function of the Council for Russian Orthodox Church Affairs;

    the prevention in the future of any action which would

violate the decree *On the Separation of Church and State* and §124 of the Constitution of the USSR. At the same time the illegal practice of registering baptisms and other church ceremonies must immediately be brought to an end.

All the churches, monasteries and theological schools which were illegally closed in 1961–64 must be returned to the Russian Church.

The right of priests to hold services in homes and requiems at cemeteries unhindered must be restored.

The callous practice of forcibly estranging children from the church, a flagrant violation of the principle of freedom of conscience, must be immediately and decisively ended. Finally, any intervention whatever of the 'civil authorities' in clergy appointments must be stopped once and for all. Moreover, the Moscow Patriarchate must inform CROCA firmly and un-ambiguously that henceforth no oral instructions from it or its officials will be carried out by the authorities of the Russian Church.

2. It is obvious that a new Synod of Bishops must be immediately summoned to revoke the uncanonical decision of 1961, which affirmed the decree which destroyed the hierarchical structure of church life.

3. Calling to mind that 'the supreme authority of the Russian Orthodox Church in the areas of doctrine, church order and the ecclesiastical courts – legislative, administrative, juridical – belongs to the General Council summoned periodically and consisting of bishops, priests and laity,' the Moscow Patriar-chate is in duty bound to make immediate preparations for the convening of a regular All-Russian General Church Council, with the widest representation.

The calling of a General Council in the immediate future is dictated by the need for the church's general appraisal of the activi-ties of the ecclesiastical administration and by the pressing need for speedy decisions on questions of church life and teaching which have arisen in the course of time. In order that the new General Council should not turn out to be a submissive tool in the hands of anti-ecclesiastical powers, it is essential that the entire Russian Church should actively participate in the preparations for this council. Parish meetings and diocesan sessions must precede it.[10] This alone can ensure attandance at the council by those members of the clergy and of the laity who, together with the best bishops of the Russian Church, truly represent the fulness of the church's conscience.

The renaissance of the life of the Russian Church, which is actively to serve the new universal rebirth of Christianity, is the great field of action with which the new General Council is undoubtedly confronted. . . .

21 November 1965.

Your Holiness!

Forseeing that certain of your malevolent advisers will press you to answer our sincerely-written letter with an episcopal rebuke, we wish to remind you of the noble words of our Lord: 'If I have spoken evil, bear witness of the evil: but if well, why smitest thou me?' (John 18:23).[11]

> Since we are sending copies of the *Open Letter to His Holiness the Patriarch* and the *Declaration to the Civil Authorities* to the bishops of the Russian Church, we consider it necessary to address the following statement to the latter.

APPENDIX

. . . . In the summer of 1965 eight bishops of the Russian Orthodox Church, with Archbishop Yermogen of Kaluga at their head, delivered to Patriarch Alexi a declaration containing a just and well-founded criticism of the 1961 Synod of Bishops.

In their declaration, the bishops remind us that the 1961 Decree confirmed the decision of the Holy Synod 'until such time as a regular General Council of the Russian Orthodox Church be convened'; they express concern and legitimate displeasure at the fact that this council has not been called as yet and that as the situation now is 'regular General Councils do not exist in the present life of the Russian Church'.

H

Further, the bishops assert that 'the measures approved by the Synod of Bishops for the improvement of parish life have brought not improvement, but greater deterioration, as three years' experience has shown'.

The bishops perceive the reason for the canonically illegitimate decision of the Synod of Bishops to be the 'manner of its convocation – unusual in the church's experience – and the extraordinary rush of its deliberations', as a result of which 'the majority of the bishops present at the synod signed the decision limiting the rights and duties of the clergy and parish councils, without taking into consideration that this decision basically contradicted the apostolic example in its division of responsibilities (Acts 6:3-6). Yet it is this very example on which the decision of the council was based.'. . . .

Addressing His Holiness the Patriarch, the bishops request that he 'look for speedy ways to rectify the abnormal situation – a situation contradicting both ecclesiastical canons and civil legislation – in which our clergy has found itself as a result of the unsuccessful and unclear decisions of the 1961 Synod of Bishops'.

The bishops, later in their declaration, point out that 'not a single bishop, if he is really a bishop, will protest against the restoration to the clergy of their legal rights'.

We do not doubt that, adhering to church canons, Archbishop Yermogen, in obtaining the signatures of the bishops for this declaration, informed the Patriarch of his action and received his approval, in accord with the 34th Apostolic Canon.

However, after the declaration with the signatures of eight bishops was delivered to His Holiness the Patriarch, Archbishop Yermogen was summoned before the Holy Synod and was presented with a resolution of the Patriarch concerning the bishops' declaration. This contained directions to the Holy Synod to clarify to Archbishop Yermogen the illegality (!) of his actions. Furthermore, the Holy Synod insisted that Archbishop Yermogen denounce the declaration and remove his signature.

To His Grace's honour, he did not do this, but took all the responsibility for the bishops' declaration on himself.

Knowing the relationship of the Holy Synod of the Moscow Patriarchate to CROCA, we can decisively affirm that the action of the supreme ecclesiastical authority aimed at the cessation of the useful church activities of Archbishop Yermogen was dictated by CROCA. The subsequent course of events leaves no room for doubt.*

In November 1965 His Holiness the Patriarch, through the administrator of the affairs of the Moscow Patriarchate, Archbishop Alexi of Tallin, expressed to Archbishop Yermogen the wish that he should request an extended and indefinite leave of absence. Archbishop Yermogen was given to understand that the 'wishes' of the Patriarch arose from the demands of the CROCA leaders, who used for this purpose the unfounded complaints of the chairman of the Kaluga Regional Executive Council.

Not wishing to cease his episcopal activities, Archbishop Yermogen declined to ask for an indefinite leave of absence. But, considering it impossible to continue as the head of the diocese of Kaluga, on 24 November 1965 he requested transfer to another diocese at the discretion of the Patriarch and the Holy Synod.

In reply to this unambiguous request,[12] the Holy Synod immediately decided to retire Archbishop Yermogen, assigning as his place of residence the Zhirovitsy Monastery. It is in this manner that the supreme ecclesiastical authority, to please atheist bureaucrats and in full view of the entire church, deals with impunity with the best bishops of the Russian Church for acting in the Christian interest.

How long?

13 December 1965.[13]

APPEAL TO THE PATRIARCH, THE HOLY SYNOD AND THE DIOCESAN BISHOPS
(Frs. N. Eshliman and G. Yakunin)

.... On 24 December 1965 His Holiness felt it apposite to pronounce the following official resolution on our *Open Letter*:

---

* For Archbishop Yermogen's own account, see pp. 239–40.

'The priests of the Moscow diocese, Nikolai Eshliman and Gleb Yakunin . . . without waiting for any decision or reply to their letter, wilfully sent a copy to all the diocesan bishops, thus attempting to destroy the church's peace and lead it into error.

'Further . . . the authors of the letter have not kept the promise (vow) made by them at their ordination "to fulfil their ministry according to ecclesiastical law and directions of the hierarchy"....

'In view of the above, His Grace Metropolitan Pimen of Krutitsy is requested to indicate to the authors of the letter its illegality and the evil of their actions which aimed at leading the church into error. Upon presentation of the latter's report, a special decision will be taken on the case of the priests, N. Eshliman and G. Yakunin. . . .'

Thus His Holiness gave no relevant answer to the substance of the charges laid by us against the supreme ecclesiastical authorities . . . . So His Holiness described as an infringement of canon law the very fact that we circulated copies of the *Open Letter* to the diocesan bishops of the Russian Orthodox Church.

Eshliman and Yakunin cite canonical authority for their method of action.

Thus our circulating of the *Open Letter* to all the diocesan bishops can in no way be described as an act of indiscipline, as does His Holiness in his resolution. On the contrary, it is an act of obedience essential to the conciliar mind of the Universal Church. It is no fault of ours that the resolution of His Holiness flagrantly contradicts the order of an Ecumenical Council.

. . . . We consider it our duty to put forward the following in this connection.

1. Unfortunately it must be stated that the resolution of His Holiness makes no distinction between the concepts of the supreme ecclesiastical authority of the church and its supreme administration. . . .

Thus, the supreme authority of the church belongs to the General Council. The supreme administration belongs to His Holiness the Patriarch, in conjunction with the Holy Synod.

Everyone who has familiarized himself with the text of the *Open Letter* can easily convince himself that it contains no critical remarks directed at the All-Russian General Church Council.

Thus the accusation pronounced against us that we 'attempted to pass judgment . . . on the actions and decrees of the supreme ecclesiastical authority' is wholly divorced from the truth. . . .

2. Before the resolution of His Holiness of 24 December 1965, we knew of no instructions from our ecclesiastical superiors, which forbade priests to fulfil the ordinances of Canon 6 of the Second Ecumenical Council. Of course, the text of the priest's vow contains no such instruction. . . .

3. . . . Having acted in defence of ecclesiastical truth and in strict conformity with canon law, we not only have not tried to destroy the peace of the church, as His Holiness's resolution groundlessly stated, but on the contrary we tried to contribute to its true affirmation.

4. The word of truth can never sow discord in the church, for truth is from God and he who sows discord is named by the Holy Scriptures as the father of falsehood.

If we have spoken the word of truth, then, undoubtedly, we have contributed to God's work. If His Holiness the Patriarch considers that there is falsehood in our letter, then he should have exposed it. If in the secret place of his heart His Holiness knows that we have spoken the truth, how can he state that we are sowing discord?

Thus all the accusations made against us in the resolution of His Holiness are completely groundless.

Five months after the first resolution of His Holiness the Patriarch, Metropolitan Pimen of Krutitsy summoned us to the administration of the Moscow dioceses and in the name of the Patriarch asked us to present a written explanation of a number of questions connected with the *Open Letter*.

We present copies of our explanation below.[14]

EXPLANATION
(Fr. N. Eshliman)

. . . . His Grace asked me, firstly, whether we regretted and repented of our letter, and, secondly, whether we intended taking further action on these lines.

Permit me to inform Your Holiness that I personally consider, and as far as I know so does Fr. Gleb Yakunin, that my part in the authorship of this letter is of the grace of God. There can be no question of any change in the ideas expressed in it.

As for repenting, neither of us considers that we were at fault over the content of the letter and the manner in which it was circulated – unless mere faithfulness to apostolic tradition and the commandments of Christ's Holy Church are a crime according to present-day 'canonical thought'! . . .

12 May 1966.[15]

EXPLANATION
(Fr. G. Yakunin)

. . . . I consider it my duty to state once more before Your Holiness my willingness to swear on the cross and Bible as a sign of the certain truth of what is contained in the *Open Letter*. . . .

In addition, the resolution of Your Holiness, without the slightest foundation, casts doubt upon the moral motives which guided us in the compilation and circulation of the letter. . . .

12 May 1966.[16]

THE METROPOLITAN OF KRUTITSY AND KOLOMNA, DIOCESAN BISHOP OF MOSCOW

I hereby communicate to you the resolution of His Holiness, Patriarch Alexi, dated 13 May 1966:*

'As is evident from the explanations of the priests N. Eshliman and G. Yakunin, they are continuing in the errant obstinacy of their actions prejudicial to the church.

'In order to protect our Mother Church from the destruction of her peace, we consider it necessary to relieve them of their

* See pp. 279–80 for Levitin's commentary.

appointments and we forbid them to fulfil their office as priests until they fully repent. In addition, they are warned that if they continue their evil activity, it will be necessary to resort to more severe action in conformity with the demands of canon law.'[17]

13 May 1966.

LETTER TO THE PATRIARCH AND THE BISHOPS
(Frs. N. Eshliman and G. Yakunin)

Undoubtedly every prohibition on a priest from exercising ministry is a matter of the greatest responsibility, because such a prohibition not only grieves the spirit of the priest, who naturally sees the whole meaning of his life in his ministry, but it is also a hard lesson for those Christian souls who, accustomed to look upon their debarred priest as their spiritual father, now feel themselves to be orphans. . . .

His Holiness the Patriarch had no right to debar the authors of the *Open Letter* from office on the following grounds: the accusations directed against the supreme ecclesiastical administration by us refer above all to the ecclesiastical activity of Patriarch Alexi himself.

In conformity with Canon 6 of the Second Ecumenical Council, His Holiness the Patriarch was bound to submit our accusations to a court of the supreme ecclesiastical authority – the All-Russian General Church Council. . . .

On the basis of all the above, it will be clear that the ban imposed upon us by His Holiness contradicts Canon Law and therefore has the character of an individual arbitrary act, which is illegitimate in the church.

Nevertheless, we consider it our duty, for the sake of obedience, to accept the illegal ban, pending trial by an ecclesiastical court.

Bowing before Your Holiness, we humbly promise that our hand will not touch the stole until a regularly-constituted church court has removed from us this unjust ban. . . .

We address ourselves to all the diocesan bishops of the Russian Orthodox Church in the name of God's truth to raise their voice in support of our appeal!

23 May 1966.[18]

PROTESTING PRIESTS SUSPENDED IN SOVIET UNION

Moscow, June 8 (UPI) – Two Russian Orthodox priests who accused the Soviet Government of suppressing religion have been suspended from the priesthood, a high church official said today....

Archbishop Alexi, chief administrative officer for the Moscow Patriarchate, confirmed the letter in an interview in the Patriarchal Palace today.

The two priests, who are 35 years old, wrote the letter six months ago, the archbishop said. They were suspended by the Patriarchate in late May – about the time the letter was disclosed in New York. He called this a coincidence and said they were 'suspended only because of their activities here'.[19]

THE PATRIARCH OF MOSCOW AND ALL RUSSIA TO ALL BISHOPS

Recently in our church life we have witnessed a sad endeavour by several clergy and laymen to sow discord and to disrupt the peace of the church.

.... In their appeal they ask that a Synod of Bishops be convened for an examination of their case: in this regard we cannot but recall that it was precisely the acts of the 1961 Synod of Bishops which are subject to censure and criticism in the *Open Letter* of the priests, N. Eshliman and G. Yakunin. We have received the opinions of the overwhelming majority of our bishops, who unanimously condemn the shameful activity of these priests banned by us. The Holy Synod will pass judgment on the matter of their appeal and will take account of the opinions expressed by the reverend bishops on this.

We decisively denounce the particular form in which the so-called *Open Letter* was sent to us, for church practice does not know of such a form of correspondence between clergy and their bishop. People who use the form of open addresses to their spiritual superior are trying to sow mistrust of the highest ecclesiastical authority among our clergy and laity and at the same time they introduce discord into the peaceful stream of church life. In their activities we perceive an aspiration to bring harm to the unity of our holy church and to disrupt its peaceful existence. Our Lord Jesus Christ, before His sufferings on the cross, prayed not only that those who believe in Him should abide in the faith, but also, more particularly, that all should be one. If anyone think himself to have the faith, but does not preserve the unity of the church, he not only remains outside the effective sphere of Christ's redeeming and omnipotent prayer, but even beyond eternal salvation. We are mindful of past schisms and their perniciousness for the holy church. Therefore its every true child is obliged, as his duty, to preserve its peace and unity as a most precious treasure; only in such circumstances is a normal church life possible.

It is a sincere joy to us that the bishops, clergy and believers of our church well understand the importance of unity and peace for normal church life and consequently efforts to sow discord in church life are not finding support; those who cause dissension in the church are in isolation and are incurring decisive censure on their activities. Furthermore, we also perceive here an attempt to slander the civil authorities. The attempt by individuals to assume the role of self-appointed judges of the supreme ecclesiastical authority and their desire to slander the civil authorities do not serve the interests of the church and set out to destroy the favourable mutual relationships which have been established.

The slanderous accusations against the supreme ecclesiastical authority can be used by certain circles abroad which are inimical to our church and our country, to the detriment of both.

We most decisively condemn those who sow strife and discord in the church and we have found it just to apply measures of censure against these clergy of our diocese; if they fail to repent and continue these harmful activities, we have warned them that we shall have recourse to more severe means of bringing them to see reason.

Further to the above, I invite all diocesan bishops to give strict attention to suppressing personally and with utmost severity the harmful efforts by certain individuals to destroy the peace of the

H 2

church and to discredit the highest ecclesiastical authority in the eyes of the clergy and laity. The dissemination of all sorts of 'open letters' and articles must be definitely stopped. It is the obligation of the diocesan bishops to attend to this. . . .

Odessa, Dormition Monastery,
6 July 1966.[20]

AN OPEN LETTER FROM RUSSIA TO FATHER VLADIMIR OF THE BBC
(a humble Christian of the Russian Orthodox Church)

Your Reverence!

Deeply respected Father!

At this moment, when the courageous statement of the Moscow priests, like an alarm in the night, is awakening the sleeping might of the Russian Orthodox Church and attracting the concentrated attention of Christians all over the world to her exalted and tragic fate, a burden of exceptional responsibility is placed upon everyone who takes the bold step of publicly expressing his opinion about the spiritual struggle which has developed in the heart of the Russian Church.

We, like many other Orthodox Christians, being deeply concerned with what is now happening in the Russian Church, are sincerely grateful to the BBC and to you personally for the attention given to our ecclesiastical affairs, for the extensive information which we extract from your broadcasts about the reaction of world Christianity to the statement of the Moscow priests and especially for the considerable support which you give to the just cause they have taken up.

However, much in the composition of the programmes and in your personal statements evokes amazement and protest in the hearts of radio listeners in Russia. In a spirit of Christian dialogue, we would like to express this to you in the pages of this letter.

1. Despite the deep spiritual interest with which we all, as Russian Orthodox Christians, regard what the representatives of foreign denominations and in particular the members of our

beloved Sister, the Roman Catholic Church, say about the situation that has arisen in our church, we are most of all interested in the voice of our native Orthodoxy.

This is something we scarcely hear in your broadcasts.

Meanwhile, we know for certain about the decisive statements in support of the Muscovite priests being made by Orthodox figures abroad, such as Archbishop Ioann of San Francisco, the ecclesiastical writer Nikita Struve and many others.

Real bewilderment is arising as to why the BBC, well known for its accuracy and objectivity in the interpretation of events, is this time depriving its listeners in Russia of sufficiently full information.

2. Father Vladimir!

Over several broadcasts you persistently have been asserting that 'a historical error had crept into' the letter of the Moscow priests to His Holiness the Patriarch.

You attempt to discover this error in the fact that there are, according to you, historical precedents for the decision passed by the 1961 Synod of Bishops concerning the transference of administrative power in the parishes into the hands of laymen, which was sharply criticized by the Moscow priests. . . .

You are completely right in your assertion that in the seventeenth century in some northern towns of Russia, and also in the Polish Ukraine, administrative power in the parishes belonged to laymen. However, in the history of Russia there has not been a case where such a practice has been confirmed by a decision of a Synod of Bishops and introduced as obligatory for the whole national church.

Thus, although the Moscow priests did not assert this, the decision of the 1961 Synod of Bishops really has no precedent, at least in the history of the Russian Church. . . .

Further, we have every reason to assert that not every precedent is worthy of imitation!

As is well known from church history, there was the Latrocinium ('Robber Council') at Ephesus and the profane 'Synod of the Oak' which condemned St. John Chrysostom; there have been usurpers of church power, Patriarchs who have introduced pernicious heresies, unworthy bishops who have helped the enemies of the church, the *Spiritual Regulations* of Peter I and much else.

3. Father Vladimir!

In one of your broadcasts you expressed the idea that the fathers of the 1961 Synod of Bishops accepted the resolution on the transference of administrative power in the parishes into the hands of laymen 'in good faith' and that this would turn out for the best.

We are bewildered on what basis you, in far-away London, can give such a crucial assessment of the moral motives by which the fathers of the 1961 Synod of Bishops were guided.

Unlike the majority of your listeners in Russia, who so far have not had the opportunity of becoming sufficiently well acquainted with the letters of the Moscow priests, you should be aware from the *Appendix* to these letters of the petition which eight of the most worthy bishops of the Russian Church, with Archbishop Yermogen at their head, handed to His Holiness Patriarch Alexi in the summer of 1965.

In their petition the bishops point to the unusual way in which the synod was convened and the extraordinary haste with which it was carried through, as a result of which, as the bishops assert, the majority of those present at it signed the resolution on the delimitation of the rights and duties of the clergy and the parochial councils, 'not considering that this resolution fundamentally contradicted the apostolic example in the division of these obligations (Acts 6:3–6), upon which it was based at the synod'.

Does it not seem to you, Fr. Vladimir, that Archbishop Yermogen and the others who signed the petition are better informed than you as to what happened at the synod?

In actual fact, could 'good faith' have motivated His Holiness Patriarch Alexi to distort the sense of a crystal-clear text of Holy Scripture?

Could 'good faith' have motivated Metropolitan Pimen to refer to the principles of 'broad democratization' in the solution of a canonical question?

Could 'good faith' have motivated the fathers of the Synod of Bishops to violate the Holy Canons?

Finally, could 'good faith' have motivated the bishops of the Russian Church to accept a resolution, the perniciousness of which was completely obvious?

Anyone who knows even a little about the state of affairs in the Russian Orthodox Church is well aware that the transference of administrative power in the parishes into the hands of the executive bodies, as effected by the Synod of Bishops, is a great tragedy for our church; therefore those who try in any way to justify the action of the 1961 Synod of Bishops are, wittingly or not, doing considerable harm to the Russian Church.

4. An insignificant factual error has crept into BBC broadcasts, about which nothing might have been said, if it were not linked with a certain idea which, though false, is persistently put forward.

This idea is that the tactics of the Moscow Patriarchate, as exposed in the letter of Fr. Nikolai Eshliman and Fr. Gleb Yakunin, permitted the restoration of theological colleges in Russia and furthermore gave the authors of the *Open Letter* the opportunity to receive theological education and to become priests. This is supposed to deprive them of the moral right to criticise the Moscow Patriarchate so sharply.

In refutation of this fabrication, we consider it necessary, above all, to say that, despite a widely held opinion to the contrary, the authors of the *Open Letter* have had no official theological education of any kind.

It is true that Gleb Yakunin, after graduating from the Wild-Life Institute at Irkutsk, entered the Moscow Theological Seminary, but the spirit of servility so forcefully propagated there and the absence of any real religious education made such a painful impression on him that Gleb left the seminary a year after joining it. After this he served for four years, right up to his ordination as a deacon, as a sexton at the Moscow church of St. Trifon the Martyr.

As regards Fr. Nikolai, as far as we know he never once crossed the threshold of any theological college.

Thus if the authors of the *Open Letter* really do have a higher theological education, they are indebted for it not to the theological colleges of the Moscow Patriarchate, but to All-Bountiful God, who gives unsparingly of His wisdom to every seeking heart.

Even if Frs. Nikolai and Gleb had graduated from the Moscow Theological Academy and therefore had reason to consider it their *alma mater*, they would still have been obliged to heed the words of Christ our Saviour: 'He that loveth father or mother more than me is not worthy of me' (Mat. 10:37).

5. Father Vladimir!

As is clear from your broadcast, very many people, including yourself, while on the whole approving the statement of the Moscow priests, reproach the authors of the *Open Letter* for an unnecessary fervour that is supposedly insulting to His Holiness Patriarch Alexi; they even suggest to Frs. Nikolai and Gleb, in the interests of the ecclesiastical affair they have begun, that, while not renouncing the basic principles of their letter, they should repent of the sharp words used.

We consider that it is spiritually unprincipled to put the question this way.

If the Moscow priests have uttered untruths, if they have outspokenly slandered the supreme ecclesiastical administration and the episcopate of the Russian Orthodox Church, then undoubtedly they deserve the most severe penalty known to the church.

But if they told the truth – and we do not for a moment doubt this – then this truth in itself is so terrible, the transgression denounced is so criminal, that it would be insulting for a Christian conscience to speak of it with indifference.

Restraint, not fervour, is the surprise of the letter of the Moscow priests!

In reading the *Open Letter*, one constantly feels that sincere reverence for the dignity of the episcopal rank has restrained the Moscow priests from displaying the degree of spiritual indignation that would have been wholly fitting to the denunciation of such a grave ecclesiastical transgression.

It is not the fact that in his venerable old age he has to listen to such sharp denunciations that evokes pity for His Holiness Patriarch Alexi, but rather the fact that such denunciations are justified. Of course, he is very old and can no longer do very much, but even when he was young and could have acted, he did precisely the same.

Did not Alexi formerly, when he was Metropolitan, together with Metropolitan Sergi, shelter within the folds of his vestments those who were destroying the church? Did not Patriarch Alexi, when in the prime of life, burn incense to Stalin, calling him, with genuine feeling, 'the great and God-given leader'?

Yes, people are sorry for His Holiness Patriarch Alexi – but they are not sorry for the great number of Orthodox souls in the vast expanses of our mother country who are deprived of spiritual food! Are they not sorry for our aged mothers, who are not strong enough to make their way to the nearest church, so rare have churches become in the Russian land? Are they not sorry for the whole long-suffering Russian Church, which those people chosen for this do not wish to defend?

People are sorry for His Holiness the Patriarch! He is especially to be pitied because what the Patriarch should surely have done has been left to the young Moscow priests who, by raising their voices in the defence of the long-suffering church, have performed a deed that in truth should have been performed by the Patriarch.

Many bitter words could be addressed to His Holiness the Patriarch! Some reproach the Moscow priests for using an accusing tone insulting to the Patriarch, but oddly enough they do not notice that the priests do not so much denounce His Holiness the Patriarch as complain to him of the illegal actions of his closest assistants, asking for his patriarchal help and defence.

Those who suggest to the Moscow priests that they offer formal penitence to His Holiness for the allegedly excessive sharpness of their accusation and fervour of their tone, and that they should display humility in the interests of the affair they have begun, do not understand that the priests do not have the moral right to such an action. It is not a question of a lack of humility, but of fidelity to the truth of Christ.

Taking upon themselves a weight of great responsibility, Frs. Nikolai and Gleb are obliged to carry this burden to a proper ecclesiastical court. Not for nothing did they seal their accusations with their willingness to swear on the cross and the Gospel.

6. Father Vladimir!

Your last talk (28 August 1966) produced a strange impression on us. Some of your statements, uttered as if they were wholly beyond dispute, create a feeling of spiritual vagueness and involuntarily force us to prick up our ears.

You say, 'Thank God for everything – for the persecution of the church, for militant atheism, and for the fact that churches are being closed . . . for sufferings purify.'

Father Vladimir!

Remember that the murmur of the long-suffering Job was more acceptable in the sight of God than the over-pious speeches of his comforters.

In truth, thank God for everything!

But tell us, Fr. Vladimir, could you in all conscience hold a thanksgiving service for the closing of a church? . . .

7. Recently from various quarters we have had to hear that the Moscow Patriarchate is supposed to have borne the Russian Church on its shoulders in the most severe years of griefs and misfortunes. There is nothing more false than this statement!

It is not by the diplomatic contrivances of the Moscow Patriarchate that the Russian Church is alive, but by the holy blood of the martyrs for Christ.

It was not the Moscow Patriarchate that preserved the finest strength of the church in the terrible 'thirties, but the Christian catacombs.

It was not the nineteen bishops of Sergi's faction, preserving themselves on the ruins of the Russian Church, who breathed new life into it, but the powerful religious upsurge of the Russian people evoked by the Second World War.

It was not Patriarch Alexi, but Archbishop Yermogen, who was persecuted by the Moscow Patriarchate; it was the courageous Moscow priests, Frs. Nikolai and Gleb, who came out in defence of the truth of the church. . . .[21]

Moscow, 31 August 1966.[22]

REPLY BY FR. VLADIMIR RODZIANKO

.... The whole matter has been based on a misunderstanding, for it was our wish to back the two priests and Archbishop Yermogen and help their cause by making public all over Russia the facts – not only their letters, but also the reactions to those letters all over the world. Obviously the reaction was many-sided and we reflected all shades of opinion, including the one expressed in the *Catholic Herald* and in *Les Informations Catholiques*: that in order to prevent a schism in the Russian Church, which would only weaken its position, it is desirable that the two priests, as an act of reconciliation with the Patriarchate, apologize for their personal attack.

I quoted this opinion with my voice and added that I personally was in sympathy with the peaceful solution. This was taken by some of the listeners who probably overheard certain passages to be an attack on the two priests, which in fact I did not make. This reaction leaked to the West and even appeared in an article in the *Observer*,[23] the whole of which was absolutely untrue. I personally have always admired the courage and purity of faith of the two priests – as well as of Archbishop Yermogen and of numerous martyrs and confessors of the Russian Orthodox Church; but of course one should not neglect the other side of church life, carried on liturgically in still-open churches, which was made possible by the present hierarchy of that church.

6 June 1968.[24]

TO HIS HOLINESS, PATRIARCH ALEXI OF MOSCOW AND ALL RUSSIA
from Christians of the Kirov Diocese

OPEN LETTER

The present open letter is addressed to all believers of the Russian Orthodox Church.

Your Holiness!

The *Open Letter* of the priests N. N. Eshliman and G. P. Yakunin, written in December 1965 and addressed to Your Holiness, has become known to the believers of the Kirov Diocese.

We support this letter *completely and in full* and on our part consider it our Christian duty to make the following declaration.[25]

The ensuing letter covers eighteen pages of printed Russian text, but in form and content is exceedingly close to that by Boris Talantov above.* Indeed, Talantov later admitted that, although twelve people signed the former, he was the principal author. It concludes:

We believers of the Kirov Diocese agree with the priests N. N. Eshliman and G. P. Yakunin, that the 'supreme ecclesiastical authority is now confronted with an unavoidable choice: either to redeem its serious guilt before the Russian Church by a decisive course of action, or finally to go over to the camp of its enemies'.

June 1966.[26]

The seven demands which follow are a summary of those made by Eshliman and Yakunin. The twelve signatories include a theological student at the Odessa Seminary, Nikodim Nikolaevich Kamenskikh.† Their full addresses are given.[27]

ARCHBISHOP YERMOGEN

ADDRESS OF PATRIARCH ALEXI OF MOSCOW AND ALL RUSSIA TO HIS REVERENCE YERMOGEN, NEWLY CONSECRATED BISHOP OF TASHKENT, UPON HANDING HIM THE CROSIER

You have confessed your good faith before the church and many witnesses. You have confessed the holy dogmas of the faith, the sacred canons of the church, the vows of your new office. Teach what you have confessed and act as you have promised. By this you will justify your election. . . .

1 March 1953.[28]

Upon his consecration, Bishop Yermogen said:

* See pp. 125–52.   † See p. 334.

When I was young, I renounced for the Lord's sake much that attracts a man in this world. I yielded my heart to Him, my thoughts worked for Him and my will served Him. If I, as a human being, have sinned, I have never forsaken my Lord, I have always been faithful to His holy church and my hand has never been proffered to any strange god . . .[29]

DECLARATION
TO HIS HOLINESS, THE MOST HOLY PATRIARCH
OF MOSCOW AND ALL RUSSIA
(Archbishop Yermogen, formerly of Kaluga) (complete text)

I have the duty to declare the following to Your Holiness.

25 November 1967 marks two years since the following resolution concerning me was published by Your Holiness and the Synod:

'The Most Reverend Archbishop Yermogen of Kaluga and Borovsk, in accordance with his request, is to be released from administration of the Kaluga diocese. In view of the fact that at the present time there is no appropriate vacant see, Archbishop Yermogen is retired. The Dormition Monastery at Zhirovitsy is designated as his residence. During the period of his retirement, he will receive a bishop's pension.'[30]

The real reason for placing me on the 'retired list', as is well known to Your Holiness and the Synod, was a demand by V. A. Kuroyedov, Chairman of the Council on Religious Affairs under the Council of Ministers of the USSR (CRA).

The above-mentioned resolution followed my enforced petition, as agreed beforehand with Your Holiness, for transfer to another see. On that occasion, Your Holiness made the promise that, following a brief period of 'retirement', I would be given a vacant see.

During the two years which have since elapsed, several episcopal sees have become vacant; prior to the last session of the Holy Synod there were four such. In spite of this, to this day I have not been offered a see, in violation of the promise given by the Patriarch of the Russian Church and the resolution of the Synod.

During the past two-year period, I have sent to Your Holiness an explanatory note and two declarations in which the groundlessness of my retirement, as regards both canon and civil law, is demonstrated with utmost clarity.[31]

My present declaration on this matter is the third and final one and I would wish Your Holiness to pay due attention to it.

My restoration to an episcopal see, given the facts stated, cannot be regarded merely as a matter of my personal disposition. It is required above all by the honour of the Patriarch of the Russian Church and the authority of the Holy Synod. It is necessary in the name of the restoration of violated canonical ordinance, by virtue of which a bishop can be deprived of his see only in ecclesiastical court or if he is condemned by a civil court for a criminal act.

Since neither applies in my case, my continuing 'retirement' can only testify to the serious abnormalities which at present prevail in the relations between our church administration and CRA. This is expressed in my case by the fact that the Patriarch has been deprived of the opportunity to be true to his word and the Holy Synod to carry out its resolution.

These abnormalities are the direct result of the current lack of definition in the relations between church and state.

During Lenin's lifetime there was complete clarity and definition, because these matters were rigorously grounded on the principle of the separation of church and state, which according to Lenin's deposition had to be applied consistently and thoroughly. Legality in these relations was ensured by the fact that all questions related to the application of this decree were assigned to the People's Commissariat of Justice, as represented by its Fifth Department, and they were resolved only from the standpoint of their concurrence with the law. Any religious associations and even individual citizens were able to appeal to the Commissariat of Justice on questions arising in the life of ecclesiastical and religious associations. The Commissariat always provided the appropriate clarifications in written form. A significant proportion of these clarifications, those defining questions of principle, were published.

Something altogether different happens today. CRA as a rule does not give written explanations and replies to declarations and complaints sent to it by religious associations and individuals, including bishops. Neither are written explanations given by its local officials and their verbal explanations are plagued with contradictions and often contradict existing legislation. Obviously one cannot consider normal a situation in which the citizen has no chance of knowing the laws that he must observe, or is left without an answer to his declarations on questions directly bearing on his activity, or, what is still worse, instead of an answer to his declarations he is deprived of the position he holds.

Essentially, the problem of the relations between church and state is a legal one. Since February 1968 will mark the fiftieth anniversary of the decree on the separation of church and state, I propose to prepare a factual report on questions of the local standing of the church, the clergy and religious associations.* This will be submitted to the Juridical Commission under the Council of Ministers of the USSR, directly or through Your Holiness, if this is convenient to you.

Here, however, I think it expedient to express several considerations of principle concerning the relation of the chairman of CRA to episcopal appointments and dismissals. This has a direct bearing on the circumstances which compelled me to write the present declaration.

Since in our country the church is separated from the state and the matters cited above fall within the sphere of internal church life, the church must have the right to resolve them independently. But since he who bears an episcopal rank is also a citizen of his country, two points must be distinguished in the ecclesiastical and civil spheres for a fundamental resolution of questions concerning episcopal appointments:

1. consecration;
2. appointment to a diocese.

The first, wholly and unreservedly, belongs to the church in the person of the episcopate.

* See pp. 244–7.

As for the second, appointment to a specific diocese, certain restrictions on the part of the state are to be expected. Moreover, depending on the nature of this secular authority and its fundamental aims, the limits of these restrictions can vary.

The church may find itself in alliance with the state, as was the case in Tsarist Russia, when the Holy Synod was not only an ecclesiastical but also a governmental establishment. Then the Ober-Procurator of the Synod had the legal right, deriving from his ecclesiastical and governmental position, to exert some influence on questions of episcopal appointments. But we must note that even in Tsarist Russia progressive public opinion reacted adversely to this 'right', particularly when the Ober-Procurator abused it.

As for the chairman of CRA, by virtue of the very same principle of separation of church and state, he cannot, without running the risk of discrediting this very principle, have the right to any active intervention in episcopal appointments, such as the Ober-Procurator of the Synod in Tsarist Russia could possess through the then-legalized relations between the ecclesiastical and governmental authorities. Therefore, at present, because of completely different principles underlying the relations between church and state, any legal intervention of the CRA chairman in the area of episcopal appointments cannot go beyond the requirement that a candidate for occupancy of a see has not been convicted by a court and has the legal status of a citizen of the Soviet Union.

As for putting bishops on the 'retirement' list, canon law provides for this only by action of a consistory for a concrete, ecclesiastical shortcoming or as a result of a personal petition. In the latter case, however, those 'handwritten petitions of resignation' from a diocese are not valid if they are given 'not of personal volition, but through compulsion, fear, or threats by others' (St. Cyril of Alexandria, Canon 3).

The civil aspect of this question is as follows: since, according to existing legislation, the acceptance by a Soviet citizen of the rank of priest does not entail any civil disenfranchisement, his dismissal from a position at the demand of civil authorities cannot be effected under any legal provision.

According to Soviet law, the right to dismiss citizens from their positions either belongs to the administration of the establishment in which the citizen works, or depends upon the verdict of a court in accordance with §§29 and 31 of the Penal Code of the RSFSR. CRA is not an administrative agency controlling the church and has been accorded no juridicial functions. Therefore, if it discovers any illegal actions in the conduct of a bishop, it must, depending on the nature of the violation, either warn the violator, or oblige him to stop the violation, or, if this includes elements of a criminal act, place the matter before the CRA chairman or his local representative. The latter would instigate legal proceedings as stipulated by law. Depending on the verdict of the court, the ecclesiastical authority is then obliged to take an appropriate decision on the bishop.

It appears to me that these considerations are in full harmony with the principles of separation of church and state.

In conclusion, I wish to touch on the question of episcopal elections on the purely ecclesiastical plane.

The procedure of installing bishops by way of appointment which now prevails in our church is unquestionably uncanonical. According to the canons of the Universal Church, the election of a bishop must be undertaken by a council, or at least by an assembly of three bishops, with a senior bishop at its head and upon agreement of all the absent bishops expressed in writing. This procedure, the only canonical one, was ratified by the Ecumenical Councils: the First (Canon 4) and the Seventh (Canon 3). Canon 19 of the Council of Antioch does not recognize as valid any decision taken in contravention of these regulations.

The Holy Canons know nothing of the procedure of 'appointing' bishops. This uncanonical procedure took root in the Russian Church as a result of the uncanonical Petrine Church Reform of 1721, which also abolished the Patriarchate.

The General Council of the Russian Orthodox Church of 1917, which restored the Patriarchate, restored also the canonical procedure of electing bishops. And one would think that the fiftieth anniversary of the restoration of the Patriarchate at the Council of 1917 could be commemorated in no better way than by the re-institution of the canonical procedure of electing bishops that was restored at that very same Council.

Zhirovitsy Monastery,   25 November 1967.[32]

THE FIFTIETH ANNIVERSARY OF THE RESTORATION OF THE PATRIARCHATE
(A historical, canonical and legal enquiry)
(Archbishop Yermogen)

.... Both the composition of the permanent members of the Holy Synod and episcopal appointments now depend on the chairman of CRA to a much greater degree than they did on the Ober-Procurator of the Synod in Tsarist Russia. ...

On 30 March 1964 Bishop Ioasaf (Lelyukhin) of Vinnitsa was appointed Metropolitan of Kiev and a permanent member of the Synod, despite the fact that all the religious activity of this hierarch had demonstrated that he should not have been appointed to these high positions.

Before his consecration as bishop he had three times been ordained priest: first in the Living Church schism; second by Bishop Gennadi in the jurisdiction of Bishop Polikarp Sikorsky during Hitler's occupation of the Ukraine; then thirdly by Archbishop Andrei (Komarov) of Dnepropetrovsk. Having been consecrated Bishop of Sumy, he helped to secure the abolition of the diocese. After this had happened, he was transferred to the diocese of Dnepropetrovsk and Zaporozhie. When he took it over it had 286 active parishes, but he was soon transferred to the diocese of Vinnitsa, by which time he had left less than forty parishes in the diocese of Dnepropetrovsk. Very soon Vinnitsa Cathedral was closed.

The very possibility of appointing completely unsuited people to responsible church posts testifies to serious abnormalities in the composition of our Synod.

.... In studying the 1945 Decrees, one clearly feels that they were not worked out by the Council, but that they were presented to it for ratification in a fully drafted version.

.... Returning to the question of the composition of the Holy Synod, we should point out that we have a full juridical possibility of electing a Synod at a General Council. This right is exercised, moreover, by the Baptists for electing their leaders at their all-union congresses which meet periodically once every three years. ...

One of the most responsible moments in the life of a church is when it elects a Patriarch.

Archbishop Yermogen then goes into precise detail of how such an election should be organized.

This procedure for the election of a Patriarch must unquestionably be followed next time, both because it guarantees a free and considered expression of the will of the council and because neither the Holy Synod nor a Synod of Bishops has the canonical right to change the decrees of a General Council.

The Archbishop then questions whether the election of the present Patriarch in 1945 was carried out in accordance with the canons.

In January 1968 23 years will have passed since the last General Council in 1945. In this time not a single council has been called, if one discounts the so-called Synod of Bishops, which lasted one day (18 July 1961) and was held in the Holy Trinity Monastery of St. Sergius on the saint's memorial day. It was not summoned, as it should have been, by a letter from the Patriarch, but by telegrams from the Patriarchate to the diocesan bishops. These contained invitations to participate in the services at the monastery in honour of St. Sergius, but there was not a single mention of the council. The bishops who arrived were informed of the intention to hold it only late in the evening after vespers on the eve of the memorial day. They thus had less than 24 hours' notice. Such a way of convening a council is unusual and cannot, of course, be justified from the canonical standpoint.

At this council a decision was taken which radically altered the structure of parish life and 'established a system of running a parish until the next General Council should be called.'

More than six years have passed since this council, but there has still not been a General Council. Yet one feels more and more the negative significance of this parish reform for the church. . . .*

It is not difficult to see that such a system has nothing in common with the Orthodox concept of a parish – it is indeed in complete contradiction to the civil legislation on the cults. . . .

Canon law states that a parish has never come into existence and received canonical status without a priest, while the latter has always been a member of the parish community with full rights. Church history knows of the existence of parishes which have had no church through force of circumstance (for example, at the time of the persecutions). However, it knows of no single instance where the priest did not stand at the head of the parish. It is not church property, nor even the place of worship, which gives life to the parish, but believers – the parishioners and the priest. The existence of a Christian community is possible only through their union and mutual action. To break this link is to destroy the idea of the parish.

According to the civil legislation, the members of the general parish meeting who have full rights are not the twenty people who signed the agreement for the use of the church, but all the local residents of Orthodox faith (decree of 8 April 1929).

Insofar as the acceptance by a Soviet citizen of the rank of priest does not deprive him of political or civil rights and does not limit his legal or functional capacity, to deprive him of the right to be a member of the religious organization, the very existence of which loses all practical meaning without him, can be seen only as an act which contravenes current legislation.

The decisions of the 1961 Council are ranked with those documents which deliberately leave everything unexpressed and unformulated, because you cannot directly and openly legalize what cannot be passed by an Orthodox Council.

You cannot legalize a position where a parishioner may not

* Cf. pp. 325-7.

approach the priest directly to request a service and the priest has no right to perform a sacrament for him upon request without charge. It is completely abnormal when the priest must unfailingly perform any sacrament or service upon being presented with a receipt from the so-called 'executive body' of the church. . . .

The author has considered it his religious duty, as a bishop of the Russian Orthodox Church, to express this dissatisfaction, taking into consideration that in connection with the fiftieth anniversary of the restoration of the Patriarchate there will not be a shortage of flattering panegyrics, such as always do disservice to the truth.

The sorry state of the Russian Church today is a direct consequence of breaking canon law and forgetting the basic principle upon which the order of the Russian Church is built and which constitutes its valuable individuality – the principle of conciliarity (*sobornost*). . . .

Zhirovitsy Monastery,   25 December 1967.[33]

TO THE RIGHT REVEREND ARCHBISHOP YERMOGEN
Zhirovitsy
(Complete text)

The office of the Moscow Patriarchate comunicates to you, Right Reverend Sir, the resolution of His Holiness made in answer to your statement of 25 November this year.

'22 December 1967. The archbishop refers to the resolution of the Holy Synod of 25 November 1965, when he was retired because at that time there was no suitable vacant diocese. A number have become vacant over the last two years, but there were more suitable candidates for them than Archbishop Yermogen, who constantly had difficulties in the bishoprics which he consecutively occupied (Tashkent, Omsk and Kaluga). Each time we had to take upon ourselves the burden of resolving these and go to the trouble of transferring him to a new diocese. No-one knows about this better than the archbishop.

'In the Zhirovitsky Monastery the most favourable situation was created for him, both as regards his personal comfort and his unhindered sacramental ministry and preaching of the Word of God. However, the archbishop was not satisfied with the conditions created for him and he several times expressed his displeasure, confounding church public opinion by pointing out the injustice which, in his opinion, had been meted out to him.

'In his statement the archbishop touches on the general ecclesiastical canonical principles of the election and appointment of bishops. According to his line of reasoning, it would seem that all the bishops not only of the synodal period,[34] but also those appointed after the restoration of the Patriarchate, were uncanonical. In the church we have an election by the Holy Synod. It is not two or three people who take part in this, as Archbishop Yermogen writes in his statement, but its seven or eight members. The resolutions of the Synod are immediately circulated to all the bishops of the church. If the archbishop considers such a form of electing bishops uncanonical, why then did he not protest against it when the Holy Synod elected him personally by this method as a bishop of the Russian Orthodox Church?

'At present the matter rests thus: the mood of the archbishop, as may be seen from the tone and character of his statement, gives no expectation that there will not be a repetition of what happened under him at Tashkent, Omsk and Kaluga. It is up to him alone to give the Synod the possibility of ending his retirement and appointing him to a diocese.'

The Archbishop of Tallinn and Estonia,
Business-manager of the Moscow Patriarchate.

22 December 1967.[35]

TO HIS HOLINESS ALEXI, PATRIARCH OF MOSCOW AND ALL RUSSIA

Your Holiness, Right Reverend Sir,

I long ago received Resolution No. 1640 of Your Holiness, dated 22 December 1967, in answer to my statement of 25 November 1967.

I hesitated for a long time over whether I ought to write to Your Holiness about this resolution. But insofar as it puts my activity as a diocesan bishop in a light which does not correspond to the facts, I consider it my true duty respectfully to offer Your Holiness my explanations in the interests of restoring ecclesiastical truth.

My statement of 25 November 1967 was provoked by my 'retirement', which had been extended in contradiction to the resolution of the Synod of 25 November 1965. This latter based my 'retirement' only on the absence of a vacant bishopric at the time the resolution was passed. Insofar as a number of dioceses have become vacant over the last two years, my continuing 'retirement' acquired the nature of a deprivation of bishopric, which, according to canon law, is legitimate only on the decision of a consistory.

Therefore I was a little taken aback to read in the resolution that my not being offered a bishopric was the result of the availability of 'more suitable' candidates for the vacant sees, since from the canonical standpoint such a consideration is quite irrelevant. It is not a question of the election of a candidate to be consecrated bishop, but of the restoration to a diocese of a bishop who had been deprived of one in a manner not permitted by canon law.

Concerning the 'complications' which arose in the dioceses which I occupied (Tashkent, Omsk and Kaluga), I should first of all point out that 'complications' may be of different kinds, as also are their root causes. In order to evaluate them correctly, it is necessary to know what lies behind them and what is their essential nature. It sometimes happens that the complete absence of 'complications' is evidence of lack of principle and of indifference to the entrusted task.

To elucidate this, I would mention here a conversation I had with the late Metropolitan Pitirim of Krutitsy and Kolomna, a permanent member of the Synod. When he met me once in the Patriarchate and found out that I was having difficulties with the CROCA official in Tashkent, he offered me the following advice: 'In order to avoid any difficulties, act thus. When you receive a priest or member of a church council on any ecclesiastical question, listen to all he has to say, then send him to the government official, so that after going there he'll come back again to you. When he reports back, ring up the official and ask what he said to your visitor. You repeat the same to him as the government official.' ...

I should especially emphasize that my church activity as a bishop has always, in every diocese where I have served, been conducted within the law, no single legal accusation has ever been brought against me and I have never been called to answer either a criminal or an administrative charge. It is true that I have had 'complications' with government officials, but in every such instance the law was on my side, while on the side of the official were arbitrary demands which were not based on Soviet legality.

The greatest number of 'complications' occurred at Tashkent – but what were the reasons for them?

Firstly, there was my refusal to 'help' Voronichev, the local CROCA official, to close the church in the village of Lunacharsky, near Tashkent. Because of the absence of legal grounds for its closure, this church has remained open to this day. During my whole tenure of the Tashkent diocese, not a single church was closed there, while in many other diocese there were mass closures, wave upon wave of them.

The second reason for the 'complications' was the construction of a cathedral in Tashkent. This was the largest building enterprise undertaken in our church in the whole of the last fifty years since the restoration of the Patriarchate. Apart from the fact that this undertaking gave believers the opportunity of praying in appropriately sanitary and hygienic surroundings, it is possible that by building the cathedral the life of more than one person was saved during the recent earthquake in Tashkent, for the old cathedral was in a catastrophic state and might simply have collapsed during the disaster.

To mark the day of the cathedral's consecration I was elevated by Your Holiness to the rank of archbishop and my activity as Bishop of Tashkent was more than once singled out by resolutions of approval from Your Holiness. I include one of these here:

'One can only rejoice at the many-sided and fruitful activity of the archbishop and of the intimate assistants under his personal leadership. One can point out much that is a model for acceptance and adoption in other dioceses. May God's blessing be upon those who are working so well to His glory and for the good of the holy church.'

During my tenure of the Omsk bishopric there were no difficulties of any kind. It certainly cannot be called a 'complication' that I was called as a witness when the warden of one of the closed churches was brought to court because a complaint had been sent to N. S. Khrushchev about its illegal closure! To censure a citizen because he is called to court as a witness is a judicial absurdity.

During my tenure of the Kaluga bishopric there were two officials in charge of religious affairs, firstly V. A. Smolin and then F. P. Ryabov. During Smolin's time there were no difficulties. All questions of diocesan life which demanded any reference to the state authorities were decided in strict accord with the legislation on the cults. After the appointment of a new official, Ryabov, however, the position became quite different. Under him legality was frequently replaced by 'expediency' or sometimes simply by his 'discretion'. Basically, difficulties began to arise over questions of replenishing the ranks of active priests in the diocese and the filling of vacant parishes.

Your Holiness must be to some extent aware how difficult it is in a number of dioceses for the bishops to appoint parish priests, for the process of appointment depends to a very large degree on the discretion of government officials, who sometimes even take it upon themselves to select the desired replacements. By no means always do they take into account the opinion of the diocesan bishop, whose role is often reduced to rubber-stamping the changes and making them official by a decree produced or demanded by the officials.

Here lies the basic disaster. The discretion of the government officials completely controls all questions concerned with their granting priests their requests for registration legally to conduct services; this right can also be rescinded from the priest by them, as can the right to participate in services of worship. This paralyses the internal church activity of the diocesan bishop and makes him completely dependent on the government official.

Moreover, § 124 of the Constitution of the USSR speaks with all clarity of the right of every citizen freely to perform religious rites. Therefore, from the civil and legal point of view, every citizen has equal right to participate in the performance of religious worship. How this is exercised by any citizen depends on the internal order of the denomination to which he belongs. From this it follows that, insofar as the right to perform religious worship constitutionally belongs to every Soviet citizen, including priests, for them no supplementary document in the nature of a request for registration should be demanded before they are enabled to conduct worship, for it is simply superfluous.

From the legal point of view, a request for registration is not a guarantee in law of the priest's right to conduct religious worship: this is provided by the Constitution of the USSR and his Soviet citizenship. In our opinion, a request for registration must provide essential information about the priest for the government authorities. In the case of any infringement of the law, the priest is here answerable administratively to a court, just as any other Soviet citizen would be.

I have deliberately emphasized the legal aspect of this question, because its judicial regulation is absolutely essential in removing all sorts of complications here.

The difficulties with Ryabov, the government official, arose because of his refusal to register priests, who had been sent by Your Holiness, according to my representations, to fill the vacant parishes in the diocese. He also tried to select candidates himself to occupy parish vacancies. Serious difficulties also arose because of the attempts of this official to remove the registration of priests without sufficient grounds. Naturally I could not remain indifferent to the fate of the clergy of my diocese. When Archpriest N. Vitun, incumbent of the church at Lyudinovo, was removed from registration without due reason, I protested about the actions of the official to CROCA and Archpriest Vitun was reinstated. No other such instances occurred, but all this, of course, aroused the displeasure of Ryabov towards me and I do not doubt that the letters of the Kaluga Regional Executive Committee were inspired by him.

If Your Holiness had had the opportunity of acquainting himself with the contents of these letters, which were the pretext of my dismissal from the bishopric, then you would have been convinced of the complete absence in them of anything which might be termed a legal finding of guilt.

My prolonged 'retirement', as is correctly noted in the resolution, is confounding public opinion in the church. But to explain this as though it arose through the discontent I had expressed at the conditions created for me in the Zhirovitsy Monastery is an assumption from false information and has no relation whatsoever to the truth. The Archbishop of Minsk can confirm that I am completely satisfied with the conditions provided for me in the Zhirovitsy Monastery and I am grateful for this both to Your Holiness and to him. Public opinion in the church is confounded by something else – the circumstances and method of my dismissal and of my continued 'retirement', contrary to the clearly expressed resolution of the Synod.

In the paragraph of the resolution a vexatious inaccuracy has crept in concerning the general ecclesiastical and canonical matters of the election and appointment of bishops. In my application there was no mention of 'two or three' people taking part in the election of a bishop. This is what I wrote, word for word: 'According to the canons of the Universal Church, the election of a bishop must be undertaken by a council, or at least by an assembly of three bishops, with a senior bishop at its head and upon agreement of all the absent bishops expressed in writing.'

Ecclesiastical commonsense and logic naturally do not demand that the canons which regulated the life of the church more than a thousand years ago in the external circumstances then obtaining should still be literally adhered to, but only that our church order

I

should be in agreement with the essence of the canons and not in contradiction to them.

In the matter of the provision of bishops, the essence of the canons demands that all the bishops should take part in the election of a new bishop. . . .

Uncanonical practices existing in any branch of the church for a certain length of time in history do not deprive it of canonical bishops, but concern to re-establish canonical order in it is the very first duty of its head and of the whole episcopate of the holy church.

With filial devotion,

The humble fellow-servant of Your Holiness in Christ,

Archbishop Yermogen.

Zhirovitsy Monastery,   20 February 1968.[36]

7 Anatoli Levitin

THE LORD IS MY SAFE STRONGHOLD
(Preface to Collection of Articles, *The Sword of the Lord*)
(A. Krasnov-Levitin)

Who are you? That is the question that has been and is being put to me by many people, and without receiving a reply they answer for me themselves.

As most of those who reply look upon me as their enemy, the answers given take the following line: each of them tries to vilify me with his most abusive swear-word.

All communists and atheists have always regarded me as a militant reactionary and obscurantist.

All reactionaries and obscurantists regard me as a communist and almost an atheist.

All churchmen think I am a sectarian.

All sectarians regard me as a churchman.

All the followers of Tikhon[1] have always looked upon me as the most avowed enthusiast of the Living Church.[2]

All the Living Church people, starting with A. I. Vvedensky,[3] have always considered me as an avowed follower of Tikhon ('saturated through and through with monastic ideology').

Every ignoramus has always thought me an intellectual.

Every intellectual regards me as a social reject and member of the proletariat.

Every Russian considers me a Jew.

Every Jew thinks me a Russian, even an anti-Semite.

And absolutely everybody has always regarded me as a kind of semi-futurist.

What are the reasons for such a strange attitude to me as a

person? There is an analogy in literature that involuntarily comes to mind. In the novel *Anna Karenina* there is a certain character, Countess Myagkaya, who enjoys the reputation in drawing-room society of being an extremely eccentric person. Her eccentricity lies in the fact that she has sometimes said things that were 'not entirely devoid of sense'. In the social circle in which she moved, this gave the impression of a very witty joke, according to Tolstoi. Similarly, my futuristic propensity takes the form of sometimes saying things that are not entirely senseless.

In present-day Russia, beclouded by a fog of dogmatism, envenomed by scholasticism and rent by artificial divisions (atheists, church-goers, sectarians), this is like a bomb going off.

I, too, sometimes say things that are not entirely untrue and since home truths are unwelcome, the reaction is yells of hatred and spite . . . 'He's an open enemy', 'He should have his neck wrung', 'His filthy articles', 'He should be kept under bolts and bars', 'I'd arrest that miserable little priest and never let him out' – those are the resounding compliments paid me (I know this to be quite true) in KGB circles; it is only a pity, they think, that their reach is not yet long enough. 'Enemy of the church', 'godless agent of the atheists', 'schismatic', 'typical tricky Jew' – those are the endearing remarks which come to my ears from church circles.

None of this worries me at all: what is the point of arguing with ignorant, stupid and malicious people? It is just as useless talking to them about the truth as lecturing brothel-keepers on morals.

All these contradictory rumours, however, do generate perplexity among honest people and they keep asking more and more insistently: Who are you?

This is my answer to them.

*   *   *

The basic facts in my biography are familiar to my readers.

I was born on 21 September 1915 in the city of Baku into the family of a justice of the peace – a Jew who had been baptized into the Christian faith. My mother was an actress, the daughter of a secondary school headmaster and the granddaughter of a priest.

In 1920 I moved with my family to Leningrad where I lived until 1942. My childhood and early boyhood were spent in a society of middle-class intellectuals.

Although my family was not a notably religious one, I was from early childhood a deeply devout individual and always belonged to the Orthodox Church. My childhood and adolescence coincided with the period of religious discord. I wavered for a long time between allegiance to Tikhon and the Living Church and finally, under the influence of A. I. Vvedensky, I joined the latter movement.

After completing secondary education, teacher-training college, the Herzen Pedagogical Institute at Leningrad and post-graduate work, I taught literature for very many years in a secondary school (and at one time in a higher educational establishment). During the war I was ordained deacon in Ulyanovsk by Metropolitan A. I. Vvedensky and I worked with him there for some time.

In 1944 I joined the Orthodox Church as a layman and reverted to teaching work. After the war I settled in Moscow.

In 1949 I was arrested by the KGB and sentenced by default to ten years' imprisonment. In 1956, after the Twentieth Congress of the CPSU, I was rehabilitated and returned as a teacher to my school.

From 1956 onwards I became a church writer. To begin with, I worked for the *Journal of the Moscow Patriarchate*, in which I published about forty articles under different names.

In 1958 I began distributing typewritten copies of my articles under the pen-name, 'A. Krasnov'. As a result, after the periodical *Nauka i Religia* had published an article about me,[4] I was deprived, simultaneously, of the right to teach in school and to work for the religious journal. Since then I have published, in conjunction with V. M. Shavrov,* *Essays on the History of the Religious Discord*[5] in

* See pp. 182–8.

three volumes, my own reminiscences, *The Decline of the Living Church* and a number of articles assembled in three collections, *The Fight for Light and Truth*, *The Fiery Chalice* and *The Sword of the Lord*. In recent years I have been subjected to attacks from official circles who want to get rid of me by dubbing me a 'parasite'.

So far, however, I am at liberty; I work as a caretaker in one of the churches in the Moscow area.

Such are the external facts of my biography.

What lies concealed behind them?

I was once asked the question in a concentration camp by a doctor friend why I had become a believer. In reply I launched out lyrically into a full apologetic for Christianity. The doctor told me in reply: 'That's all stuff and nonsense. You haven't answered my question at all. When, as a boy, you chased around churches and monasteries, you had no conception either of Einstein or of the theory of relativity or of physical idealism. So it has nothing at all to do with it.' I fell silent. He was perfectly right. Everyone's view of the world always originates with emotion and only with emotion; the arguments come later on.

Accordingly, I shall offer no reasons for or defence of anything. I shall talk about my own feelings. These feelings can be summarized under three headings: 'My religion', 'My socialism' and 'My Russia'. All these three ideas combine to form another idea which I can designate by the pronoun, 'I'. If I talk briefly about my feelings, maybe I shall be answering the question: 'What kind of person am I?'

1. *My Religion*

As a child I learned about God and I strove towards Him. What was it that drew me to God? His omnipotence? No. That made no special impression on me. I knew, even so, that I depended on everyone and everything, beginning with my strict father and ending with nature. His majesty? Not that either. As a natural individualist, a city dweller, I knew little about nature as a child, could not appreciate its beauty and seldom thought about miracles (in our milieu people took a sceptical view of them).

His sanctity, justice and truth? What does a boy of five or six understand about that?

I always apprehended God in the image of Christ. I had an endless love for Christ and was wont to look upon him as Friend, Brother and older Comrade. The comparison is exact. As a child I felt the same feeling for Jesus Christ that small boys feel for an elder brother: I was enraptured by His deeds, I loved Him with that adoration peculiar to a child, I gloried in His triumph, I grieved for His sufferings and firmly believed: come what may, He will always stand by me; He is always and everywhere beside me; He is my 'safe stronghold'.

The solemn phrase which I have put at the head of this essay had no portentous implications for me; on the contrary, it was something quite humdrum, ordinary and to be taken for granted.

This intimate, childlike, almost familiar relationship to Christ has remained with me all my life. At the most difficult moments I have always felt the powerful hand of a Friend, a Friend who has never deserted me. Later on, I began to look more intently at my Friend's face. And I discerned that it was not a face, but an Image. I discerned Truth, mighty wrath, the Love of God. Then, too, I had a feeling of fear for my unworthiness. But still the feeling of the Friend's nearness remained and the conviction did not desert me that with the Friend everything was easy and simple.

From early childhood I used to go to church, as one goes to visit a friend – and as I took communion I felt with a quiver of love that my Friend was near me – I was meeting Him. I loved the Mother of God because she had given birth to my Friend and I loved the saints because they were His friends. In the same way, little boys love the friends of their elder brother as being brave, clever and strong, almost like the elder brother himself. That was how I felt, too, about priests. Until I was fifteen, I revered all of them, seeing them as friends of the Friend, until I discovered that not all of them were His friends.

Thus, from childhood onwards, I got accustomed to living with Christ and in His church, but at the same time I saw that people offended, reviled and attacked my Friend.

For my Friend and His friends to be offended? – no, that must never be allowed! Even at seven years of age I was crazy about religious disputes: I argued with both my parents, with my teachers, with Pioneers and *Komsomol* members and with comrades at school. I always and everywhere defended my Friend, finding that He was really stronger than everyone and everything. The faint lamps of human falsehood paled and grew dim before the sunbeams of my heavenly Friend's Truth.

I could never reconcile myself to the fact that people are evil; if they are, they have to be made good; if they make mistakes, they must be taught the truth. The whole of life must be transformed, renewed and changed.

That was how I reasoned. Even as a child, I began thinking about the fate of the world. I would be walking along from Vasiliev Island, where I lived, to Petrograd Street to see my cousin Seryozha and thinking – was there anything I did not think about: the Revolution, the church, politics, socialism? Grown-up people talked about all these things and I listened in avidly to their conversations and had already begun to read books.

2. *My Socialism*

How intensely I always disliked any kind of higher authority: I hated teachers, headmasters, politicians, bishops, tsars, generals, sovereigns and policemen. And Stalin, and all rulers of every kind. Any kind of pompous, bloated, earthly grandeur always seemed to me to be incredibly ridiculous and those who displayed it something half-way between wizards and madmen. I feared them as one fears madmen and in my heart laughed at them as one does at clowns. From childhood I revolted against all kinds of barriers fabricated by people.

I remember once when my father and I were in a theatre we saw there an officer (at that time they were called commanders) – a

Chinese with a Russian woman. My father was indignant: 'Just
imagine, what a bitch! Taking up with a Chinese.' I suddenly
began quarrelling with my father and defending the Chinese
('Aren't they just people like us, after all?').

'All right, then – that's enough of your philosophizing,' said
my father, and I realized that it was useless contradicting him.
But from then on I realized that all people were equals. Grandmother – a convinced Tolstoyan – had impressed on me when I
was only five years old that simple people ('louts', as my father
called them) were many times superior to intellectuals. My
Christian nurse and the simple, good women whom I saw in
church were always very much closer and more akin to me than
intellectuals.

And as a child, I was already emotionally a socialist. What I
liked best about socialism was the idea of the disappearance of the
state, its complete destruction, the idea of the equality and brotherhood of all peoples. As a tireless disputant, a sufferer from adolescent negativism, I was a supporter of revolution, but was always
repelled by its atrocities. I had a feeling that my Friend would
disapprove of them: and so it turned out.

3. *My Russia*

The question of nationality burst in upon me as a child. As I
have already said, I am half Jewish. My mother, though, was
fiercely anti-Semitic, while my father was a man who terribly
disliked referring to his nationality; he used to recount Jewish
anecdotes and refer to Jews as 'Yids', but at the same time adored
his Jewish mother. I loved her, too, and this affection of mine for
grandmother was my only link with Jews. Other Jews I disliked;
they were always terribly remote from my Friend (they were all,
you see, business people or lawyers – colleagues of my father). I
did not like Russian intellectuals, either, and always felt them
deeply alien and uninteresting to me. On the other hand, I adored
servants, nurses and the people who came to visit them – soldier
boy-friends, peasants and country-folk, women-friends and village

girls. In this way I acquired as a child a love for Russia and for simple Russian people.

Much later I understood the immense tragedy of the Jewish people (principally under the influence of S. M. Mikhoels)[6] and I learnt to respect them. But the feeling of kinship remained only towards simple Russian people (I never did have any love for intellectuals of any kind – neither of the old school, nor the contemporary, re-educated or the new semi-educated type).

So Russia – my own Russia, kindly, warm-hearted and simple – continued to be part of my very soul. Russia was somehow close to my Friend, a country of justice, overflowing with love – one that had nothing in common with government officials, false, soulless and empty-minded people.

In speaking of myself, I have intentionally harked back to my childhood. In childhood a man lives by his emotions; the emotional foundations of manhood are laid down in childhood.

Unfortunately – or fortunately (I really do not know) – I have hardly changed at all since childhood. I believe in Christ as God and Man, the Divine Friend of mankind. I believe in the church, that mystical society of the friends of Christ, both alive and gone before. I yearn for the transfiguration of the world. I consider one of the forms of approach to it to be the period (call it what you like – socialism or something else) when any kind of coercion or organized rule over people will disappear. I understand, of course, that it is, at the moment, impossible to abolish the state; it is, however, possible to confine it to its natural functions. The way leading to this is democracy – placing the state under control of the people.

There can be no socialism without democracy, for where democracy is lacking, there is no equality, freedom or brotherhood of man. Wherever there is no democracy, there will be arbitrariness, lawlessness and misuse of power. . . .

The best guarantee against bad legislative practices is democracy, which must be the foundation of a socialist society. Such a society – a society of full democracy, brotherhood, equality and freedom – will be built in our Russia by the simple, good-hearted Russian people.

I have briefly stated my conception of the world. Maybe it will now be easy to understand what kind of person I am – a Christian, a socialist and a democrat . . .

It only remains to say just a few words about the church. I have already mentioned my dislike for everything that is pompous, exaggerated or reflecting earthly grandeur. This applies also to the church hierarchy. I am prepared to respect it and obey it, if it is guided by Christ's Spirit. If, however, all that differentiates it from the rest of officialdom is merely mitres and pallia, then my attitude to it is the same as to any official caste. That is the explanation of my bitter polemics with princes of the church.

* * *

When I was in the concentration camp I had a dream: I was travelling in a boat along the Neva at night-time and there were many stars in the sky. I stepped out of the boat and walked barefoot on the water; the sensation was so realistic that even now I can still recall the coolness of the water under my feet and the thought crossing my mind: 'Surely I'll drown – after all, it must be three times deeper than a man.' Then I reached the bank and someone, invisible in the darkness, stretched out his hand to me.

And I still feel this hand in mine, the hand of my Friend.

Moscow, 9 October 1966.[7]

'DIALOGUE' WITH THE ATHEISTS

This article was written in answer to various charges against believers made by *Nauka i Religia* in 1960–61.

DEGENERATION OF ATHEIST THOUGHT
(A. Krasnov-Levitin)

In direct contradiction to this decree (§4 of the 1929 Law on Religious Associations[8]), we now find that the principle of compulsory 'registration' of priests is accepted by CROCA – or rather by its local officials. Not one priest may begin his ministry without being registered. Moreover, the least whim of these officials (who are usually former employees of the MGB, as it used to be called) can remove the priest's registration. In a number of cases, a libellous secret personal report flies in pursuit of the priest whose registration has been suspended and sometimes he spends long months travelling with his family from town to town, nowhere finding refuge.

As a rule, these officials compile registers of the people who are unacceptable to them. On these appear the priests who most assiduously preach the Word of God and enjoy popularity among the people. 'Suspension from registration' is a marvellous tool for blackmail: using threats to influence irresolute and wavering priests, the officials force them to leave the priesthood by terrorizing them. Under Beria the all-powerful MGB used 'registration' to post its agents and recruited weak priests as secret collaborators, forcing them to write false reports.*

As the reader will see, these methods which were introduced during the time of Stalin's despotism completely contradict the laws of the USSR. Moreover, they irreconcilably contradict the Soviet Constitution and its principle of the separation of church and state. It is not difficult to establish that the 'registration' of priests entails nothing other than their appointment by the state authorities. If one adds that not only priests but also bishops have to be registered, we are confronted by a monstrous paradox: a state church in an atheist governmental system. It goes without saying that such a terrible perversion of the freedom of conscience could come into being only in the stinking atmosphere of the cult of Stalin and the omnipotence of Beria's scum.[9]

FREEDOM OF BELIEF AND OF ATHEISM: FACE TO FACE
(A. Krasnov-Levitin)

In Moscow on 21 May 1965 I met with representatives of anti-religious opinion in a room of the Zhdanov District Executive

* Cf. p. 190.

Committee on Taganka Square. Members of a great variety of organizations participated in this meeting. There were two important officials of the KGB, the managing director of the State Political Publishing House, the deputy editor of the journal, *Nauka i Religia*, the deputy director of the House of Scientific Atheism, representatives of the regional committee, an official of the Council for Russian Orthodox Church Affairs and the secretary of the Zhdanov District Executive Committee.

My literary activity was the subject of discussion, although a number of general questions were also raised. Since the contents of this discussion are of definite interest for our readers, we are publishing it, together with our brief commentary.

Major Shitikov (representative of the KGB): Anatoli Emmanuilovich! We would like to have a friendly conversation with you and would like to ask you a number of questions. Representatives of public opinion are here. By the way, next to you is Alexei Alexeyevich Trushin, whose name must be familiar to you.

Levitin: I'll answer all your questions with pleasure.

Shitikov: It's well known to us, Anatoli Emmanuilovich, that you publish your articles by any means and with unusual persistence. If any evidence is needed, here it is: you know Gleb Pavlovich Yakunin well. He states . . .

Levitin: Not necessary. I know.

Shitikov: Oh, he told you. A citizen leaves his briefcase in a telephone booth. It's brought to the police and in it your article is found.

Levitin: Who was it?

Shitikov: You want to know? Ivan Petrovich Nedoshivin, who lives in the Izmailovo district.

Levitin: Never heard of him.

Shitikov: You're leading your typists into error by saying that your articles are very good . . .

Levitin: I know that you've got my typists under surveillance.

Shitikov: . . . . You ought to know the laws and obey them, but instead your actions contradict all generally accepted norms.

Levitin: I've reached the age of fifty (*Voices*: You haven't had your fiftieth birthday yet.) That makes no difference – I was only using a round number. In fifty years I've formed unshakeable and clear convictions and I express them in my articles. I write the truth in them. You yourselves don't claim that they contain anything untrue. I protest against the barbarous persecution of religion which finds its expression in the destruction of churches and the humiliation of believers. I protest against a situation which reduces the church to the scum of the earth, while Comrade Trushin, who's present here, is the dictator of the Moscow church. He, a non-believer and a communist, assigns and removes priests as he pleases (this is nothing personal, but a comment on the present state of affairs).* This is wholly contradictory to all norms and even to Stalin's constitution. I protest against all this in my articles which I've been disseminating. I'm continuing to do so and intend to carry on, using my right to freedom of speech. By the way, Russian literature has always defined the word 'citizen' as someone who is fighting for and upholding the truth, not as someone who crawls on his belly before the authorities. I'm not afraid of anything and never have been. This is even more true now at fifty, as I approach the limit beyond which any kind of threats cease to be effective.

Shitikov: No one is frightening you. We want to talk to you as a comrade.

A citizen (unknown to me, sitting at the end of the table – he seems to be a representative of the regional committee): Anatoli Emmanuilovich! You've got a very prepossessing appearance.

Levitin: Thanks.

Unknown citizen: You make a sympathetic impression – which surprises me. Your articles create a completely different impression. They're full of anger and hatred. You take isolated facts and generalize from them. You say that this is the policy of both party and government and allege that certain directives have been given for a fight against religion using force. If your articles should fall into the hands of our enemies, they can make use of them, of course. But it's all untrue. You yourself know that the party has always

* Cf. pp. 327–8.

fought against these distortions and that Khrushchev protested against them several times.

Levitin: That reminds me of Stalin's admirers, who always refer to Beria when speaking of violence and say that Stalin had nothing to do with it. . . .

Romanov (deputy director of the House of Atheism): Anatoli Emmanuilovich! Your 'literary' works hardly deserve the name. . . . You say that from propagating atheism one gets the same benefit as from spreading syphilis. That's indecent. You hate atheists, you slander them, you tear open an abyss between them and believers. You're offending all of us. Judging from your articles, you hate fascism. But it was non-believers, mostly, who defeated fascism and have just celebrated the twentieth anniversary of their victory. You can't deny that.

Levitin: I didn't want to insult anyone personally. If anybody's feelings are hurt, please accept my apology. I was writing about consistent atheism. Luckily, not all atheists are consistent. Furthermore, in my letter to Nikodim I give examples of those who, though atheists, were good and honest people (such as in particular, Mikhail Yurievich Shavrov, the father of my friend Vadim). . . .

Grigorian (deputy editor of *Nauka i Religia*): Anatoli Emmanuilovich! I like your articles. I like them because of their breadth of vision. That is why I was astonished at your attack today on atheism. You've written extensively on the monks of Pochaev. May I bring to your attention that I heard about these shocking things going on in Pochaev earlier than you and that I've done more to stop them than you. At that time, I telephoned about this to the Central Committee and also spoke to its members about it. You will also know that our journal recently attacked that odious person, Alla Trubnikova.* I myself have many friends among believers. One simply has to be unbiased towards atheism.[10]

Levitin: I know you maintain an honourable attitude in the fight against religion. . . . and I would meet with you with great pleasure. . . .

* See pp. 56–7.

Chertikhin (head of the Political Publishing House): . . . . You write that the Declaration on Human Rights adopted by the delegates of Eisenhower and Churchill is the basis of socialism.

Levitin: I didn't write that.

Romanov: I quote from the letter to Nikodim: 'It is necessary to publish the Declaration widely, to bring all legislation into correspondence with it and to structure all daily activities according to it. That is the basis of socialist democracy.'

Levitin: That's something quite different; it's about socialist democracy. What democracy can actually be meant when the most important document setting out the principles to have been signed and ratified has not only not been put into practice, but has not even been published? . . .

Major Shitikov: . . . . You called our Constitution Stalinist. It may perhaps be so, but it still is in force. You well know the article which allows all citizens to disseminate anti-religious propaganda and which restricts the preaching of religion to special premises and special people. Apart from the Constitution, other legislation exists which one must respect. Of course, nobody can forbid you to write what you want, but if you continue to distribute your work in the same manner as before, you may not be meeting with us again, but with another public body, who will confront you with §162 (the transaction of illegal trade).

Levitin: That's all your affair; mine is writing. Yours is to react to it.

Shitikov: Now to the second question: about your work. You insist that you must necessarily work as a teacher. But that's exactly contradictory to your convictions. With us the school is separated from the church and all education is built on an anti-religious foundation.

Levitin: How are my convictions relevant here? Of course, I will never say anything anti-religious, but I love making people literate and teaching them Russian literature. In more than twelve years of teaching, I have given new insight to countless people. They all know literature now, but I didn't discuss religion with them.

Romanov: In your *Degeneration of Anti-religious Thought*, however, you recount how once you couldn't communicate with a class until the pupils understood you were a believer.

Levitin: Now what's wrong with that? I've never made a secret of it.

Grigorian: Anatoli Emmanuilovich! You should devote yourself to scientific work. For the present, your best course would be to become a bibliographer.

Chertikhin: Anatoli Emmanuilovich! You know about atheism better than anyone else. We need a bibliographer on atheism. You'd get 150 roubles.

Levitin turns down the offer and the meeting breaks up.

Honourable atheists who sincerely wish to understand religious problems and who suggest a dialogue on an equal level with believers do exist nowadays: and they will in the future probably play an even greater role. One can have a serious and sincere discussion with them, respecting them as honest people and comrades without, of course, retreating one iota from one's own convictions. Incidentally, the conversation with B. T. Grigorian, which took place the following day and went on for nearly five hours, convinced me of this.

It was not a diplomatic exchange, but the most ordinary human talk of two writers expressing their opinion in a free and unrestrained manner. It recalled to me vividly my student days, when, strolling through the town, I had just such witty (and often abstruse) conversations with my friends.

The establishment of a full – not an illusory – freedom of religion in our country will destroy the artificial barriers between atheists and believers; then there will be created an atmosphere of friendship and collaboration which will enable them to search for the truth together.

The struggle for freedom of religion, for freedom of atheism and for full freedom of conscience is the olive branch which I proffer to my friends, both believers and atheists.

With that I wanted to finish, but after some consideration I thought that my appeal to fight for freedom of atheism would astonish many people; others might consider it as demagogy.

But no, this is not so – it is the truth of life. For with us atheism is not free, just as religion is not free. The situation of atheism at present strongly recalls the situation of the Orthodox Church in pre-revolutionary Russia.

Orthodoxy at that time was, as is well known, the official ideology. All disputes with it were categorically prohibited. 'Our priests are unfortunate people: one must not argue with them, wrote V. S. Solovyov. The church was not free because it was under compulsion.

Atheism is not free in the Soviet Union precisely because it is under compulsion, obligatory and not open to discussion. (One can conclude this even from the material of the above discussion, since all the participants were convinced that a believer could not possibly be a teacher.)

Therefore the struggle for religious freedom is also a struggle for the freedom of atheism, for methods of compulsion (direct or indirect) are compromising atheism, depriving it of all ideological significance and all spiritual fascination.

Therefore, long live free religion and free atheism!

30 May 1965.[11]

DECLARATION TO THE CENTRAL COMMITTEE
OF THE CPSU
(Anatoli Emmanuilovich Levitin-Krasnov,
23, 3rd Novokuzminskaya Street, Moscow, Zh-377)
(Complete text)

In the course of the current year organs of the KGB have made several attempts to take repressive action against me. In February the KGB summoned a number of people as witnesses, in order to prove that I was engaged in a 'specially prohibited trade'. This attempt was given up after I sent an open letter to Semichastny, Chairman of the KGB. Thereafter, the KGB decided at all costs to turn me into a 'parasite'. In May this year the KGB special commissioner for the Chekhov district of the Moscow region categorically demanded that the warden of the Trinity Church, Vaulovo village, where I was working as an accountant, dismiss me immediately on the grounds that the church was located in a region subject to 'special conditions'.[12]

On 22 September I was summoned by the district commissioner of the 72nd Police H.Q., Moscow (my place of residence), and, although I submitted a document to show that I was employed as a watchman at the Dormition Church in the hamlet of Veshnyaki, I was served with notice in writing to get myself fixed up in a job within a month, which gives them the right on 22 October 1966 to deport me automatically to the depths of Siberia.

In this connection I beg to make the following statement:

1. I do duty as watchman in the Dormition Church (at Veshnyaki) three times a week: from 8 p.m. on Monday to 12 noon on Tuesday; from 8 p.m. on Wednesday to 12 noon on Thursday; and from 8 p.m. on Friday to 12 noon on Saturday.

I invite all honest people to come to the church at these times and testify to this fact.

2. I shall go on working in this church as long as I have not been dismissed from it. Dismissal may be effected only by order of the KGB, since there can be no other reasons.

3. Last year I requested the Central Committee of CPSU to help me to obtain employment corresponding to my qualifications. Nevertheless, no place was found for me either in the Lenin Library or in the Book Chamber, to which I had been directed by the municipal committee of the CPSU.*

In August this year the Ministry of Education refused to reinstate me to my post as a teacher. In spite of this I renewed my application, stating that I was prepared to work in any teaching, library, museum, literary or art-history job that should be offered me.

4. The method of punishing honest high-principled opponents by proclaiming them parasites cannot possibly convince anyone and can merely serve to disgrace those who resort to such methods.

26 September 1966.[13]

* Cf. p. 269.

THEOLOGIAN-PROVOCATEUR
(G. Vasiliev)
(Complete text)

A. Levitin, who writes under the pseudonym of Krasnov, is a prolific author. Theological treatises flow from his typewriter one after another. I have in front of me his latest work, *The Ailing Church*,[14] in which he harshly criticizes the prelates of the Russian Orthodox Church. According to him, many bishops of the Russian Orthodox Church 'are a dead, barren and useless fig tree'. He goes on to say that the church contains 'a large number of gangrenous members who play a pernicious role in its life, poison it with their putrid exhalations, infect and inject cadaverous poison into its most secret depths. That is why the Russian Church is ill – seriously ill.'

I shall not argue with Krasnov-Levitin; after all, this is not an atheist bearing witness. What I find interesting and noteworthy is something different: in what cause is he breaking his lances? What appeal is being made by the author of this theological treatise? Levitin's brief diagnosis of the ailment yields a great deal of enlightenment: 'The most important ailment – the primordial and most ancient – is that of Cæsaropapism (subjugation of the church to narrow, nationalistic interests and to the secular power).' Note – the 'secular power'.

What has happened, then? Why is a defender of religion making an attack on churchmen?

The secret is very simple: Levitin is trying to represent a regular, normal crisis of religious life as a consequence of the harmful actions of individual negligent prelates of the Russian Orthodox Church. In order to overcome this crisis, he proposes to activate religious life by surrounding the Orthodox Church with an aureole of martyrdom.

Levitin-Krasnov produces in scrupulous detail a list of particular cases where local bodies and individuals have violated the legislation on the cults and tries his utmost to present this as the general policy followed by our state towards religion. But at the same time he is obliged grudgingly to concede the fact that 'The opponents of religion themselves are usually disgusted by these facts, since they run counter to the most elementary norms of the law on separation of church and state'.

Where is the logic in this? On the one hand, the theologian admits that the state punishes violations of the law by safeguarding the rights of citizens to practise any form of religion. On the other hand, he endeavours, with a zeal worthy of a better cause, to provoke the prelates of the Russian Orthodox Church into protesting against persecutions he has himself invented.

Discarding any unnecessary pretence of modesty, he launches out into a tirade: 'Is it not really reprehensible that these lines are being written not by a member of the hierarchy or the Synod, but by an ordinary layman, a schoolmaster? I am writing because you are not carrying out your duties. You should be ashamed!'

Levitin is dissatisfied with everything: that Orthodox priests are not engaging in unlimited missionary work, that pillars of the church are not sufficiently 'aware of their duties as citizens' and that the theological seminaries are not training fanatical 'beacons of the faith'.

Levitin goes on to expound what it means to be a 'one-hundred-per-cent citizen' and deluges the reader with the names of Brutus, Marat, Riego, Bulgarin, Grech, Herzen, Ryleyev . . .[15]

At one pole we have Marat, Riego and Ryleyev, at the other Bulgarin and Grech, 'classical examples of civic valour' directly set against 'the submissive man in the street, ready to obey any orders laid down by authority'. According to Levitin, citizenship has no other connotation than protest against the existing order. The valorous toil of millions of Soviet people he regards, of course, as not coming under the category of civic virtue.

The theologian counts on our respect for the names of Marat, Riego and Ryleyev. But we respect them because they fought selflessly for the ideals of the social system under which Soviet people live and in which Levitin feels so uncomfortable.

No wonder then that he names as his ideal of a present-day citizen Cardinal Stefan Wyszynski, the Primate of the Catholic

Church in Poland, who is well known as a violent anti-communist, an active opponent of the socialist changes in the Polish People's Republic, and who dreams of Poland's returning to the old capitalist system.

In accusing the Russian Orthodox Church of 'grovelling' to the state, Levitin-Krasnov recalls the liquidation in 1946 of the Union of Brest.[16] 'Gavriil Kostelnik, the traitor from Lvov,' he writes, 'whose hands were stained with the blood of his former brethren, was received with the highest honours by the Patriarch in Moscow.'

Really, though, the facts of the matter for which the 'truth-lover' Levitin is so hotly contending are quite different: it was the hands of the Uniates which were stained with the blood of the patriot Gavriil Kostelnik. The real truth (on which the theologian is silent) is that the Union of Brest was always used in the service of oppressing the Ukrainian people. The truth is that Count Andrei Szeptycki, Metropolitan of Lvov, who dreamed of becoming the second (eastern) Pope, delivered a pastoral message in 1 July 1941 in St. Yuri's Cathedral, in which he said: 'We welcome the victorious German Army as a deliverer from the enemy!' The truth is that Andrei Szeptycki, Iosif Slipy and a number of other prelates of the Greek Catholic Church set up the closest union between the cross and the swastika during the war.

It is well known that, on a proposal by a committee headed by Kostelnik, the Synod of the Greek Catholic Church at Lvov unanimously decided to secede from the Union.

Those are all facts and Levitin, of course, knows them.

The theologian has adopted an anti-social stand by trying to place the Russian Orthodox Church in political opposition to the state. In order to cover over his outspoken assertions, he endeavours here and there to don the fig leaves of a pretended concern for the development of socialist democracy. But, as the saying goes, 'even a wise man stumbles'.

In his fight for civic virtues, Levitin is really trying to sever the social links between believers and the 'world', to separate them from the society in which they live. He is seeking to erect an im-

passable barrier between believers and society and to sow antag-
onism between believers and non-believers.

Levitin does not confine himself to admonitions – he utters
threats! If, he declares, the prelates will not rise up and oppose the
state, then they 'should remember that the patience of Orthodox
people is not unlimited and their unworthy conduct may easily
lead to schism'.

Well, well – the theologian is really going too far! This is the
kind of case that Kozma Prutkov had in mind when he wrote:
'Zeal sometimes gets the better of commonsense.'

All Levitin's vain efforts to organize a religious group hostile to
the state are doomed to fail. For us the words 'democracy' and
'freedom' are concrete words replete with class significance. In
our case it is not 'democracy' in general, but socialist democracy –
the popular rule of the labouring class. Our society has laws in
operation which protect the interests of all Soviet citizens, ir-
respective of what religion they belong to – both believers and
non-believers. And we are entitled to expect each and everyone
to comply with these laws – including even people like Levitin.[17]

Despite this clash in 1966 with the authorities, Levitin was still a
free man at the trial of Yuri Galanskov and Alexander Ginzburg in
January 1968. The accusations here contained that Levitin is inciting
the Russian Orthodox Church to political activity against the state
are extremely serious. That nothing seems to have come of them
suggests a hesitation in the state's present policies. This article is unique
in quite clearly representing to atheist readers the drift of an underground religious publication and giving the widest publicity to
Levitin's ideas.

THE PATRIARCH AND HIS STAFF

WITH LOVE AND ANGER
(A. Krasnov-Levitin)

Love and anger are the world's redemption. Love and anger
were brought by Christ to earth. Love and anger are sisters and
where there is no anger, there is no love.

The sayings of the ancient prophets were full of a mighty wrath precisely because their hearts were filled with a great love for their own people – and love brought forth anger not only against the oppressors of the people, but also against the people themselves, because they were not following the paths of truth.

There was a mighty anger in the words of the Saviour when He looked upon the Scribes and the Pharisees, as they poisoned with their man-made lies the life-giving springs of Divine Revelation: 'And when He had looked round about on them with anger, He was grieved for the hardness of their hearts' (Mark 3:5). . . .

1. *Patriarch Alexi*

Levitin prints the text of Patriarch Alexi's ban on Frs. Eshliman and Yakunin.*

As I read, I feel a flush of shame flooding over my face. Nine years ago I took part in the preparation for the Patriarch's eightieth birthday celebrations. I wrote an article, 'The Primate of the Russian Church', dedicated to Patriarch Alexi. It was published in the *Journal of the Moscow Patriarchate*, occupying almost the whole of the jubilee number, two quires in all (No. 11, 1957).[18] Two quires – more than forty pages, forty shameful pages, which I regard as the great sin of my life and of which I deeply repent. However, repentance and disavowal are but a trifle; one must finally realize who this old man is, who for 21 years has been occupying the patriarchal throne of the Russian Orthodox Church.

The Patriarch is really proud that he was born into the aristocracy. His late sister, Anna Vladimirovna, loved to talk about the velvet books in which the Simansky lineage was recorded. As I discovered when I was working on the Patriarch's biography, the Simanskys achieved the rank of nobility under Catherine II and produced an admiral, all of whose descendants held office at court. When Alexi Simansky was consecrated in May 1913 as Bishop of Tikhvin, an article appeared in the Synod's official gazette,

* See pp. 226–7.

Kolokol ('The Bell'), written by Ye. Poselyanin (the famous conservative writer on religion). . . . In it he lauded the aristocratic
origins of the new bishop. He looked upon this as a great advantage *vis-à-vis* those bishops who were 'sons of sextons'. A bishop
from the nobility, you see, would be able to hold his own with
representatives of the government with greater dignity than a
priest's son from a seminary!

Was Poselyanin right? I would be the very last to bow and
scrape to the Russian nobility, but in all fairness it has to be
admitted that it produced many bold, honest and incorruptible
characters. A nobleman had an inborn sense of honour which
obliged him not only to fight a duel, but also to refrain from the
most dishonourable kinds of behaviour. In the old days an aristocrat was, above all, a man of honour.

Sergei Vladimirovich Simansky, I respect your years but truth
compels me to tell you to your face: you are a very bad aristocrat
and you are completely devoid of a sense of honour. Remember
how you behaved to Metropolitan Nikolai when you compelled
him on 15 September 1960 to sign a petition for resignation![19]
You assured him then that he could go off without worrying and
rest for a couple of months at Sukhumi, since the Synod would
not in his absence consider the petition at its autumn session. Yet
when Metropolitan Nikolai arrived at Sukhumi, he found there
a telegram from you notifying him that his petition had been
considered by the Synod and his resignation accepted. Was not
that a dishonourable action?

Later on, when Metropolitan Nikolai after his dismissal was
living in quiet retirement in Moscow during the last year of his
life, did you not do everything in your power to make his life a
misery? You refused to allow him to take a service; you did not
invite him to the Patriarchal Cathedral and did not allow him
even to say the paschal liturgy, thus embittering his last Easter.

In the days when churches were being closed down *en masse*,
when unfortunate monks were being thrown out of the monasteries, when thousands of priests and Orthodox laymen were appeal-
ing to you in prayer, with faces full of trust and hope – did you

utter a single word in their defence? Did you even lift a finger to help them?

When your assistant, Metropolitan Nikodim (he was foisted on you and you well know what he is worth), made lying statements about persecutions of the church, did you refute him by as much as a single word? No. You more than once made similar declarations.

You are not a man of strong will – and, of course, you cannot be blamed for this. Still, can one explain by mere weakness of will the disgraceful favouritism which has been flourishing under you and which never occurred under any other Patriarch? Whoever heard of such a situation where casual individuals, not in holy orders, whose only merit was their personal loyalty to the Patriarch, should be the real dictators, interfering in everything, slighting metropolitans and appointing bishops?

In your ruling on the case of Frs. Eshliman and Yakunin you make a reference to church regulations and canon law. Yet the whole of your activity is a crass violation of just this. I say nothing about the gross violations of canon law which were pointed out in the petition of the two priests. Anti-canonical behaviour has become such a standard feature of your activities that every day brings further fresh instances of it.

It is well known that canonical rules pay very great attention to the procedure for the nomination of bishops. This is done by all the bishops of the province concerned and provision is also made for the people to be consulted. . . . But who was it who decided to appoint to an episcopal see a person to whom the whole diocese had unanimously objected – an absolute majority of clergy and laymen?

Yet this is what occurred three months ago when Metropolitan Antoni Krotsevich returned to the bishopric of Tula, not withstanding the universal protests of the whole community of believers without exception.* This bishop, who was unanimously and quite deservedly despised by his flock, was forcibly enthroned and is at present obliged to conduct divine worship under police guard. All the numerous requests of the people not to appoint

* Cf. p. 144.

this unpopular bishop to the see of Tula have gone completely unheeded.

In a similar breach of canon law, without any consultation at all with the people and even without hearing the views of the Ukrainian bishops, you deferred to the pressure exerted on you and agreed to appoint the young Bishop Filaret as Exarch of the Ukraine, although there were worthier candidates available, superior in every respect to the said bishop.*

Equally anti-canonical, also, was the resolution adopted by you on 24 December 1965 on the petition of the two priests.† In it you cast doubts on the right of priests to appeal to a synod of bishops and you censured the priests for having circulated copies of their petition to the bishops. Yet the church regulation states clearly and definitely: 'Should any persons, not being heretics, excommunicated people, convicted persons or under a preliminary charge for any kind of offence, make a statement or clearly have something to report against a bishop on church matters, such persons shall be ordered by the council firstly to submit their charges to all the bishops of the province and produce to them evidence in support of their charge against the bishop. The latter is then bound to enter a reply' (Canon 6 of the Second Constituent Council).

The numerous protests sent in from all quarters evidently played their part. In your resolution of 14 May 1966[20] you do not once mention your former accusation, but you blame the priests for 'actions prejudicial to the church'.‡

But how are these prejudicial actions expressed?

Is it that they attack the notorious evils in the life of the church? But you have not uttered a single word in refutation of any of the statements contained in the petition. Furthermore, according to completely irrefutable information in my possession, you yourself in private conversation confirm the correctness of what the two priests have said. Or, possibly, do the 'prejudicial actions' consist in the attack made by the two priests against the anti-canonical

---

* That, incidentally, is not the worst variant (Levitin's note).
† See p. 224.   ‡ See p. 226.

synod of 1961? But even you yourself cannot deny the anti-canonical character of that synod . . . . – in fact you do not deny it, as you have not raised a single objection to the arguments adduced. But you talk of the 'errant obstinacy' of the priests. What form did this assume and what was the origin of this accusation?

It started from the same origin from which all the actions of our supreme ecclesiastical authority begin and end.

On 12 May 1966 Metropolitan Pimen of Krutitsy and Kolomna was summoned before the Council for Religious Affairs. When he returned from it to the Novodevichi Monastery, the Metropolitan immediately summoned the two priests and demanded that they should without further delay explain in writing whether they had changed their opinions. Both priests, as honest men, naturally confirmed their adherence to their views. The following day the Patriarch placed them under interdict.

The question arises – when and how could the Patriarch be convinced of the 'errant obstinacy' of the two priests? In the six months that had elapsed from the date the petition was submitted, the Patriarch never once summoned them or sent them any notification. Metropolitan Pimen, too, never once saw these priests after 25 December nor talked with them. Clearly, neither dignitary regarded the matter as urgent.

Why did they both suddenly take alarm and 'cook up' the interdict so hurriedly in 24 hours? There can be only one reply. Because on 12 May Metropolitan Pimen was called before the Council on Religious Affairs and was there given the directives relevant to this matter. More about these later, but now let us address the Patriarch.

Your Holiness!

You have by God's grace attained a ripe old age. Every one of us, including the present writer, hopes you will continue to live many years longer and celebrate your hundredth birthday.

Nevertheless, however many birthdays you may celebrate, the day is not far distant when you too, like the poorest pauper standing in the porch of the Yelokhov Cathedral, will stand before that court which no one has ever yet avoided. This is the awful, righteous Judge who attaches no significance to pompous titles, episcopal vestments, golden mitres and other trappings which, even here on earth, are the commonest of trumperies if they are not matched by the spiritual and moral elevation of him who wears them. That will not be on earth, but in the life beyond the grave, in a world that for us is still hidden. Yet that is a real world, which we who are advanced in years can already very clearly discern.

What will happen on earth? Here the court of history will intervene – a court that is also stern and incorruptible. What a sorry, defenceless figure you offer as you stand even now in presentment before that court. If you look carefully around you, you will see sorrowful, wrathful glances directed at you by all honest people. If you will take a look at your inner self, you will find there an unquiet conscience which will keep on pricking you if you cast your eyes upwards. There you will find the sword of divine justice already suspended over your grey head.

In the words you address to bishops on the day of their consecration, you always remind them that they must 'cherish within them the grace of a bishop's office' – and these words do really have a deeply religious meaning, since grace does not operate apart from a man's will; it has to be achieved by constant effort.

Make an effort of will, also; shrug off the chilly sleep that holds you fettered and may you renew your youth as the eagle!

The first act of your spiritual rebirth will be to retract your resolution and to have a fatherly talk with the two young priests, whose honesty and good intentions even you yourself do not question.

2. *Conversation with the Civil Authorities*

Our reference to the Council for Religious Affairs was not a chance one. No one doubts that this body played no small part in the whole business.

Let us now turn our attention to it. In the press, in announcements and in the speeches of government officials the expression 'moral and political unity' often features.

Moral and political unity certainly does represent a vitally important problem for all patriots. Its achievement (if we speak not of assertions but of real and genuine unity) is a difficult business. You have to work on it constantly and keep on creating it.

I would like to put a question to all Soviet people: 'Can there be unity when thirty million people (that is roughly the figure of the religious population of the USSR) consider that their rights have been infringed?' What should be done to achieve unity with those people? It is very little – implement systematically, completely and entirely the law on the separation of church and state. What needs to be done is to see that in our society a religious man does not feel himself a pariah, that all paths and doors are open to him. That is the kind of system that exists in many socialist countries – in Poland, Rumania and Yugoslavia – countries where power is in the hands of unbelievers, but where there is not the slightest indication of religious discrimination. . . .[21]

Why do we not take advantage of this experience? It might not be a bad idea to learn something from these countries, either. Of course, one should not mechanically transpose their experience into our environment. We make no demand whatsoever for the state to supply funds for religious education (as is done, say, in Poland). That would not only be impossible; it would even be undesirable, since it would strengthen the dependence of religious conscience on the state. We support the complete and systematic separation of church and state and therefore we have no need of any privileges or advantages – we merely want to be ordinary free citizens in a free socialist state. We raise no question about religious instruction for children, since at the present time and in present circumstances that would be unrealistic.[22] We desire one thing only – the free and independent existence of the church and all other religious organizations. We want guarantees against any kind of administrative duress or violence towards religious people.

The petition of the two priests makes minimum demands (seven in number) which could form a basis for negotiations between the state authorities and the religious community. Apparently, though, the state at the present time rejects such negotiations. Why? Evidently, because they consider their contacts with the church authorities to be entirely adequate: needless to say, it is an easier matter to deal with servile officials in cassocks and white cowls than with manly, sincerely convinced people. Nevertheless, the interests of the Soviet State itself urgently call for contacts with the people who express the point of view of wide circles of believers. The church is a living popular organism and all attempts to create substitutes for it always end up in failure.

I will venture to cite a few examples from the recent past.

In the 'twenties the government officially recognized a holy synod consisting of 'Living Church' bishops. In all official documents the synod figured as the official representative of the Orthodox Church. Government departments conducted negotiations with it; churches were supervised by it and the former official residence of the Moscow Patriarchs – the Trinity Palace – was handed over to it. Patriarch Tikhon (referred to as the 'ex-Patriarch') and his successors were simply ignored by the state authorities who refused to regard them as legitimate. That was the authorities' decision, but not the people's. The latter stood aside from the Living Church, whose representatives remained alone in the magnificent empty churches and in their residences – and so in 1943 the Soviet Government was obliged to disown it and agree to the restoration of the Patriarchate.

A more recent example can be cited. It is well known that Metropolitan Nikolai played a large part in post-war times in the fight for peace. There were, of course, many mistakes in what he did (only people who do nothing make no mistakes); but on the whole, what he did was positive. In any case, there can be no doubt that it was very useful for the Soviet State. All Metropolitan Nikolai's speeches at international gatherings achieved an extremely wide effect and brought religious folk together in the fight for peace. It should, moreover, be said that the metropolitan did the work completely by himself, as he had only two or three assistants.

Metropolitan Nikolai, however, took an independent stand

during the period of pressure on the church which began in 1958 – and paid the price for doing so by losing his high position. He was replaced by the complaisant Metropolitan Nikodim who accommodated himself to everything. The new metropolitan organized a foreign department consisting of a few dozen parasites who compile card-index records that nobody needs and reply to unnecessary letters. He holds splendid banquets and receptions on a very pretentious scale. And what is the outcome of it all? The outcome is that the peace movement, in its religious sector, that took so much effort to organize, has wholly and entirely collapsed (all that is left of it is a mere miserable remnant in the form of the Prague Christian Peace Conference).

Metropolitan Nikodim travels around in first-class compartments, flies all over the world in the company of his hangers-on and reads out his typewritten speeches, roughly and clumsily composed as they are; he engages in intrigues, plays at being a diplomat – and no one at all pays him the slightest attention. If people really failed to notice him it would not matter, but sometimes it is worse, for he has become a target for malicious pranks and an international laughing-stock.

The question arises: has the state gained anything by placing at the head of church government such an odious personality as Metropolitan Nikodim? In spite of his abilities and great intelligence, he has failed to acquire any authority and has ruined an important and useful cause. This Metropolitan Nikodim is extremely talented. What can one say about his untalented comrades-in-arms? One thing should be said: the coefficient of their useful work in favour of the state can be designated by inscribing a round zero.

The state needs an urgent settlement of the problem of religion, based on the widest consultation not only with the official organs of the church authority, but also with religious and social circles. As we stated above, the petition of the two priests could be a basis for negotiations. Furthermore, in the very near future I intend to submit (like any other citizen of the Soviet Union I have such a right) to the Presidium of the Supreme Soviet of the USSR and to the Central Committee of the CPSU a draft of the legislative acts needed for the settlement of the religious problem.

What is to be said about the current situation?

Any thoughtful observer will readily notice the existence of conflicting trends and insufficient reflection in religious (or anti-religious) policy.

The last Decree of the Presidium of the Supreme Soviet of the RSFSR, dated 18 March 1966, contains an article which, in principle, cannot but be welcomed:

'The refusal to accept citizens at work or into an educational establishment, their dismissal from work or exclusion from an educational establishment, depriving them of privileges or advantages guaranteed by the law, and similarly any material restrictions on the rights of citizens in respect of their religious adherence . . . constitute an infringement of the laws on the separation of church and state, incurring criminal responsibility under §142 of the Penal Code of the RSFSR.'[23]

We propose to test the reality and serious intention of this regulation by applying to the Director of Working Youth School No. 116 of the City of Moscow and to the Ministry of Education of the RSFSR with the demand to reinstate the present writer to the post of teacher in that school. Complete and unconditional compliance with this regulation would mean the end of religious discrimination in our country and would be a great step forward in the religious problem, the settlement of which is in the interests both of believers and of the Soviet State.

3. *With Anger or with Love? Schism or Difference of Opinions?*

In his first resolution of 24 December 1965, the Patriarch accused the authors of the petition of trying to violate the peace of the church. The present writer has also had to suffer quite a few similar reproaches.

An especially large number of charges have been laid against me by people from the Moscow Theological Academy, the teaching staff of which were apparently upset by my remarks

K

about the poor quality of their instruction and the low standard of knowledge attained by some of their students. A noisy campaign against me started up in the academy, in which his reverence the Rector joined, suggesting to the teachers during a routine break for tea in the senior common room that they find out whom I was influencing in the academy.

I must confess that I didn't lose much sleep over this stupid fuss and bother. As A. K. Tolstoi has said:

> 'I don't fancy myself a Laocoon
> Reclining in the snake's embraces,
> But modestly discern I am beset
> By none but earthworms.'

While the personal allegations can be laughed off in this way as a joke, I must repudiate the reproaches that I am disturbing the peace of the church. On the contrary, this problem is in every respect highly serious. As everyone is aware, I took an active part in the Living Church schism, observing it for many years from within its very core. More than any other person I know what an awful evil schism is. With hand on heart, as Almighty God is my witness, I declare that neither I, nor any one of the people who think like me, wants schism. I think that it is desired least of all by the priests who wrote the petition; they are God-fearing, submissive, obedient sons of the church. Nevertheless, when we are denied the right to criticize the obviously disastrous actions of princes of the church, actions which constitute a direct perversion of all ecclesiastical and canonical practice (and all this, allegedly, for the sake of the peace of the church), then we reply that to put the question this way means a proposal of suicide for fear of death. Moreover, it means a betrayal of Orthodoxy. As everyone knows, what differentiates the Orthodox from the Catholic Church is that the former does not recognize the dogma of infallibility – neither the Pope's nor the Patriarch's. Moreover, people who deny our right to expose the palpable faults of the rulers of the church are offering us an inferior brand of papism. As is well known, the dogma of papal infallibility calls for unconditional acceptance only of those statements of the Pope which refer to problems of belief and morality and which are made *ex cathedra*. This does not, however, inhibit the occasional expression of very severe criticism of Vatican policy in Catholic circles. Both Pope Pius XII and Pope John XXIII encountered such criticism more than once. They were sometimes proffered petitions and open letters and it never once occurred to either of them to reply to such criticism by any kind of interdict.

The historical paradox is that in the twentieth century the Popes of Rome calmly listen to criticism, while the Orthodox Patriarch replies to it by an interdict and threats, considering any kind of criticism of his actions as 'harmful to the work of the church'.

No, Your Holiness, you will not succeed in foisting the dogma of infallibility on Orthodox Russia – and, in any case, certainly no one will regard you as infallible.

Patriarch Alexi makes a reference in his resolution to the canons. Let us also say a few words about them. All law represents a special kind of agreement between the state and its citizens. The latter must obey the laws, but the state must not abuse them. These are also the grounds on which Christian morality is based and on which its greatest exponent, St. Paul, took his stand. . . .

Canon law exists for the good of the church, for its defence, for reinforcing its moral basis. When it is utilized for clearly immoral purposes – in order to pervert and debase the church – it is a mortal sin to obey it. It is a perversion of the spirit of the Gospel, a victory of falsehood over truth, a service to Satan.

The Patriarch threatens in his resolution to lay fresh interdicts on Frs. Eshliman and Yakunin for having spoken the truth. We do not know, of course, what attitude the two priests will adopt in face of these threats; we are not empowered to speak on their behalf and we cannot anticipate their actions. We must, however, say that, no matter what the Patriarch decides, we shall never recognize these priests as unfrocked and shall never recognize that the Patriarch's decision or decree carries any weight.

The Holy Spirit is not the Patriarch's servant – he is the servant of the Holy Spirit. And if he, as Patriarch, is a bad and unworthy servant, the Holy Spirit will possess more worthy servants as bishops, for the world is too vast to be confined to Chisty Lane.[24]

Having given vent to our anger and indignation, we could sign off at this point. But this is where love takes over and asserts its rights. No, we want no schism, we want brotherly unity with the whole church. Such unity is possible even where there is disagreement and the Catholic Church of the present day can provide an example of this: a church in which two trends, an integralist and a modernist, exist peaceably side by side. Surely we Orthodox Christians will not be found to be less imbued with the spirit of love than the Catholics.

May the Patriarch have the patience and the humility to listen to the honest criticisms made of him and may he reply to them not with interdicts but with explanations.

All his addresses will be met with love.

So we are left with the alternatives of anger and love. Either there will be a patient smoothing over of differences or interdicts will be uttered which will inevitably lead to schism.

The choice lies with the Patriarch.

Moscow, 21 May 1966.[25]

LISTENING TO THE RADIO:
AGAINST PASSIVITY IN DEFENDING THE FAITH
(A. Krasnov-Levitin)

I have never been a conservative either in political or church matters. I am more the rebel or revolutionary type. Any generally accepted attitude has always aroused in me, from childhood onwards, a passionate desire to question it – for the single reason that it is generally accepted. I had a special dislike for attitudes or formulas that were officially adopted. In ordinary daily life, though, I am a terrible conservative, even a completely recalcitrant one. Quite apart from television, the mere mention of which makes me feel I am on the point of being sick, I simply cannot get used to either cinema or wireless. I very seldom go to the cinema (a couple of times a year when friends insist) and I have never in my life even had a radio in the house. I acquired a special distaste for it in the camps where from 1951 onwards (as a token of specially liberal treatment) loudspeakers were installed in all the barracks, broadcasting at full blast all round the clock. I remember one occasion (in the camp at Gavrilova Polyana, near Kuibyshev) the lads with me decided to switch off the radio, but one super-patriotic comrade (he was the production rationalizer and the camp stool-pigeon) suddenly announced that there had been a mass counter-revolutionary attack. The radio must not be switched off. They would immediately be starting to transmit a speech by comrade Molotov. And so there is not a single one of the rights I recovered in 1956 of which I am so happy to take advantage as the right not to listen to the radio.

I don't like foreign broadcasts either. Every time I am urged to listen to the BBC I always reply: 'If anything happens in the world that is worth hearing about, I shall find out about it even without the BBC and I can comment on the events myself just as well as they can.'

Well, on 31 July 1966 an acquaintance told me: 'Yesterday I heard about you on the BBC and they'll be putting it out again today; come along and listen.' So, of course, in such circumstances even the most fanatical hater of radio could not resist. I went along and listened.

The reader, of course, will have understood that I am referring to the British radio broadcast of 30 July (repeated on 31 July) about the petition of Frs. Eshliman and Yakunin. The broadcast took the form of a review of the reactions abroad to the petition of the two heroic priests. According to the radio broadcast and to other sources which have come to our knowledge, the petition shocked the whole world. It is very gratifying and comforting to realize that the world still knows how to pay tribute to heroism and to appreciate a genuine case of self-sacrifice. That this is the position is something of which we are daily being convinced even here in Moscow. It is no exaggeration to say that the overwhelming majority of Russian priests and laymen warmly endorse the petition of the two heroes. True, people are keeping quiet for the

time being and confining themselves to expressions of very warm
and touching sympathy towards the authors of the heroic document. No matter – they will speak out tomorrow. Only mercenary-minded people who are directly connected with the existing church structure, people who profit by the ailments affecting
the church and who are building a career for themselves by
betraying the church's interests – only they are making angry
noises. So, too, are leading members of the hierarchy whose
activities have been exposed in the petition of the two priests.
Angry noises are also being made by officials of the Foreign
Department of the Patriarchate, where the petition has thrust
right home; and by priests who sullied themselves during the
Stalin and Beria regimes by deliberately betraying their parishioners.

We have decided, however, to talk about the broadcast. Let
us listen to it . . . First of all, the question arises of how the petitions
of the two priests and my articles came to the knowledge of the
people abroad. Neither the two priests nor I have ever looked in
the face of a single foreigner or of any person connected with
other countries; even the very term 'abroad' seems almost fantastic
to us. When I was having a talk about my articles in the spring of
last year in the premises of the Executive Committee of the
Zhdanov District of Moscow, I asked how it was that the people
present were so well acquainted with my articles.* Major Shelkov[26]
of the KGB told me: 'Through your readers, Anatoli Emmanuilovich, through your readers.' . . . Well, that cuts both ways:
evidently there are various kinds of readers, or possibly not.
Which of my readers take my articles to foreign correspondents?
Could they be the very same ones who take them along to the
KGB? I think it is very possible. But that is not the point.
Although, in general, sympathies have been expressed for the
two priests' petition, attempts at censure have also been emerging.
Many people abroad have been shocked by the 'harsh tone'
('heated abuse') adopted towards the Patriarch. This is succeeded
by panegyrics in his praise, for he 'bore on his shoulders the burden

* Section omitted from p. 269. See Levitin, *Zashchita Very v SSSR*, p. 98.

of the Yezhov persecutions'. This is an objection that needs to be noticed, for with us, too, a great deal is now being said about the Patriarch. Only in our case people go to the other extreme: many people refuse to give the Patriarch any credit at all for past services. In this respect I hold a certain advantage. The point is that I lived in Petrograd throughout the 'Yezhov persecutions' (1936–39). I used to see the Patriarch at that time (he was then Metropolitan Alexi of Leningrad) every Sunday in church and can give an objective opinion of the part he then played.

In the first place, the metropolitan was at that time really in a very difficult situation. His suffragan, Bishop Nikolai of Peterhof (the future metropolitan), used to keep by him at home a small bag with two changes of clothes, two sheets and a towel – in case he was arrested. I think Metropolitan Alexi also had a similar bag at home. Every two or three months brought some kind of un-pleasant surprise – the arrest of a group of priests. By 1937 there were only fifteen of them left in the whole of the Leningrad region, whereas in 1930 they had numbered more than a thousand. In the spring of 1937 the metropolitan was turned out of his rooms in the Novodevichi Monastery at the Moscow Gates and found shelter for himself in the bell-tower of the Prince Vladimir Cathedral in the cramped and gloomy accommodation formerly occupied by the caretakers. Metropolitan Alexi took church ser-vices along with Archdeacon Verzilin, the only deacon left in Leningrad.[27] After Verzilin's death in 1938 he celebrated without a deacon. At that time the metropolitan put on his robes at the altar, not in the middle of the church, and celebrated in a way very little different from a priest. His Grace's whole way of life at that time was essentially modest. I remember once, as I was walking along Nevsky Prospect, near Morskaya Street, I noticed the metropolitan clad in civilian garb. A threadbare light-weight overcoat, galoshes, an ordinary grey cap – all this, in conjunction with his aristocratic face and subtle elegance of gesture, gave him the appearance of a bankrupt landlord. As I passed I made him a deep bow and the metropolitan acknowledged it with a slight nod. He was very resigned and never made a single attempt to

resist or protest against the palpably illegal actions of the authorities. In 1936 Metropolitan Alexi signed a diocesan decree forbidding the giving of communion to children and giving an order 'to
see that children were not admitted to the Holy Sacrament, since
they had no understanding whatsoever of what was being done
to them'.*

It is, of course, completely ridiculous to assert that the church
is indebted for its revival during the war years to the actions of the
Metropolitans (later Patriarchs) Sergi and Alexi. As we have more
than once written in the past, the church owes its revival, as well
as to Divine Providence, to its own strength as exhibited in war-
time, a strength which compelled Stalin to reckon with it. One
cannot deny the services rendered by the prelates of the time,
including Metropolitan Alexi. He did not forswear either God or
his high office, as did the Living Church Metropolitan of Leningrad (Nikolai Platonov) – and such proposals were probably made
to Alexi; moreover, the prospects in case of refusal were very
terrible. The metropolitan did not leave his post and did not
cravenly withdraw into retirement, as many bishops at that time
did, more especially among the Living Church camp, who ran
away from their flocks. The metropolitan, finally, did not sully
his name by treachery, as did many unworthy members of the
priesthood at the time, with N. Kolchitsky at their head. (In
Leningrad the principal agent of Yezhov's NKVD was Archpriest
Lamakin.) It may be said that these are all negative virtues and
nothing to boast about. The problem, however, will assume quite
a different aspect if we remember the kind of sanctions that could
follow a refusal to give up church work or engage in outright
treachery: arrest, terrible tortures, death in the dreadful Yezhov
camps.

Thus it is to some extent correct to say that Metropolitan (later
Patriarch) Alexi bore the Yezhov terror on his shoulders. But
without wishing to offend His Holiness the Patriarch, it has to be
said that tens of millions of believers did the same; they all faced
the danger at that time and yet they did not renounce God. I

* As happened again under Khrushchev. See p. 160.

shall cite at least one case from the history of those years. In
January 1937 a census of population was taken in Leningrad (as,
of course, in the whole Soviet Union also). Among the questions
put to citizens was this: 'Religious denomination?' to which
'hundred-per-cent citizens' should have answered that they were
non-believers. I was at the time a school teacher and simultaneously a student at the Institute. As my father pointed out, the reply
'Believer (Orthodox)' could entail arrest, which at that time involved deportation of the whole family from Leningrad. 'You'll
ruin yourself and us', said my father. Nevertheless, I declared
myself as Orthodox, as did tens of millions of others. Such
instances occurred constantly at that time. These were times when
to go to church, to have icons in your room, or to wear a crucifix
round your neck, meant that you were labelled as a 'churchman' –
with all the terrible consequences that entailed. And yet we all,
several tens of millions of people, did not renounce God and
carried on our shoulders the 'whole burden of the Yezhov terror'.
Moreover, none of us, after all, derived any advantages whatever
from membership of the church: neither money nor honours nor
a brilliant rank. Metropolitan Alexi was our spiritual leader then
and it would have been hard on us if he had left us. But what could
he have done if we all, the members of his flock, had left him? I
fear that he would have found it not only difficult but even impossible to carry on. Consequently, we all at that time carried on
our shoulders the burden of the Yezhov terror (I also carried the
burden of the Beria terror from 1949–56) and none of us has
anything to boast of over the other.

Does this, however, entitle all of us (or any one of us) to behave
badly now? No, it does not.

Levitin draws a parallel with General de Gaulle, who repudiated
Marshal Pétain's capitulation to the Nazis.

What we are talking about now is not our motherland, but our
church. We are fighting not against our country's enemies, but
against the abuses that arose during the years of Stalin's and
Khrushchev's rule. Those years gave rise to an unnatural situation

when the church found itself under the domination of atheists who were acting as complete dictators over the priesthood, appointing to posts people (sometimes complete unbelievers) who toadied to them and bossed the church as they liked. Who encourages all this unlawful behaviour? For twenty years now, and longer, it is Patriarch Alexi who has been countenancing all this in clear violation of the Soviet Constitution. He is covering up unlawful actions by remaining silent, bewildering or confusing people by his lying refutations (see, for instance, the Patriarch's interview published in the *Journal of the Moscow Patriarchate*, No. 4, 1966),[28] upsetting all attempts to rectify mistakes and punishing honest priests who defend the church. He it is who is protecting with his authority anonymous characters who, by making use of their shady connections, have pushed themselves forward into senior bishoprics. It is he who is betraying the church to the godless. His role at the present time is fully analogous to that played by Philippe Pétain in France in the 'forties, except that he has not defended Verdun and has rendered no special services to the church in the past. Yet someone is being reproached for 'heated abuse' of the Patriarch. No, if anyone can really be reproached for anything, it would actually be for not being heated enough, for only beginning now to talk in proper terms about the Patriarch and openly requiring him and his counsellors to explain their toleration of the illegalities and of the innumerable breaches of the separation of church and state.

All the while we do love the Patriarch; we pray for him and we do not break off canonical association with him. We come out with our accusations openly and honestly, but we hear not a word in reply. All that is heard is a doleful muttering by officials about 'forms of address', with every care being taken to evade the root problems of church life referred to in the petition to the Patriarch. Incidentally, a new 'argument' has recently appeared, one that was first brought up by Archbishop Alexi Redigear in a conversation I had with him and which was later given worldwide publicity by Metropolitan Nikodim, when he declared in Geneva: I do not deny that individual abuses have ocurred in

some places, but as soon as these became known to the Council
for Religious Affairs (formerly the Council for Russian Orthodox
Church Affairs) they were instantly stopped.'

What can one say about that? Only this – that people who
advance such an argument evidently have nothing better to say.

Kuroyedov, it is suggested, knew nothing about the closure of
the Pecherskaya Lavra in Kiev,* about the barbarous destruction
wrought by hooligans at Glinskaya Pustyn, the mockeries perpetrated on the Pochaev monks which have gone on for six years
in full view.† Or perhaps CROCA knew nothing about the
barbarous way in which the Transfiguration Church in Moscow
was destroyed (despite the protests, appeals and invocations of a
thousand parishioners who, for almost a whole day, refused to
leave the church).[29] Or possibly CROCA was unaware that out
of four hundred churches in the Odessa diocese only ninety remain; of 39 churches in the Novgorod diocese only ten; of the
innumerable monasteries in Moldavia – not one. Maybe you
church leaders knew nothing about it either? No, you knew
about it, because every closure of a church was approved by a
bishop's signature and the closure of the Transfiguration Church
was preceded by a telephone call from Metropolitan Pimen
directing the church to be handed over. When he was told that
there was no order in writing, the metropolitan replied: 'There's
an oral direction.'

So, if you, Father Nikodim, have no other arguments, you
have wasted your time going to Geneva – with arguments like
yours you might as well have stayed quietly at home. As always
happens with people who know they are telling lies, our prelates
seem to have a terrible fear of publicity. In July the Patriarch
issued a special decree making it obligatory for bishops to ensure
that there should be no dissemination in their dioceses of 'open
letters or articles aimed at disturbing the peace of the church'.‡
Archbishop Ioann of Pskov in his order to the prior of the Caves
Monastery near Pskov, Archimandrite Alipi, enjoins him to see
to it that no 'open letter' is circulated in the monastery. Lastly,

* See p. 85.   † See pp. 98–115.   ‡ See p. 228–30.

a meeting was held in the Foreign Department, in the private office of Metropolitan Nikodim, with Archbishop Alexi, Bishop Pitirim and others participating, at which they discussed through whom 'information was being leaked'. You would have thought they were talking about a military plant or an atomic station. Like everyone who finds the truth distasteful, our prelates have turned to repression. Everyone knows of the uncanonical, quite unjustified, ban that has been laid on Frs. Eshliman and Yakunin. This has disgraced the Patriarchate in the eyes of the whole world and has dealt its authority a heavier blow than thousands of such petitions. That is not all, however; threats are re-echoing louder and louder in the lobbies of the Patriarchate to have the two priests who wrote the petition unfrocked.

We have already stated in our previous article* that we would never recognize such a barbarous decision, nor would it be recognized by large numbers of believing Christians. We have, of course, no idea what exactly these two priests will do if they are unfrocked. One thing, however, is beyond doubt: whatever action they do take, the Patriarchate will have to face up to many bitter surprises and will be convinced of the truth of the old proverb: 'Sow the wind and reap the whirlwind!'

Our prelates, however, are not going to leave it at mere spiritual interdicts; louder and louder demands are being heard from their midst for more tangible coercive measures to be taken. In July, for instance, Frs. Yakunin and Eshliman were told at CRA that the bishops had made representations to this organization and were demanding that it should 'protect them from the attacks of these priests'. It is easy to understand what precisely they have in mind when they call on a government department 'to protect them from attacks'. In private conversations many partisans of the official line of policy warn about the possibility of arrest. In so doing, the cowardly prelates are judging by their own reactions. For them personally arrest is the culmination of all disasters; they simply cannot understand how it is that people are not afraid of being arrested. None of us has any grounds for

* See p. 287.

fearing arrest, since our only offence lies in the fact that we are defending the separation of church and state and are supporting the observance of the Soviet Constitution. But if it comes to talking about arrest, may I, as an old jail-bird, be allowed to remark: 'Don't be upset, friends; it's better to be imprisoned and speak the truth than to walk around in freedom, drive round in *Chaika* cars and gabble atrocious lies.'

Incidentally, the international hubbub which has blown up round the two priests' document has obliged the Patriarchate to get busy on producing a refutation. On this occasion, as they placed no reliance on their own forces, they have turned to the 'leader of the band'. At the present moment, in the inner recesses of the *Journal of the Moscow Patriarchate* a lengthy 'refutation' is being fabricated under the guidance of the notorious political adventurer, A. L. Kazem-bek.[30] There is probably no need to say anything more. The name of Kazem-bek speaks for itself. This lordly large-scale adventurer might really have sprung from the pages of Sukhovo-Kobylin.[31] He is a Krechinsky[32] from head to foot – without the slightest extraneous admixture. Krechinsky, as we know, operated with imitation diamonds.* Kazem-bek has done nothing all his life but manufacture ideological imitation diamonds. Nowadays, however, there are not many simpletons around: for all his ingenuity, no one has fallen for Kazem-bek's bait or taken his diamonds for genuine. I think the same will happen with the diamonds which are at present being produced in the Novodevichi Monastery.[33]

We have become so carried away with our internal problems that we have forgotten about the London broadcast. And quite naturally, too. What interests us is Russia and Russia alone. Even

---

* In comparing Kazem-bek with Krechinsky we are referring to his political activity, his methods, his procedures and publicity schemes, but we have no desire whatsoever to cast any aspersion on his private life or moral image. We would not, incidentally, have considered writing about him in such terms, had we not had exact information that he is intending to direct public insults against the two priests. That is perhaps below the Krechinsky standard and quite ungentlemanly. Are you trying in this way to demonstrate your political reliability, Mr. Kazem-bek? Actually, no one has any doubts about it (Levitin's note).

so, let us return to London. Out of the fogs of London we hear
the voice of Fr. Vladimir Rodzianko.* His talks on the faith are
talented, profound and of a very high standard. He has attracted
the attention of our theologians and earned himself universal
recognition and respect. It was all the more disagreeable to hear
Fr. Rodzianko's talk given on 31 July 1966 when he plunged into
what is apparently to him unfamiliar territory – church politics.
He considers the accusations put forward in the two priests'
petition to be exaggerated and advises us to await in patience the
forthcoming free council of the Russian Church. Allow us to
judge how far these accusations are exaggerated. Here in Moscow
we have a clearer view than you in London. And as regards the
invitation to await the 'free council', which will meet heaven
knows when, that recalls the similar invitation of the Russian
liberals, headed by Fr. Vladimir's deceased grandfather, addressed
to the Russian peasants to wait for the emergence of the Constituent Assembly. Well do we know the results of those exhortations.
Anyway, let us look at the facts. In order to understand whether
the accusations made by the two priests are exaggerated or not,
let us cite just one example from the life of the Smolensk diocese.
One could cite hundreds of similar cases.

At the beginning of 1965 a new bishop, Antoni (Vikarik), was
appointed to the diocese of Smolensk. Although this bishop did
not enjoy much of a reputation in Moscow during student and
post-graduate days, he started laying down a sane, healthy church
policy in Smolensk. The situation which confronted him there
was catastrophic. The local priests hardly even bothered to conceal the fact that they were working for certain departments and
even boasted openly to one another at the altar about their ex-
ploits. The proto-deacon, Alexei Petrovich Zhirov, is an especially
colourful figure. He was so notorious all over Smolensk for his
shameless behaviour and had become such an odious character
that all the anti-religious propagandists always cite him as an
example and every time his name is mentioned it evokes a thunder-
ous outburst of laughter from an audience. Alexei Petrovich

* Cf. pp. 230–7.

makes no secret of the fact that he is an unbeliever. The files of the diocesan administration contain several documents testifying to his atheism: a report by Fr. Nikifor Prysk and another by Fr. Yevstafi Vasliko. Finally, no one knows whether Alexei Petrovich is an ecclesiastic at all – how and when he was ordained – or whether he was ordained at all. In three questionnaires which Alexei Petrovich completed at various times (they are to be found in the files of the Smolensk diocesan administration) he has given three different dates of his ordination and three different names of bishops who ordained him. Over a period of several years all the efforts made to remove this disgraceful character from the church have failed. It all comes to nought every time because of the support extended to this miserable proto-deacon by the CROCA officials, Alexei Gavrilovich Anishchenko (since replaced) and his successor Citizen Navozov (who considers himself an extremely literate exponent of Marxism). Moreover, neither of these officials has any illusions whatsoever about the moral qualities of Zhirov: they say right out that they tolerate him because he is useful to them. The dean of the cathedral was wiser and more cunning than Alexei Petrovich, but in matters of morals, it seems, not so very superior, and was favourably regarded by many highly-placed bodies. The bishop realized that it was impossible to work under such circumstances; he began by dismissing the dean and then he set about choosing more respectable personnel. Gradually three decent priests made their appearance in the church: a new dean, Archpriest Anatoli Demianovich Aukhimik, Priest-monk Pavel Maximenko and a young priest, Fr. Nikolai Chernetsky. Finally, the bishop decided to dismiss the omnipotent proto-deacon himself. On receiving the requisite report, the bishop forbade him to take part in church services. A little while later the bishop was urgently summoned to Moscow to appear before CROCA. After a two-hour conversation, with Navozov present, the bishop returned and immediately removed the three priests: Frs. Anatoli Aukhimik, Pavel Maximenko and Nikolai Chernetsky (the first two were dismissed from the diocese). He reinstated Zhirov to all his rights and revoked all the measures he had taken to make diocesan life healthier. The bishop has now lost absolutely all authority, the diocese is completely dominated by the CROCA official (no-one goes to the bishop at all) and a gang of unbridled louts exercise absolute control of the cathedral. That is where you need to look, Fr. Rodzianko. It would be interesting to know whether you would find the charges made by the authors of the petition exaggerated and whether you would wait with Olympian patience for the convening of a 'free council'.

The most disgusting feature of the whole of this business is the cowardly behaviour of the bishop. What was Your Reverence afraid of? Were you beaten or tortured? After all, what was the worst they could have threatened? Well, they would have sent you into retirement – that and no more. You would not have died as a result, you know. I have no doubt, of course, that Your Reverence is a Godfearing and honourable monk. But let me put the question – suppose an unbeliever or someone not bound by a monk's vows were in your place – how would he have behaved? Precisely as you did, of course. He too would have held on to his job and accepted any compromise whatever with his conscience in order to keep it. Fr. Rodzianko, of course, is entitled to accuse us of 'using heated insults', but when Jesus Christ saw people committing abominations in the temple, he went beyond a display of anger. He snatched up a whip and drove the money-changers out of the temple. But maybe these are the antics one expects to find in the provinces. Smolensk is just a provincial place. Let us have a look at what goes on in Moscow.*

. . . . The participation of the laity in church affairs is an essential factor and highly desirable. I do not propose to deny that the system that prevailed from 1944 to 1961, when the parish priest had the uncontrolled disposal of church property, was a throughly wrong system which, in practice, resulted in many abuses, Incidentally, that system was a reflection of Stalin's personality – he had a pathological terror of any kind of communality (even in its most rudimentary form).

We are not criticising the 1961 Synod at all for placing the

* See pp. 305–6 for the extract omitted at this point.

parish priest under the control of the congregation. The whole trouble is that under the present system the churchwarden is not elected, but is appointed by the district executive committee (an atheistic body) from people who are often entirely outside the church, even non-believers, and of highly suspicious morals (not to mention that they are completely illiterate). So you have these illiterate upstarts ordering the clergy about, stuffing their pockets, making fortunes at the church's expense, rapaciously exploiting the property of the church for their own benefit, while the parish priest has to stand by helplessly watching it all. Not only is he not the head of the community – he is not even a member of it. He is merely a hired servant (on the same level as the caretaker and the stoker). Let us again turn to concrete examples.

In the town of Pushkino, near Moscow, some years ago St. Nicholas' Church had a parish priest, Fr. Vladimir Rozhkov (at present on the staff of the Foreign Department). In this church the warden was a mercenary-minded, rude fellow, of dishonest habits and an unbeliever. The parish priest called a meeting and proposed dismissing the churchwarden, as everyone knew about his malpractices. What was the result of the priest's action? He was immediately removed from his post. Archpriest Rozhkov (one of the most zealous officials of the Foreign Department) will now, of course, deny this fact. It will not work; I can produce tomorrow several dozen witnesses.

Here is another fact from the experience of Fr. Nikolai Eshliman, one of the authors of the petition. Two years ago Fr. Nikolai was serving in the Grebnevo village church, Moscow region. It is a magnificent church, built by General Bibikov with the co-operation of Kazakov, and it is a wonderful work of art. This church was in the hands of ignorant and mercenary-minded people who were looting and destroying it. Fr. Nikolai proposed holding a meeting to elect a new churchwarden, but this proved to be not so simple a matter. In order to hold a meeting of believers, you need permission from the district executive committee. Over a period of several months the believers tried to secure this, but without success. The secretary of the executive committee referred them to Trushin (at that time the CROCA official) and he referred them to the secretary of the executive committee. In the end, after many tribulations and a big row, they managed, through the regional *soviet*, to obtain permission for the meeting. The churchwarden was dismissed, but a few days later, by decree of His Holiness the Patriarch, Fr. Nikolai Eshliman was transferred to another church as assistant priest.

We have cited examples from the experience of two very energetic people. What do priests do who have not got the energy of Fr. Vladimir Rozhkov (at the moment it is not – momentarily, I hope – properly directed) and the exceptional devotion to principle of Fr. Nikolai Eshliman? Nothing. They sit and watch how the churchwardens lord it over everyone, forcing people to comply obediently with all their orders, even their caprices. Incidentally, parish priests are not authorized to take any kind of action against, or even to address any reproof to, a churchwarden, for Metropolitan Pimen in one of his diocesan orders has forbidden priests even to 'interfere in domestic problems', threatening to take the severest measures if there is any kind of interference here, 'not stopping short of dismissal from the diocese'. No; if one looks for historical analogies, then they should be sought not in Novgorod or Pskov but in the Ukraine in the seventeenth century. Here the Polish magnates farmed churches out to Jewish money-lenders who did absolutely as they liked in them. This was written up, incidentally, by Nikolai Vasilievich Gogol. Of course, it does not follow from all this that every churchwarden is some kind of monster. There are among them some splendid, deeply religious and fine men. I am simply referring to the general system. . . .

The broadcast from London deplores schism and says that 'mutual reproaches can only make the situation of the Russian Church worse'. . . .

In my opinion, unfortunately, a situation may arise where schism could become unavoidable. This will occur if the high-ranking prelates call upon everyone to bow down before lies, to disown the truth and unconditionally tolerate all the outright brazen breaches of canon law which are actually occurring. Moreover, anyone who objects to this will be banned from office. Unfortunately, there are some grounds for believing that the high-ranking prelates are preparing to take this line. They are being driven to do so by godless people who do not understand the church and think even less of its good. In any case, the people in Chisty Lane and on Ryleyev Street[34] must clearly realize the direction that is being taken.

We do not want schism! We do not want it at all! The one way to avoid schism is to hold patient negotiations, in the course of which the differences that have arisen must be settled. I can, of course, speak only for myself, but I am quite sure that the authors of the petition also think on similar lines. As for me, when I handed my last article over to Archbishop Alexi of Tallinn, I told him I was prepared to recant everything I had written against the Patriarchate on one condition: let them show me that I am wrong. The best way of refuting me is to prove that we are dealing not with soulless officials who know only how to issue circulars, but with leaders of the church who have its interests at heart, who are prepared to give their opponents a full hearing and agree to their suggestions when there is nothing to be said against them.

19–21 August 1966.[35]

8 Archpriest Shpiller and His Parish

ABOUT CHRISTMAS AND EASTER
(Archpriest Vsevolod Shpiller)

In spirit the eyes of Orthodox Christians today are once again fixed on the picture of the divine Child in the manger at Bethlehem. Before him kneel the wise men with their gifts of love and wisdom of all ages; above shines the star which has shown them the way, while the angels bend down to earth and praise God.

How we long to see this star in the sky today! It is so difficult to find the way to the manger by electric light! We would like to kneel at the manger with the shepherds and the wise men in order to share in the joy of Christmas. For we know how great that joy is!

Our earthly joys pass and are gone, and how often do they end in pain and distress. But the joy of Christmas (we are told), the joy proclaimed by the angels, will never pass away (John 16:22). No one can take it from us either in this life or the next.

In the midst of modern life, how often do we stand confused, overwhelmed by the changes, the naked facts and the old mysteries which remain unsolved. We cannot find our place in this world. One explanation presents itself: that we belong to Christ, whereas the world is not Christian and does not want to be. What seems to us to be a fact is regarded by many people only as a dilemma: either to accept the de-Christianized world and adapt oneself to it, or else to withdraw from it and reject it as strange and hostile to our way of thinking and feeling.

The joy of Christmas saves us from this dilemma. No explosion of nuclear weapons under the earth or up in the infinite realms of space can drown the Gospel words, 'The Word was made flesh' (John 1:14). 'The Word was God. The same was in the beginning with God. All things were made by him . . . In him was life; and the life was the light of men.' (John 1:1–4.) This Word entered the created world for all in the miracle of the incarnation. This marks the centre and the culmination of the creation and we know that nothing in the world can alter the fact: 'In this was manifested the love of God toward us, because that God sent his only begotten Son into the world, that we might live through him.' (I John 4:9.) This infinite love cannot be withdrawn, nor can that which it has bestowed upon us.

Let us banish the thought of death. The idea of death and the thought of his own inevitable end fills man with sadness. Is death the end of everything that we love, everything that we cherish in ourselves and in others, all the values, everything by which the soul lives? If all this were to end in the terrible emptiness of the grave, life would be emptied of all value, because this void may open at any moment. Involuntarily our imagination pictures total annihilation (for me death will be the end of everything) and all our joys are destroyed by the picture of death.

But God became man. His incarnation is the beginning of the liberation of all men and of the whole creation from the power of death. . . .

January 1963.[1]

THE PARISH CLAIMS ITS RIGHTS

LISTENING TO THE RADIO*
(A. Krasnov-Levitin)

Is there anyone who does not know the church of St. Nicholas-in-Kuznetsy[2] in Moscow? Who does not know the revered icon of the Virgin with the wonderful name, 'Soothe my sorrows'? Is there anyone, finally, who does not know the incumbent of that

* This extract was omitted from p. 300.

church, one of the best respected and most enlightened priests in
Moscow, Fr. Vsevolod Shpiller? The life of that Moscow parish,
whose clergy make an excellent impression by their piety and
intelligence, was flowing peacefully and quietly. That was the
position until last year, when the warden of the church was killed
in a car crash. His successor (a singer from the Maly Theatre) immediately adopted a new policy. He dismissed all the church
workers (candle-sellers, cleaners and so on); the persons newly
appointed saw no need for even making the parish priest's acquaintance; they treat the clergy rudely and provocatively and order
everyone about as if they were in a conquered country. The new
churchwarden, anxious to show what an especially trustworthy
person he is, not content with following the usual routine for
checking the documents of parents of children brought for baptism, began demanding that fathers produce also their army cards,
which is quite illegal. Finally, the churchwarden introduced still
another new departure: he allowed 'public-spirited' anti-religious
people from the neighbouring Foreign Trade Institute to gad
about the church. They come in, check documents and attend all
the meetings of the *dvadtsatka*. Finally, they began to suggest to
Fr. Vsevolod that he discontinue his sermons. These suggestions
were made both directly to him and through his relatives. What
happened when Fr. Vsevolod began to protest against such
actions? He was removed by a personal decree of the Patriarch
and in his place was appointed a certain priest, Konstantin
Meshchersky, who died last Saturday (13 August 1966) just when
he was about to begin his duties as incumbent. The judgment of
God had fallen on him. We shall therefore not say much about
a dead man – only that Azev and Malinovsky (the notorious pro-
vocateurs of old Russia) were angels compared with Meshchersky
(they still had some humanity left).

The Patriarch is aware of all this and he also knows these two
priests and their comparative moral character. Yet, on the insist-
ence of CROCA, he does just this: he dismisses one and appoints
the other.

19–21 August 1966.[3]

A DROP UNDER THE MICROSCOPE
(A. Krasnov-Levitin)

When I was eleven and in the fourth form at school,[4] our biology teacher, Marya Kirillovna, a tall, plump woman with short, grey hair, brought into the biology laboratory a bright, shiny, metallic object – a microscope.

'Tolya Levitin,' she ordered, 'come up here, take a little piece of glass, let a pure, cold, limpid drop of water from the tap fall on it and place it under the microscope. Now look,' she added. And I looked . . . Good Lord, what I saw! The drop turned out to be a whirlpool, a den filled with monsters . . . 'Those are microbes,' said the teacher. Thus was revealed to me the fearful inner life of the drop of water.

*   *   *

In Moscow, off Novokuznetskaya Street, in Vishnyakovsky Lane there is a church: white, bright, clear as a drop of water in the winter. . . .

A drop. Yes, one drop. For is not every church and every parish a drop, a single minute drop, in the bottomless ocean which is the Universal Church? It is a blessed drop in a blessed church. This is why miracles of faith and of God's love occur every day in the church. Sinful people are spiritually renewed, the sick are healed and tired, withered souls receive here life-giving water – here their sorrows are relieved and they feel the joy of the resurrection.

But this is also a part of the Russian Church. It is a drop in a sick church and that is why it is terrifying to examine it with a microscope. One is frightened by all the ills of the Russian Church reflected in this drop.

I distinctly remember the feeling of fear and paralysing anxiety which I experienced as I looked into the microscope. But I also recall the kind, ironic smile of the elderly teacher: 'Don't be afraid, my child. In spite of all these microbes, water is still water, the water which sustains us. But you must also realize what is hidden even in pure water so as not to catch typhoid.' So now I fearlessly bring the microscope into the church with me, firmly convinced that the lifegiving water of Christ's teaching can sustain us. But one must also keep in mind the microbes. Let us therefore examine the drop and not fear these microbes.

. . . . The role of the wardens in the parishes of the Russian Church today is peculiar and we should know more about it than we usually do. That is why it is he, the warden of this church, who will be the principal hero of our article.

On 1 January 1966 S. I. Plyashkevich took up the duties of warden (at Fr. Shpiller's church, St. Nicholas-in-Kuznetsy). Such an event, of no historical importance whatsoever, is, nevertheless, under present conditions, a very important episode in the life of the parish. According to the new order of church life established in 1961,* the warden is the virtual master of the church. He is the head of the executive body, in fact he hires and dismisses employees, signs contracts with the clergy and effectively controls the entire parochial life. In these matters he is in no way subordinate to the church authorities. He is absolutely and in every sense independent of the church hierarchy. He is completely independent both of the parish priest and of the diocesan bishop.

What sort of a man is he, this new master of this prominent Moscow parish?

Plyashkevich is 73 years old. He himself graduated once upon a time from a theological seminary and his family had always been close to the church. It was precisely these reasons which, apparently, prompted his promotion to the office of warden. One must point out, however, that Plyashkevich had never taken any great part in church life; for many years he worked as a chorister at the Maly Theatre and sang in the church for money.

Now, after his first year in the parish, there has arisen the following legitimate bewilderment: it goes without saying that the warden of an Orthodox parish must be a member of the community and an Orthodox Christian. The basic obligation of every

* See pp. 44–6.

Orthodox Christian is to take part in Holy Communion. Any member who, in the course of a year and without valid excuse, has not been to confession or Holy Communion is cut off by the church like a withered branch, like a dead member who has lost connection with the source of life. He loses the right to call himself an Orthodox Christian until he returns to the church with sincere, heartfelt penitence, until he cures himself of his dark folly – for in truth he is mad who rejects the Chalice of Life.

But the fact remains that, during the whole of 1966, Plyashkevich never once went to confession or to Holy Communion. Indeed, no one can ever remember when he last did so. What is more, when he attends divine worship, citizen Plyashkevich behaves, even in the choir, as an unbeliever, thus introducing temptation into the congregation through his provocative behaviour.

The question arises, is he an Orthodox Christian? It should be stated with regret that, since he does not take part in the sacraments, Plyashkevich is not, at the present time, in eucharistic fellowship with the church and cannot, therefore, be regarded as one of its full and equal members: it is impossible (until he receives the sacraments) to bestow on him divine grace and other rites and he should do penance according to the instructions of his confessor. Since he does not take part in the charismatic life of grace in the community, he cannot be regarded as a member of it. The tenure of the post of warden by a man who is not in eucharistic communion with the church is of itself a scandal which vividly characterizes the contemporary condition of the Russian Church.

But how does Citizen Plyashkevich rule the community which has fallen to him?

It is not entirely fair to reproach him with indifference to all the mysteries. Indeed, to one of them he devotes a great deal of attention. The illegal, unconstitutional procedure of recording baptisms, which requires the passports of the parents, is well known. This procedure forces the church to assume the completely unnatural role of a policeman. Even this did not seem 'civic-minded' enough to Citizen Plyashkevich. Driven by servile zeal, he thought of checking the military documents of the fathers in addition to passports. But this was still not enough. He went even further . . . and it suddenly came to light that Citizen Plyashkevich was a man of immense talent, a man with a special vocation . . . Oh, yes, this is no joke. Plyashkevich does have a vocation . . . and what is it? Is he a singer? No, the singer in him turned out to be of little importance – he never went further than a chorister in a dramatic theatre. Is he a good church worker? No, and if he is a worker at all, he is definitely not a church one. Who is he then? What sort of bird is he? About this there can be no doubt. Citizen Plyashkevich is a secret policeman by vocation.

His principal duty is to receive money for religious ceremonies. It is true that at the same time the surnames and addresses of the parents of the baptized babies are taken down. Citizen Plyashkevich, however, acts like a true secret policeman . . . The very next day after the baptism our Sherlock Holmes sends to all ends of the Moscow region and even beyond messengers who roam through the *soviets*, house managements, police stations, where they check, search and demand information . . . and suddenly it emerges that some parent has given his name or profession incorrectly. When questioned about the motives of his actions, Citizen Plyashkevich usually answers, not without bravado: 'I act according to the dictates of my civic conscience.' We, of course, admire your civic conscience, Citizen Plyashkevich, and offer you our congratulations, but allow us also to ask an indiscreet question: why, as a matter of fact, does your civic conscience dictate you to act in this way? And why do you assume that the parents of the baptized babies would give an incorrect name, profession or address? Is the baptism of one's children a crime? Can it really be followed by some kind of punishment? Do we not enjoy individual freedom of conscience and of practising religion? Why are you silent, Citizen Plyashkevich? Do you not know how to answer?

We, too, are silent and do not know how to answer.

*   *   *

Citizen Plyashkevich behaves like an autocrat. The auditing commission requests him to present the financial accounts. He fails to do so. Without any explanation and disregarding the Labour Code, he dismissed all the church workers who had been there for years and replaced them with people never seen in the church before, unknown to anyone and who do not even bother to pretend they are believers. Indeed, Plyashkevich does not even greet the incumbent when they meet and he addresses the other priests in the insolent, haughty tone of an army officer. He has insulted them more than once. 'Who are you? Some little seminarian?' he asks, in the presence of worshippers, the second priest of the parish who has served here for eleven years. The employees hired by Plyashkevich have adopted approximately the same attitude. 'Tell the priest to come and introduce himself,' the new book-keeper informed the incumbent through a third party. The priest is an elderly man, a venerable Moscow archpriest, who enjoys authority in both Russian and international religious circles.

Levitin describes the attempt of the parishioners to persuade the church authorities to intervene on their behalf and oust Plyashkevich. Metropolitan Pimen's negative replies are quoted in full.

As is evident from these documents, His Grace answers all requests in a highly laconic fashion: 'It does not depend on me', 'It does not lie within my powers', 'I do not have the right.' The question arises: what matters do actually lie within the metropolitan's powers and what are his rights? Are there not, perhaps, reflected in this insignificant episode the paralysis of the church authorities, their cowardice, uselessness, total lack of initiative – the very features which represent the tragedy of the Russian Church? Unpleasant? Repugnant? Painful? Never mind, observe – this is a drop under the microscope.

In any event, the people became convinced shortly after this that it was foolish to appeal to the church authorities.

So they turned to the civil ones, namely to the Kirov District Executive Committee of the city of Moscow.

Arguments developed over the administration of parish finances.

Who can settle all these disputes? None other than a general parochial meeting. But Citizen Plyashkevich does everything he can to prevent this. . . .

The secretary of the Kirov District Executive Committee, N. G. Bryzgova, firmly supports Plyashkevich. She completely ignores all the petitions of the parishioners who turn to her with requests, supplications and categorical demands to authorize the calling of a parish meeting, as required by the law.

There was the parishioners' appeal to Bryzgova of 9 September 1966, signed by 170 people, fifteen of whom were members of the *dvadtsatka*. The reply: deathly silence.

These same parishioners appealed to the same committee for the second time on 23 September again making the same request. The reply: deathly silence . . .

Finally, on 18 October of the same year a petition with 44 signatures was handed in to the secretary of the district executive committee. Again silence.

Then on 16 November 1966 a complaint signed by forty parishioners and ten members of the *dvadtsatka* concerning Bryzgova's unlawful action was lodged with the Procurator of the city of Moscow, Comrade Malkov.

Levitin quotes the official reply received.

As is evident from the document quoted above, the Procuracy believes that a meeting of the parishioners must certainly be called and both CROCA and the district executive committee have been informed accordingly. Nevertheless, there has been no meeting. Why and for what reason is there such a flagrant disregard for the law?

All this is because of a desire to retain Plyashkevich. . . . With the help of people like him, it is much easier to deal with troublesome clergymen and to put into practice all the illegal measures directed against the church. Through his like it will be possible at a future General Council to force upon the church an unsuitable candidate for Patriarch.[5] For there our Plyashkeviches will depict themselves as 'representatives of the people' and vote for passive and cowardly princes of the church who even now are shielding all the former's lawlessness. . . .

* * *

Now that we have examined the drop, let us put away the microscope. Let us try to analyse what we have seen. There are microbes in this lifegiving, beneficial water: lawlessness, the apathy of church authorities, their total passivity and the cynical arbitrariness of the chance people who have penetrated it.

This is only one drop, but in it is pictured graphically and in a documentary fashion the state of the entire Russian Church. After all, did not two Moscow priests, Yakunin and Eshliman, testify to this when they wrote?

What must be done, then, to keep this water pure, lifegiving and able to quench spiritual thirst?

It must be boiled and the microbes destroyed.

12–14 December 1966.

Postscript

This article had been completed when new information came from Vishnyakovsky Lane.

Having refused to authorize a meeting of the parishioners of St. Nicholas-in-Kuznetsy Church and having failed to reply to the petition sent by the members of the *dvadtsatka* requesting such a meeting, the district executive committee authorized Plyashke-vich to form a 'new' *dvadtsatka*, so that it would 'legalize' his position in this parish, which is fighting for its rights. Individuals unknown to the congregation, joined in all by only five parish-ioners, were authorized to meet in the church and the warden then declared them the 'new *dvadtsatka*'. Yet, in defiance of all church canons, neither the incumbent of the church nor the Patriarch, as bishop of the diocese, was even informed of this 'meeting' (if such it may be called).

Levitin appends the texts of five further appeals by the parish to the authorities, the fourth of which makes these legal points:

True, the law does grant the registering authorities the right to dismiss individuals from membership of the executive body of the *dvadtsatka* after their election (§14 of the Statute*) – but it says nothing on the right to dismiss individuals from the *dvadtsatka* as such.

The registration of the individuals presented by the warden as members of the *dvadtsatka* and the total disregard of our petitions by Bryzgova constitute a breach of the law. It is not difficult now to foresee the subsequent course of events. To the fraudulently elected *dvadtsatka* and to it alone, Bryzgova will ultimately give permission to call a meeting, which will elect the members of the new auditing commission to replace those who have resigned in protest.† A scandalous infraction of the law will thus have been legalized. . . .

The month's term since we submitted the petitions signed by us (on and after 30 October 1966) has long passed. Within this time-limit, according to §7 of the law of 8 April 1929,[6] Bryzgova was obliged to register us as members of the *dvadtsatka* or to inform us of the reasons for her refusal, but so far she has failed to do this.

As if to lay bare her illegal actions, she has not allowed us to call a general meeting for about four months (although the RSFSR NKVD Instruction No. 328 of 1 October 1929[7] requires her to do this within seven days). . . .

The question arises of how long our community of believers will be prevented from implementing the rights granted to it by the law.

We are confident that the Procuracy of the city of Moscow, on the basis of the statute concerning the procurator's supervisory powers of 1955, will instruct the Kirov District Executive Com-

---

* Of 1929. See p. 17.

† Permission for such a meeting to be held was given on the very day after this was written. See p. 316.

mittee to register us immediately as members of the *dvadtsatka* and to authorize a general congregational meeting in the very near future. . . .

(Signed by twenty parishioners who requested recognition as the *dvadtsatka*).

15 December 1966.[8]

PETITION TO THE CHAIRMAN OF THE COUNCIL
OF MINISTERS OF THE USSR,
ALEXEI NIKOLAEVICH KOSYGIN
(*Dvadtsatka* of the Parish of St. Nicholas-in-Kuznetsy, Moscow)

Dear Comrade Chairman,

Allow us to address you in the final but firm hope that you will protect us from the administrative duress of those officials in authority who, even in this fiftieth jubilee year of our state, in their official dealings with us in the course of their duties make a show of legality to conceal their illegal actions. . . .

We are no alien body within our state and society. Neither do we desire to become such. Not by words, but by deeds, both during and after the Second World War, believers testified, and continue to do so, to their loyalty to our socialist fatherland, the common fatherland of all citizens, both non-believers and believers alike. For this reason we most strongly protest against the restrictions on our rights which are guaranteed by the laws of our country.

Perhaps the present law on religious communities of 8 April 1929 is outdated: it was passed at a time when some religious communities and their leaders often held reactionary views. Nevertheless, even this law, passed in the very special conditions of that time – which happily no longer exist – guarantees us certain rights which, although very limited, are nevertheless definite. Consequently we are assured of a definite legal status within the formal framework of the state.

We are forced to ask you to protect these rights which are being shamelessly violated by certain responsible officials, in spite of the fact that at the present time everything is being done to strengthen our socialist legal system.

We are extremely dissatisfied with the way in which the executive body of our parish of St. Nicholas-in-Kuznetsy – an important Moscow church often visited by foreign church leaders and thus well known abroad – has been conducting its business. . . .

Having illegally prevented a general meeting of all the worshippers of our parish from being held, the secretary of the Kirov District Executive Committee and the Moscow CROCA official gave permission on 16 December 1966 for a meeting to be held in our church of some 'new' *dvadtsatka* which had suddenly appeared, consisting of the same executive body (Plyashkevich, the warden, and Popov, the treasurer), together with several persons engaged by it for work in the church and several other persons, of whom so little is known that it is not even possible to say whether or not they even belong to our faith.

At the same time the warden informed the members of the real *dvadtsatka*, who had long been registered as such with the Kirov District Executive Committee, that he, together with the secretary of the executive committee and with the agreement of the CROCA official, had 'dismissed' them from the *dvadtsatka*. This organization of a false *dvadtsatka* is an incredibly arbitrary act. The removal of legally registered members of the existing *dvadtsatka* is a crass violation of the rule of law.

. . . . We very much appreciate the general aim and spirit of the existing legislation on religious cults, even though in many ways it may be outdated.

For this reason it was with a feeling of special satisfaction that we read quite recently in the newspaper *Izvestia* (No. 204, 1966) an interview with the Chairman of CRA in which he said: 'The ideological struggle with religion must not violate the rights of believers. A series of decisions by the party and government very clearly point out the inadmissibility of administrative measures . . . The necessity of strictly observing the laws on religious cults is equally incumbent upon both religious organizations and local government bodies.'[9]

However, at the same time as *Izvestia* publishes for the whole world this declaration of the Chairman of CRA here in Moscow, in the church of St. Nicholas-in-Kuznetsy, in Vishnyakovsky Lane, the exact opposite of what is being officially declared is going on, as we have just set out in detail. . . .

If it is possible, would you kindly inform us of the measures taken by your department at this address: A. P. Krushinskaya, Flat 19, 9 Tatarskaya St., Moscow. . . .

17 February 1967.[10]

THE CHURCH WAITS TO HEAR WHAT HIS HOLINESS THE PATRIARCH WILL SAY ABOUT THE EVENTS IN THE CHURCH OF ST. NICHOLAS-IN-KUZNETSY, MOSCOW
(A Chronicler)

In the summer of 1965 eight bishops of the Russian Orthodox Church, with Archbishop Yermogen of Kaluga at their head, handed His Holiness the Patriarch a declaration in which they testified that the decrees of the Synod of Bishops had led to the 'disruption of church life in the parishes. . . .'*

The bishops consider that the 1961 reform destroyed 'the unity of the hierarchical principle' and testify that, according to the present regulation, 'it is forbidden for priests even to be present at meetings of the *dvadtsatka* and generally to give any pastoral advice' to the members of the executive body, for now this is regarded as 'interference in the economic affairs of the parish, which is forbidden by the decree of the synod'.

Expressing in connection with this 'a deep anxiety about the future fate of the Russian Orthodox Church', the bishops asked His Holiness the Patriarch 'quickly to find ways of righting the abnormal situation which is contrary to the ecclesiastical canons'.

Six months after the statement of the eight bishops, the whole church resounded with the voices of two young Moscow priests, Frs. Nikolai Eshliman and Gleb Yakunin. . . .

* Cf. pp. 221-2.

L

If we compare their *Open Letter* with the petition of the eight
bishops, we see that, notwithstanding the undoubted difference
in the degree of spiritual protest, they have both taken up essentially the same position in their canonical evaluation of the 1961
reform. They understood clearly that the decisions of the Synod
of Bishops completely removed control of the administrative and
economic life of the parish from the ecclesiastical authorities and
established a system by which the parochial council (the executive
body) has become a purely lay organization, acting without
pastoral blessing.

A rather different position with regard to the 1961 reform has
been taken up by that grand old Moscow archpriest, Fr. Vsevolod
Shpiller, incumbent of St. Nicholas-in-Kuznetsy Church.* Being
a deeply committed churchman and not as much as allowing the
idea that in the church there could exist a body acting without
pastoral blessing, he apparently understands the decrees of the
Synod of Bishops in the sense that they do limit the pastor's
power, but do not deprive him of the 'right and duty' to exercise
spiritual control over the actions of the executive body and to
sanction these actions by means of pastoral blessing.

'The intelligent incumbent,' said the Patriarch, 'as a reverend
celebrant of services and, which is very important, a man of
irreproachable life, will always be able to preserve his authority in
the parish. His opinion will be considered, while he will be calm
in the knowledge that administrative burdens no longer rest on
him and that he can give himself wholly to the spiritual guidance
of his flock.'[11]

As is clear from the official letter of Fr. Vsevolod Shpiller
written at the beginning of April 1966 to Metropolitan Nikodim
of Leningrad, a member of the Holy Synod, Fr. Vsevolod bases
his understanding of the significance and extent of the reform
precisely on these words of His Holiness the Patriarch.

Considering the Orthodox Patriarch to be the living organ of
the 'ever-present expression of the canonical conscience of the
church', Fr. Vsevolod sees in the words of His Holiness the

* See pp. 321-8.

Patriarch the key to the correct understanding of the decisions of the Synod of Bishops: the weight of spiritual and moral authority in all spheres of parochial life remains with the parish.

This position taken up by the incumbent determines to a large extent the spiritual significance of the conflict which has arisen within the congregation of St. Nicholas-in-Kuznetsy Church. . . .

For spiritual dissociation from the ecclesiastical authorities, for an insolent attempt to violate the conciliar unity of the parish and for systematic grave violation of church discipline, Fr. Vsevolod Shpiller has inflicted an ecclesiastical punishment on the warden and his like-minded friends.

In his official report to His Holiness the Patriarch about the prohibition imposed on the churchwarden, Fr. Vsevolod writes:

'I have considered it necessary, as I reported in person to Your Holiness on 16 December last, to impose a ban on the parishioners S. I. Plyashkevich and I. P. Popov. Until they recognize their guilt and carry out corresponding penance, I shall not permit them the pastoral blessing which they themselves have disdained in such insolent fashion; nor may they venerate the cross at the end of the liturgy, according to custom; nor may they be anointed. Neither do I allow them entry within the altar during services.'

The events in St. Nicholas-in-Kuznetsy Church reveal with exceptional force the wretched condition in which the Rusisan Church has found itself as a result of the 1961 reform. The warden is subject to an ecclesiastical punishment from his parish priest, he is repudiated by the conciliar will of the parish and yet he continues to be warden. . . .

We know for certain that the authorities which determine the affairs of the Moscow Patriarchate have demanded of the supreme authority of the Russian Church that it should immediately extinguish the conflict that has arisen in St. Nicholas-in-Kuznetsy Church.

But who can compel a priest who is deeply aware of his ecclesiastical duty to depart from the truth?

Who can compel parishioners who preserve ecclesiastical unity to submit to transgression?

According to canon law, only the diocesan bishop (in this instance His Holiness the Patriarch of Moscow) can lift the ban imposed by a parish priest.

So it is now up to His Holiness the Patriarch to speak! . . .

The noble idealism of Fr. Vsevolod Shpiller, as has been revealed in his effort to understand the words of His Holiness the Patriarch in the very best sense and to act according to that understanding, presents His Holiness Patriarch Alexi with the possibility of testifying by word and deed that he has really tried, to the utmost of his personal strength, to deaden the sting of the anti-ecclesiastical reform.

If, however, His Holiness the Patriarch undertakes any action directed against Fr. Vsevolod, if he by his supreme episcopal power lifts the ban imposed by the parish priest on the insubordinate warden and his followers, if he takes Fr. Vsevolod's fellow clergy away from the parish because they support their parish priest or do something similar to what Archbishop Yermogen and the priests who wrote the *Open Letter* have done, then he will completely lose his spiritual and moral authority among the people who have remained faithful to the church's truth. This would antagonize even those who are still trying, for the sake of his high dignity, to see him as the spokesman of canonical conscience, to regard him as the man who takes the church's sorrows upon himself. . . .

The church waits to hear what His Holiness the Patriarch will say.

19 March 1967.[12]

As far as is known, nothing was said up to the autumn of 1968, but neither was Fr. Shpiller removed from his parish.

FR. SHPILLER SPEAKS

This document offers a clear illustration of how certain members of the Patriarchate are assigned to foreign visitors. They report back on their contacts and conversations.

TO HIS GRACE METROPOLITAN NIKODIM
OF LENINGRAD AND LADOGA

(Archpriest Vsevolod Shpiller)

Your Grace,

You suggested that I offer you, in the form of a letter, some explanation of the official report of Archpriest A. Koznovetsky who accompanied Archbishop Antony (Bloom) when he came to Moscow on a visit from London last December. Having heard the extracts you quoted me from this report referring to my conversation with the archbishop, which took place in my official residence attached to the church on 10 December last, after the liturgy conducted by the archbishop in our church with the blessing of His Holiness the Patriarch, I have quite readily accepted your suggestion.

Allow me, though, to remark that Archpriest Koznovetsky's exposition of my conversation with Archbishop Antony is (or so it seemed to me) outwardly accurate and in places so detailed that one cannot but be surprised at how well he managed to remember it all. But the archpriest evidently found difficulty in getting to its core . . . Consequently, it now behoves me to recall once more the actual meaning of the conversation, which suffered somewhat in the archpriest's report of it. I shall try to do so in the explanation which I now offer Your Grace, setting out, as you wished, the opinions I then expressed, and placing them, as far as possible, in their broadest context.

*   *   *

Two subjects dominated the conversation. As far as I understand, it is precisely these which also interest you. One was our church's 'young episcopate', some aspects of its service and activity, and in what esteem it is held by our clergy and believers (insofar, of course, as I know about this). The other theme was the parochial life of our church in the conditions brought about by the Synodal Resolution of 18 April 1961, the subsequent decisions of the Synod of Bishops of the same year and the directives and demands which also came from the civil administration.

I have had occasion to speak a good deal on these matters, which are of vital interest to representatives of many churches and countries. Among the churchmen with whom I have spoken on this theme have been people who hold the most diverse positions in their churches and, as Your Grace is aware, sometimes even the highest positions in the ecclesiastical hierarchy. With the consent of my church authorities, I have also had occasion to write on the same topics, in various connections, at the suggestion of some of our central state and civil institutions, for example CROCA and the Soviet Press Agency, APN. As an example I can cite my article, 'The Orthodox Church in the Soviet Union', written for the *Comparative Encyclopædia of the USA and the USSR*, published in Paris by American and APN agencies. The article was accepted for publication in that encyclopaedia in January 1964.

In my conversation with Archbishop Antony on 10 December last, I expressed the same views as I did during my trips abroad and on the occasions of all those meetings with churchmen and public figures who have visited us from Europe and America in recent years. I adhered to the views I have put down in writing more than once, for different reasons, in articles, lecture notes and explanations of this type. But my meeting with Archbishop Antony took place at a time when comments were being made in Moscow, among the clergy and believers with whom he associated, about the circumstances in which the former Archbishop of Kaluga, Yermogen, had recently been retired. Frequent heated discussions were taking place on those difficulties in the inner life of our church, well known to Archbishop Antony, which a few days later formed the subject of an *Open Letter* by the priests N. Eshliman and G. Yakunin. . . . which at once gave rise to a hubbub of publicity. I realized what significance my conversation with our Acting Patriarchal Exarch in Western Europe could have in such circumstances and for that reason I considered it necessary to express my opinion and attitude on what is happening in our church, not so much on the surface of its life as deep down, where everything is in a state of flux. This seems to me to portend many changes. These are not necessarily changes for the worse, as many think, but in my opinion changes for the better. . . .

Of course, Archbishop Antony has no need at all to prove how groundless are the discussions, not only still going on, but perhaps even at this moment being fomented by anti-Soviet political propaganda, about how present-day bishops of the Russian Orthodox Church are nearly all 'agents of the KGB', people who have been 'sent into the church as saboteurs or the like', with the task of destroying it from within. . . .

Once I chanced to meet a young bishop, Nikodim, who now holds office somewhere in South America,[13] but who then was Bishop of Kostroma, in the church offices on Ordynka Street with Archbishop (at that time Bishop) Kiprian (Zernov). . . . I told Archbishop Antony that I well remembered what a profound and strong impression their conversation made on me, because Nikodim apparently had no feeling for this most complex problem of the relationship between two legal orders, the church and the state; indeed, the problem seemed to him quite inconceivable. It was outside his ecclesiastical and legal consciousness. What is more, this does not apply only to Bishop Nikodim.

An acknowledgement that the social order takes precedence over the ecclesiastical, that one is necessarily superior or subordinate to the other, in no way obliges the bishop or priest to stand to attention before a representative of the secular authorities, whatever position he might hold in the state administration. Even when both are engaged on business belonging to the sphere of so-called 'overlapping affairs' (where it is hard to establish when the competence of the state ends and that of the church begins, and vice-versa), the secular power absolutely must not (and most often does not want to) hear from a bishop's lips a mere obsequious, 'I obey'. This applies especially when the matter belongs to the realm of 'internal church affairs', even though this concept is also relative and has been variously defined at different times, both by the church and by the society in which it has existed and continues to exist. But as I listened to that conversation between the two bishops, I became finally convinced that for some of our 'young bishops' (for example, Bishop Nikodim, who made such a strong impression on me) all this is quite incomprehensible. . . .

One should not think that the meeting of these two spheres, in the profound and important process which is taking place at this moment in our church's inner life, must necessarily mean their clash. Nor that, in the course of church life, their clash will engender (or is already engendering) conflicts which threaten the inner life of the church. There are no such conflicts and I am sure that on this ground there will be none. It was this opinion of mine, which I put forward extremely energetically in my conversation with Archbishop Antony, that Archpriest Koznovetsky omitted to convey in his official report. . . .

As is well known, the Synodal Resolution of 18 April 1961 consists of ten points with introductory remarks – a sort of pre-amble – and a conclusion which warns of certain dangers.[14] These are somewhat unexpected in a document of this sort. It contains a call to the clergy and believers to hold their ground against disorders which might arise as a result of the execution of this Synodal Resolution. What a strange confession of the doubtful expediency of such a measure, even if we assume that the reference is to disorder which might result from an incorrect local interpretation of the resolution! . . .

Later, whenever I sent in my report with a request for leave – up to and including this year – Metropolitan Pimen demanded, and to this day continues to demand, an endorsement on it, signed by the warden, to the effect that the latter grants me, the incumbent of the parish, ... my leave; that he, the warden, has no objection to the metropolitan's granting me this . . . Is it surprising that even representatives of the civil administration have begun to view the office of priest in the same way – as a position subordinate to the executive body of the community and its chairman, the warden? . . .

I told Archbishop Antony, in a considerably milder form than

I shall now tell you, how a few days after I received the Synodal Resolution of 18 April 1961 I went to see Archbishop Pimen, who was then administrative officer of the Patriarch and who is now Metropolitan of Krutitsy and Kolomna. I reported on the execution of the resolution in my parish: at the head of my parish there was now an executive committee of three men; I had assumed the subordinate role of a civilian employee under a labour contract with them specifying my official duties. I reported that, although the resolution considered me the 'spiritual leader' of the community, according to the strict letter of the resolution, which allowed of no other interpretation, I was not even a member of that community: that is, I no longer belonged to its canonical composition. I was right outside it. . . .

A few days after my report to Archbishop Pimen, I was admitted to the CROCA headquarters by the head of its department of external relations, P. V. Makartsev, on a matter which had nothing to do with the parochial changes. Now everything was different. Archbishop Pimen had received me very politely and warmly, of course, but gave no response to what he heard from me. Here, however, I was asked only casually and *en passant* what my attitude was to the Synodal Resolution and how it had been received in my parish. Yet my answer to a question which had been asked almost by the way was listened to not only with extreme politeness, as always, but with obvious interest. They evidently sought to get right to the heart of the view which I was able to develop to the full. . . .

Nowadays the supreme ecclesiastical authority is under reproach for its deviation from canon law. This is not out of consideration for the church's needs. Yet in the eyes of our believers – not to mention people abroad – not only our ecclesiastical, but also our civil, authorities stand openly accused of direct interference in the church's inner life, cutting across all the existing legislation of our country in this sphere. . . .

From the few remarks that Makartsev made when he was listening to me very attentively, I realized that the essence of the problem, as it has just been presented here, had not been put before CROCA by any of our church authorities. This amazed me. As I left Makartsev's office I did not conceal my astonishment: it was not for me, in my extremely humble position in the church, to discuss such an important church matter, which also had a political aspect, with a responsible executive of a state institution, even if it were in a chance private conversation.

. . . . In the Foreign Relations Department of the Patriarchate there is a pamphlet in French, published not long ago in Paris by François Mauriac's committee. It is entitled *Situations des Chrétiens en Union Soviétique (Part II: Documents*)* and in it Olivier Clément, who observes our ecclesiastical life from a far greater distance than Archbishop Antony, comments upon those difficulties in our parishes which result, in his words, in 'the priests' loss of control of their parishes' and 'their subjection to the arbitrary authority ("au bon plaisir") of the executive bodies under the chairmanship of the wardens' (p. 67). Far from needing to hear of this situation from us, let alone from me, Archbishop Antony could no doubt have told us of cases where some hapless civil servant, acting in his administrative capacity in a spirit of unbridled 'subjectivism and bureaucracy', dispatches an official order to the executive body of the church community (let us say in the Tula region), demanding that within three days 'the public entertainments in the building occupied by the community must stop' and the building be cleaned out. This means that divine worship must stop and the church be closed. Such an incident occurred, by the way, not long before Archbishop Antony's arrival in Russia, or perhaps even while he was here in December last year.

It was not the facts themselves which interested Archbishop Antony. He was not, so to speak, 'collecting' them; what interested him was our, in particular my, interpretation of those facts.

. . . . 'God's people' do not raise objections to the 1961 decisions, no . . . they simply wait. Judging by what is now happening, not on the surface, but deep inside the church, we all know what they are waiting for. . . .

The church is waiting, 'God's people' are waiting for the Holy

* Quoted pp. 59–60, 117–18.

Synod to remove all ambiguity from the decisions of the Synod of Bishops and inject precision into them, banishing those shortcomings which are causing the church so much acute pain and damage. . . .

As for those political circumstances on which a great deal in the course of the church's parochial life naturally depends, there was no need to discuss them at great length with Archbishop Antony. In the relationship of the civil administration (at all its various levels) to the church, the departure from Lenin's standards observed in the time of Ilichov[15] is now undoubtedly coming to an end. Then administrative measures concerning parochial life were often disguised in words as 'a return to Lenin's norms', but were, in fact, something quite different. Now the tendency to re-establish socialist legality in reality is undeniable. And it is more than just a tendency.[16]

We are fully aware that official functionaries of the vast administrative machine who deal with various aspects of measures concerning the church (for example, during the period called in the West the 'normalization' of church and state, then, in the same terminology, 'the time of Ilichov', and finally the present day) are by and large the same people. How can one expect from them an instantaneous reorganization and change from certain bureaucratic methods to others which are fundamentally different? This requires time – and from us long-suffering and patience. I think we have these qualities.

I remember how, even before 1961, someone from CROCA came into my church, accompanied by A. A. Trushin, the Moscow representative of this organization. They were checking, among other things, to see if we kept a record of those who married in church and whether we examined their documents before the ceremony. I replied that we did. Trushin and I received a reprimand: the church had no right to demand any papers or to keep a record of them (that is, to 'register' them).

A little while later Trushin accompanied yet another official, a new one, from the same CROCA on a visit to our church. To his question as to whether we asked couples who married in church for their documents and whether we kept a record of them, I replied that we no longer did. Trushin, who remained silent all this time, and I yet again received a stern reprimand . . . It turned out that this, too, was a breach of some unknown 'norms' or other . . .

Of course, I did not tell Archbishop Antony of this incident. . . .

Nowadays the tendency that we have been describing has manifested itself quite plainly. Adherence to the Soviet laws is obligatory for all. Their infringement by the clergy and believers is prevented legally in the same way as their infringement by official functionaries in the civil administration. . . .

Moscow, March 1966.[17]

LETTER FROM ARCHPRIEST VSEVOLOD SHPILLER TO ARCHBISHOP BASIL (KRIVOSHEIN) OF BRUSSELS

You will certainly have met Metropolitan Antony since his return from Moscow. During this visit he had a very large number of meetings and he must surely have returned home very tired. I played a part in his meetings with the two priests and then with Archbishop Yermogen – and this was with the knowledge of Metropolitan Nikodim. We can say, therefore, that he has met the 'opposition' – an opposition which does not exist, however.

In my opinion, there is no opposition in our church to anything, but only . . . positions. Let us call them attitudes of dissatisfaction. This is very often expressed: sometimes in a form completely unacceptable to canon law, or at least to church tradition; sometimes in a completely acceptable, even irreproachable, way from this point of view. In all this, much depends on temperament and even more on theological intelligence – or the lack of it. Basically, this dissatisfaction has really contained nothing frightening up to now. By 'frightening' I mean the transition from these positions of dissatisfaction to a genuine opposition which could threaten the church with division or schism.

. . . . This explains the broad expansion of the dissatisfaction which is gripping an increasing number of believers and parishes.

But I am personally convinced that, even in 1967, a return to our normal parish organization is possible. . . . Not only can no problem be correctly solved, but it cannot even be precisely formulated, if one does not approach it with sufficient self-control, putting aside the tension which, often artificially, is created around it. One of the most important pastoral functions which I continue to exercise in my parish . . . . is to relieve the tension created by the difficulties of our internal church life. The little room in the bell-tower, well known to Your Reverence, where I live and from where I observe what goes on around me, is not very big. You cannot see much from it. But what I can see, if it does not make me an out-and-out optimist, at least it gives no grounds for an exaggerated pessimism. . . .

2 January 1967.[18]

Epilogue

This is a brief selection from the documents which reached us in 1968. It demonstrates quite clearly that the various movements in the Soviet Union which are fighting to establish human rights are making closer contact with each other. Further, there seems to be a particular significance in the new links between the young intellectuals and religion.* No words express this more clearly than Alexander Solzhenitsyn's prayer, which has remained almost unknown since its publication in Paris in 1966.

'SERGIEVSHCHINA' OR COMPROMISE WITH ATHEISM (THE LEAVEN OF HEROD)
(Boris Talantov)

Nikita Struve's book, *Christians in Contemporary Russia*,[1] has been published in England. He, like others in the West, approves the activity of Patriarch Sergi, even comparing him with St. Sergius of Radonezh[2] and Patriarch Yermogen.[3] In the West Patriarch Sergi is almost considered to be the saviour of the Orthodox Church in Russia. Such an incorrect evaluation results from the fact that Western students of the subject do not know the hidden facts and circumstances of the life of the Russian Orthodox Church. The roots of the serious religious crisis which has now evolved were laid by none other than Patriarch Sergi. . . .

What did Metropolitan Sergi save by his compromise and monstrous lies? By the beginning of the Second World War there were only between five and ten churches remaining in each region (out of many hundreds), the majority of the priests and almost all the bishops (except for a very few who had co-operated with the authorities like Metropolitan Sergi) were being tortured in the concentration camps. Thus Metropolitan Sergi's actions saved nothing except his own skin. He lost all authority in the

* Cf. p. 36.

eyes of the faithful, but acquired the good will of Stalin, 'the father of the peoples'. The greater part of those churches which remained did not recognize Metropolitan Sergi. . . .

The opening of the churches (during and just after the war) within strict limitations was not due to Patriarch Sergi or Patriarch Alexi, but it was done by the atheist authorities themsleves under pressure from ordinary people and to appease them. . . .

From what we have set out, it is clear that not only did the *Sergievshchina*[4] during Stalin's despotism not save the Russian Orthodox Church, but on the contrary it contributed to the loss of genuine freedom of conscience, turning the ecclesiastical authority into an obedient tool of the atheist state.

Cardinal Wyszynski's categorical refusal to compromise with the atheist state and his resulting powerful struggle for the truth of the Gospel and genuine freedom of conscience has had the following result: now in Poland the church is in reality separated from the state and enjoys a significant degree of freedom.

The church cannot be defended by lies.[5]

(This next document must have been written after May 1967, the latest date quoted in it.)

SECRET PARTICIPATION OF THE MOSCOW PATRIARCHATE IN THE CPSU'S FIGHT AGAINST THE ORTHODOX CHRISTIAN CHURCH (CRISIS IN CHURCH LEADERSHIP)
(Boris Talantov)

The activity of the Patriarchate is directed towards using lies and false presentation of evidence to set the Christian movement in the whole world on a false course and thereby undermine it.

Such, for example, was the suggestion of the Moscow Patriarchate, at the Rhodes consultation of Orthodox Churches,[6] that Christian apologetics and the ideological struggle with modern atheism should be renounced. The activity of the Moscow Patriarchate abroad is a conscious betrayal of the Russian Orthodox Church and the Christian faith. The Patriarchate appears on the world platform as a secret agent combating world Christianity.

Metropolitan Nikodim is betraying the church not out of fear, but out of conscience; a full unmasking of what he and the Patriarchate are doing would mean the end of his undercover enterprise. The time has come to unmask the betrayal by the Moscow Patriarchate abroad; Metropolitan Nikodim's hour has struck....*

A universal unmasking of the betrayal by the princes of the church will inevitably lead to a crisis in church leadership, but not to a schism (as is maintained by some ill-wishers of the church and others who unconsciously follow them).

The faithful must cleanse the church from false brothers and false pastors[7] (according to the command of St. Paul: 'Put away from among yourselves that wicked person')[8]. Only after such a cleansing will a true rebirth of the church be possible.[9]

TO THE PROCURATOR-GENERAL OF THE USSR
From Citizen Boris Vladimirovich Talantov,
Flat 1, 12 Uritsky Street,
Kirov 2.

COMPLAINT

On 31 May 1967 the newspaper *Kirovskaya Pravda* printed an article by O. Lyubovikov, 'No Punches Pulled', which contains libellous assertions, coarse threats and baseless insults directed against me. . . .

In August 1966 twelve believers in the Kirov region (including myself) forwarded to Moscow . . . an open letter addressed to Patriarch Alexi of Moscow and All Russia.†

Following this, I wrote a second letter to the editors of *Izvestia* entitled 'The Soviet State and the Christian Religion'. . . . This letter was received by the editors of *Izvestia* on 19 December 1966, as was seen from a post-office notification. . . .

On 14 February 1967 I was summoned to the Kirov KGB headquarters in connection with the aforesaid letters, where it was suggested to me that I should officially disclaim having signed the *Open Letter of the Kirov Believers* which had become known abroad.* In a written declaration I pointed out that as author of both letters, my signature was genuine. I was also ready to prove that the contents of both letters were true, but that I had absolutely no idea how the *Open Letter of the Kirov Believers* had been sent abroad.

On the very same day a KGB official removed from the flat my professional files, consisting of synopses of various philosophical works with my notes on them. The KGB officials promised to return them after inspection, but have not so far kept to this.

Later, on 25 February I learnt from a BBC broadcast that at the very same time as I was asserting the genuineness of my signature at the KGB headquarters, in London Metropolitan Nikodim had been declaring the letter to be an anonymous communication and therefore quite untrustworthy.

On 22 March, therefore, I sent a letter to Patriarch Alexi refuting Metropolitan Nikodim's assertion about the anonymous nature of the *Open Letter of the Kirov Believers* and confirming the authenticity of its contents.†

In addition to myself, seven other citizens of the city of Kirov signed this *Open Letter*. At the beginning of April they were individually called up before the Kirov City *soviet* in connection with this. The interrogations there were conducted by the secretary of the city *soviet*, L. Ostanina, who described me as 'a dangerous person with foreign connections' and threatened with imprisonment any one who signed such a letter in future. Despite the threats, they all confirmed that they had signed the *Open Letter* voluntarily and deliberately; four of the people in question (including Ye. M. Khalyavina) sent a letter on 20 May to Patriarch Alexi, confirming that they had consciously signed the *Open Letter* which had become known abroad and pointing out that the local authorities in the Kirov region were continuing as before to persecute believers and were refusing to open churches which had previously been illegally closed.

* See pp. 153–4.   † See pp. 153–4.

At the same time, KGB officials kept intimidating certain believers who had appealed for a second church to be opened in the city of Kirov, accusing them of being in league with me, a 'dangerous political criminal', as they called me. Finally, a lecturer in the Polytechnic Institute, where I had worked in 1955–58 as a teacher of higher mathematics, publicly called me an 'enemy of the people', in the style practised in Yezhov's time. . . .

One of the people who signed the *Open Letter of the Kirov Believers* was Nikodim Nikolaevich Kamenskikh, a student at the Odessa Theological Seminary and a permanent resident of the town of Nolinsk, Kirov region. The Inspector at the seminary, A. N. Kravchenko, called upon Kamenskikh to renounce in writing his signature under the *Open Letter*, threatening that, if he did not do so, he would expel him from the institution. On 19 May 1967 Kamenskikh officially declared in writing: 'Once again I confirm the authenticity of my signature and my agreement with the contents of the document.' Thereupon, the inspector, as well as the CRA official, summoned N. N. Kamenskikh to report to the Odessa KGB headquarters at 43 Bebel St. . . . . Kamenskikh, however, refused to comply with this demand unless he received an official notice from the KGB. Thereupon he was, on 29 May 1967, removed from the student register of the Odessa Theological Seminary for 'incompatibility with its spirit'.[10] Thus Kamenskikh decided it was better to suffer than to disclaim agreement with the *Open Letter*. But this was not the end of his sufferings. On 20 June the chief of police of the town of Nolinsk refused on various pretexts to register him at his place of permanent residence. . . .

These facts reveal the indubitable connection between the actions of Metropolitan Nikodim and those of the state security organs. This constitutes a violation of the law on the separation of church and state.

Such are the indisputable facts which must be borne in mind in order to understand Lyubovikov's article properly, for it was deliberately worded obscurely.

I now proceed to analyse this article. . . .

On 18 July 1957 I sent a registered letter from Kirov to the

newspaper *Pravda*. . . . It contained a protest against the arbitrariness and lawlessness of Stalin's time and was not intended for
publication, but was an appeal to the CPSU. I and my close relatives suffered greatly from the lawless and arbitrary actions of the
state security in Stalin's time. In 1937 my father, at the age of 62,
was sentenced by a tribunal. Despite his age and ill health, he was
sent to the Temnikov camps, where the writer Yu. Daniel now
is. On 5 February 1940 I petitioned the Procurator's office of the
RSFSR for his early release from prison because of his illness.
After a great deal of red tape, it was not until 19 December 1940
that the ministry informed me that my father had died in the
camps on 12 March that year. The only reason for his arrest and
imprisonment had been that he was a priest. My brother, Serafim
Vladimirovich Talantov, who was working as a hydraulic engineer at Vologda, was arrested in 1930 at the age of 22. He was sentenced for no reason at all and died in the concentration camps on
the Baltic-White Sea Canal. Thanks to my origins, I was myself
under constant threats from the security organs from 1930 until
1941. In 1954 I was dismissed from the staff of my teachers'
training college because of my religious convictions, although
ill health was given as the formal reason for my dismissal. . . .

I have no idea whether my letter reached the editors of *Pravda*,
but it eventually turned up in the Kirov KGB headquarters.
. . . . On 14 August 1958 I was dismissed from employment
at the Kirov Polytechnical Institute 'at my own request' and
on 21 September of that year *Kirovskaya Pravda* published O.
Lyubovikov's article, 'Out of the Gutter'. This article, containing as it does filthy language, threats and slander, is the best proof
of the truth of the basic idea in my letter to *Pravda* – namely that in
the USSR non-party people have no rights and are subjected
to severe persecution even for writing a letter to a national newspaper. If my letter and Lyubovikov's article were to be published
simultaneously, then it would be Lyubovikov and not I who
would be ashamed to face the public.

As is proved by the closed trials of A. Sinyavsky and Yu.
Daniel in February 1966 and of Yu. Galanskov, A. Ginzburg, A.

Dobrovolsky and V. Lashkova in January 1968, and by the appeal of P. Litvinov and L. Daniel to the Soviet and international public, as broadcast by the BBC on 12 January 1968, the state security organs and the courts of law in our country are behaving even today in an arbitrary and unlawful fashion. It is accordingly a regrettable fact that my letter to *Pravda* is topical even now. I therefore consider it my duty to register yet another determined protest against the arbitrary way in which in these days trials are held in camera; people are being persecuted for their beliefs and political detainees are being held in prisons and camps in inhuman conditions.

Most of the article 'No Punches Pulled' is devoted to the *Open Letter of the Kirov Believers to Patriarch Alexi*, which was broadcast by the BBC on 8 December 1966. If it had not been broadcast, nobody in the USSR would have known about it, since we have no chance of reading foreign newspapers. . . . Soviet newspapers sometimes print articles by foreign writers sharply criticizing their own governments and nothing is heard of these writers being persecuted in their own country as a result. Accordingly, the campaign of slander and threats organized against me, because of a collective letter sent to Patriarch Alexi which has somehow become known abroad, constitutes an inadmissible relapse into the lawless practices of Yezhov's time. . . .

Fom 1959 the Slobozhanin family lived in the village of Onunchino. . . . Kirov region. It consisted of Mikhail Lavrentievich, Tatiana, his wife, and four children, Alyosha, Kolya, Vova and Dusya. The eldest is a boy of twelve, the youngest a girl of three. . . . They brought up the children in the Christian faith and in their house they spread a religious outlook among their fellow-villagers. Believers who called themselves members of the True Orthodox Church prayed in their house, sang psalms and read the Bible. Their only difference from other Orthodox Christians is that they do not recognize Patriarch Alexi and the other bishops appointed by him, considering them to have betrayed the church. In June 1961 a people's court condemned M. L. Slobozhanin as a parasite and sent him into exile for five years.

Later reports in the newspapers claimed he had been sentenced to six years' imprisonment for anti-Soviet propaganda. It was nowhere explained what the substance of this propaganda was. At the end of 1962 the same court deprived Tatiana Slobozhanina of parental rights and sent her as a parasite right away from the district. The children were forcibly removed to a home. . . .

We have no law which punishes people for believing in God, yet doctors, teachers, engineers and even ordinary workers and employees have been and are still being dismissed 'at their own request' or for some other formal reason, as soon as it becomes known that they attend church and perform religious rites. . . .

In 1963, after the plenary session in June of the Central Committee of the CPSU, special *Komsomol* teams in the towns and villages of the Kirov region carried out inspections for the purpose of discovering icons. If these were found in the flats of workers and employees, the party and trade union organs suggested that they should remove them, on pain of being dismissed from employment.

We have no law which punishes people for believing in God and yet many articles have been and are being published in national and local newspapers which openly declare the teaching of religion by parents to children to be a crime. For instance, *Kirovskaya Pravda* on 8 June 1967 published an article by P. Rozhnev entitled 'If not these hands'. The writer makes the following reference to K. M. Martianova (a member of the sect of Evangelical Christians and Baptists), who is bringing up her daughter Nadya in the Christian faith. It says: 'You are forcibly compelling your adolescent child to pray. Even that is a violation of our laws and regulations.' Yet it is clear from the article itself that Nadya, a pupil of the seventh class in School No. 40, Kirov, attends worship of her own free will. . . .

Finally, the persecutions suffered by believers and the severe punishment meted out to them by the law courts are mentioned in the complaint lodged by the Evangelical Christians and Baptists with the United Nations and broadcast by the BBC on 16 December[11] 1967. The facts described here, as well as those described in my letter to *Izvestia*, prove irrefutably that in the USSR Christian believers are social pariahs. At the present time they are deprived even of the limited rights which were extended to them in the latter years of Stalin's life. . . .

In his article Lyubovikov states: 'Atheism – writes Talantov maliciously – engenders terrible destructive wars.' However, he does not mention the source of this sentence. I surmise that he took some such assertion from my files confiscated by a KGB man on 14 February 1967. Their contents were known to no-one and they are my working materials dating back many years.

I do not deny that I have always protested against the forcible implantation of nihilistic atheism which, in my opinion, is one of the reasons for the increase of crime in the USSR. However, nowhere and on no occasion have I ever made an assertion like that cited by Lyubovikov. Therefore I categorically protest against the illegal use of my personal files.

I absolutely repudiate Lyubovikov's unsubstantiated charge that I have, as he alleges, transgressed any Soviet laws.

Nowadays people who openly defend their religious and philosophical convictions and criticize the arbitrary and illegal actions of the authorities are, without any justification, charged with being in illegal contact with the bourgeois West. In Yezhov's day they were accused of imaginary espionage – nowadays of being linked with NTS[12] and the CIA.

. . . . Russian people in our country are not parrots who can only repeat what is said in the West. Practical experience of daily life generates new thoughts and ideas in their heads and stimulates scientific progress. Marxism-Leninism is undergoing a practical testing – not in the West but in the USSR. It is, therefore, only in the USSR that it can be given a scientifically based critical assessment. On one point we believing Christians, on the strength of fifty years' experience of life in a socialist society, have become convinced that the widely propagated teaching in our country about the rise and the decay of religion is erroneous. Our belief derives from actually living in a socialist society and is not based on bourgeois propaganda from the West. Accordingly, we Christian believers suggest to the atheists in our country that we start an open and friendly discussion on the problems that interest us, as is done in certain socialist states.* The sixth section of my letter, 'The Soviet State and the Christian Religion', has this aim. However, Soviet atheists like Lyubovikov prefer to 'root out' religion by means of threats, slander and violence, but ideas cannot be conquered by force.

My wife, Nina Agafangelova Talantova, a sufferer from high blood pressure, was unable to endure the threats and libellous accusations in Lyubovikov's article, couched as they were in the tone of the abusive attacks written against imaginary enemies of the people in Yezhov's time. On 7 September 1967, as a consequence of the grievous experience endured, she had a seizure and died on 16 September.

The day she died I wanted, at her request, to have the last rites administered by the church, but the priest of the only church in Kirov told me that the local authorities forbade such rites being administered in a private home. This lamentable fact shows that Christian believers in Kirov are nowadays deprived even of those rights which were provided for them by Stalin. This is irrefutable evidence of the way believers continue to be persecuted. What kind of freedom of conscience is it if a dying person is not entitled to be granted his last request of receiving the last rites at home?. . . .

I have been delayed in handing this complaint because of the death of my wife and my own illness.

26 April 1968.[13]

FR. SERGI ZHELUDKOV WRITES TO PAVEL LITVINOV

Flat 6,
14 Pskov St.,
Pskov.

Among the reactions to what you have said in defence of your friends,[14] I have somehow not heard the name of a single servant of the church. Allow me to associate myself in sincerest sympathy

* Cf. Levitin's call for dialogue, pp. 269-70.

with your sorrow. Alas, it is not too late – your friends continue to suffer innocently. Together with this sorrow, however, I experience a spiritual uplift. All honour to you! I long to make your personal acquaintance.

I have heard that you are an atheist. That in no way qualifies my admiration. In the most recent directions of Christian thought we come to an idea of the church as the mystical Body of Christ. It consists of cells – people of good will and deeds, whatever their superficial rational so-called 'convictions'. . . . Today in Russia many call themselves atheists only because of a shortcoming in their education.

This could not be said of you, but I hazard the guess that even with you there are conditional and chance factors bound up with it. I do not intend to preach Christianity to you here, but I am extremely glad to write to you that you yourself are a living proof of the truth of Christianity. Every Christian who hears about what you have said will, I believe, experience the presence and action of the Spirit of Christ among mankind. I hasten to establish a common language with you: if everywhere that I pronounce the name of *Christ*, which is most sacred to me, you put the principle of spiritual *Beauty*, which is most sacred to you, this will be sufficient for our practical unity. For Love, Freedom, Truth, Fearlessness, Loyalty are all names of our Lord, whom you honour without knowing it, and whom you have so marvellously proclaimed in your noble and brave declarations.

Your poor friends are continuing to suffer, however. We thank Stravinsky and others for their support, of course, but this has not been enough. Among people of good will there should have been collected not ten, but ten thousand, a hundred thousand, a million signatures in defence of Christ, who has been suffering in the person of your friends. 'I was in prison, and ye visited me not.' I am especially sad that in this instance these words are addressed to the Christians of the whole world, who have remained so strangely indifferent to the fate of your friends.

In saying this, I beg you not to apply this reproach to the organization of the Russian Church. I want to use this sad occasion to 'justify myself' in general terms before you in particular, for you are in a certain sense the conscience of the Russian intelligentsia. You know that our basic mass of believers are mostly little-educated and aged women. They have heard nothing about what you have been doing and know nothing of it. As for our priesthood, its past social activity has been paralysed since time immemorial. Today the organization of the Russian Church is in indescribably difficult circumstances, such as have never before obtained in human history. You know that from time to time our Patriarch signs documents declaring that the Russian Church enjoys the most complete freedom. It would not be wise to treat this seriously and it would simply be unfair to reproach us for this, for we cannot make ourselves understood publicly.

. . . . Socialist society should . . . find a viable combination of public discipline and creative freedom. Together with the need to preserve peace, this is the central problem of our time. It is obvious that the absence of freedom is the death of creativity in all aspects of life. It is equally clear, however, that freedom without the other principles of Christianity would turn to anarchy and hooliganism . . . In truth, 'Without me ye can do nothing'.

It would appear that the first step towards a regulated freedom should be to give back to words their proper meaning, to adhere to the laws as written. In this context one may say that your friends are suffering for all of us, for all who love the truth. May God help them. May I express the hope that you will not weaken in your efforts. 'Knock, and it shall be opened unto you.'

30 March 1968.[15]

HUMAN RIGHTS YEAR IN THE SOVIET UNION:
CHRONICLE OF CURRENT EVENTS
(anonymous)

The trial of seventeen intellectuals from the city lasted in the Leningrad court from 15 March to 5 April. Guseva was the prosecutor and Isakova the judge (the latter being deputy president of the Leningrad City Court).

All the accused were charged under §§70 and 72 of the Penal Code of the RSFSR. The substance of the accusation was that they had participated in the All-Russian Social-Christian Union for Liberation of the People.

Brief exposition of the programme of the union:

Establishment of a democratic order. The head of state is elected by the whole people and is accountable to parliament. The controlling body is a council consisting of representatives of the clergy, which has the right of veto over the head of state and parliament. The land belongs to the state, but is leased in plots to individuals or collectives (exploitation is forbidden). Labour is hired only on an equal footing. The majority of enterprises belong to workers' collectives, while the main branches (transport, electronics, and so on) belong to the state. The basic principle of the economic structure is personalism.

The constitution of the union:

Strict secrecy with division into 'cells of three'; each person knows his cell leader and its second member. Besides this, each recruits new members and creates a new cell of three, of which he is the leader. The members do not know the head of the organization. If necessary they address him in writing through the leader of the cell.

The organization has practically engaged in only the following:

1. recruitment of new members;

2. circulation of literature. (During searches the following books and copies were found: Djilas, Berdyaev, Vladimir Solovyov, Rauch's *History of Soviet Russia*, Tibor Meray's *Thirteen Days that Shook the Kremlin* (on Hungary, 1956), Gorki's *Inopportune Thoughts*, etc. – even Ginzburg's *Into the Whirlwind* was included.)

The organization was founded in 1964, approximately. By the middle of 1965 it consisted of about ten members. Already the Leningrad KGB headquarters knew of its existence at this time, but it did not cut short its activities. Rather the KGB allowed it to develop and increase in numbers. (Alexander Gidoni appeared as a witness at the trial, having denounced the organization to the

KGB in 1965, after which he had been advised to continue his contacts with its members.)

In February–March 1967 about sixty of its members were arrested (not only in Leningrad, but also in Tomsk, Irkutsk, Petrozavodsk and other places).

In November 1967 the Leningrad City Court sentenced four leaders of the organization under §§64, 70 and 72 as follows:

Vladimir Ogurtsov (translator from Japanese, 30 years old) – fifteen years.

Mikhail Sado (orientalist, 30) – thirteen years.

Yevgeni Vagin (specialist in literature from the Pushkin House, 30) – ten years.

Averochkin (lawyer, 28) – eight years in a strict-regime corrective labour colony.

The trial mentioned at the beginning ran from 14 March to 5 April. The difference between those who were accused and those who were brought as witnesses was basically that the former had recruited at least one person into the organization. All the accused pleaded guilty (apparently in the sense of admitting the facts of the accusation), but they did not retract.

Seventeen further names are then listed. All the accused were born between 1935 and 1943 and were sentenced to between one and seven years' imprisonment.

This trial, like the one in Moscow, infringed the legal norms:

1. Some of the accused had been under arrest for longer than the permitted period.

2. Entrance to an 'open' trial was by passes only, while the courtroom remained half empty.

3. Most of the witnesses were removed from the courtroom immediately after they had given evidence.

Neither is it known why the leaders of the organization were tried separately, nor why they were also accused under §64 (high treason), as well as §§70 and 72. Was the programme they had compiled construed as a 'conspiracy to seize power'? If so, this was a blatantly illegal charge. Any illegality might have occurred during the trial of the first four, because the fact that it had taken place became known only after it was over and it was, apparently, completely closed.

It is known for certain that no-one was sentenced for links with the NTS, nor for speculation, nor for being in possession of fire-arms.[16]

PRAYER
Alexander Solzhenitsyn (Complete text)

How easy it is for me to live with You, Lord! How easy it is for me to believe in You! When my thoughts get stuck or my mind collapses, when the cleverest people see no further than this evening and do not know what must be done tomorrow, You send down to me clear confidence that You exist and that You will ensure that not all the ways of goodness are blocked.

From the summit of earthly fame I look round with wonder at that road through hopelessness to this point, from which even I have been able to shed abroad among men the refulgence of Your glory.

And You will grant me to express this as much as is necessary. And insofar as I am not able to do it, that means You have allotted the task to others.[17]

1975 POSTSCRIPT

Seven years after this book was compiled the problems set out by the various Christian writers represented are every bit as actual as they were originally. One document with totally ,fresh information has emerged since publication relating to the 1959–68 period which this book covers. That is an account, in the minutest detail, highly personal and with acerbic character evaluations, of the controversial 1961 Synod of Bishops by an anonymous participant. It is so long that it is impossible to work it into the present text. Never having been published, it deserves to see the light of day in its entirety. Yet had it been possible to include this, it would have merely confirmed the opinion of that Synod expressed, among others, by Frs. Eshliman and Yakunin (pp. 204–7 and 220–2) and Fr. Shpiller (pp. 326–8).

There has been one major event since publication, to which several writers represented looked forward: the *Sobor* (council) of the Russian Orthodox Church which met for less than a week in May-June 1971 to elect a new Patriarch after the death of Alexi the previous year. It would be overstating the case to call it a "major non-event", but the fact is that it did not discuss, only confirmed, the controversial decisions taken in 1961, which then became official. It took some new ecumenical initiatives on closer relations with the Roman Catholics and the

Old Believers, it was an occasion on which church leaders were able to meet and this meant much spiritually to many of the more isolated ones, but it could not tackle the basic restrictions of the state on parish life and its interference in the internal life of the church. It has elected Pimen as the Patriarch, but left unsatisfied the urgent requests of the writers of this book for justice and religious liberty.

Solzhenitsyn's name would figure large in a second volume of *Patriarch and Prophets* which, it is hoped, will be compiled before long to cover the years from 1969 to the present day. Other names of note would be added to his, such as Fr. Dmitri Dudko, Fr. Alexander Men and, among the younger generation, Yevgeni Barabanov and Fr. Pavel Adelheim.

As well as Solzhenitsyn, another of the greatest writers represented here is now in the West after lengthy imprisonment: Anatoli Levitin. He has supplied enough new material to provide whole volumes of his own and one such will appear in English. Another remarkable figure, Boris Talantov, died in prison in 1971. So did Yuri Galanskov, at the age of 33 in 1972.

Perhaps most significant of all is the emergence of a Christian literature on the experience and the martyrdom of the Russian Orthodox Church in the twentieth century. This is not new, in the sense that it was written at various times in and after the 1930's, but now it passes more openly from hand to hand and copies are reaching the West. The present publishers plan a series of such works in English, which could not only add infinitely to our knowledge of the spiritual riches of the Russian Church, but will also replenish the resources of a church in the West which is so often on the defensive.

Internationally, the response of the churches in the West to the challenge offered by these pages and similar literature on the Russian Baptists has begun—which one could not really claim before 1970. The British Council of Churches sponsored a most impressive study of religion in Eastern Europe, *Discretion and Valour* (1974). The World Council of Churches has intervened in certain cases of persecution. The Baptist denomination has done likewise. The Anglican General Synod passed a resolution in February 1975 expressing solidarity with the church in the East.

Most importantly of all, there is now, under the direction of the present author, an organization, Keston College, which assembles and publishes the full range of information. The second impression of this book and the publishing plans mentioned above are associated with it and will form a loosely-linked series of "Keston Books". The College itself publishes a journal, *Religion in Communist Lands*, information about which may be obtained from Keston College, Heathfield Road, Keston, Kent, England. The ground-work established in the compilation and publication of this book has now been put on a permanent basis and Christians in the Soviet Union have already expressed their gratitude for this.

Notes

INTRODUCTION

1. For a discussion of the evolution of this constitutional principle, see B. R.
   Bociurkiw, 'Church-State Relations in the USSR', *Survey*, London, January
   1968, pp. 4–32; also RFR, pp. 106–13.
2. *Konstitutsia (Osnovnoi Zakon) SSSR* ('The Constitution [Basic Law] of the
   USSR'), Moscow, 1964, pp. 27–28.
3. See RFR, pp. 109–10.
4. *Ibid.*, pp. 14–16.
5. *Law on Religious Associations*, 8 April 1929 (henceforth LRA), §§4–9; *Instructions of the People's Commissariat of the Interior*, 1 October 1929 (henceforth
   NKVD), §§62–4. Both these enactments are conveniently set out in English
   in W. B. Stroyen, *Communist Russia and the Russian Orthodox Church, 1943–*

1962, Washington, D.C., 1967, pp. 121–35. For a full discussion of registration, see RFR, pp. 3–6.

6. LRA, §8.
7. NKVD, §§54–59.
8. LRA, §14.
9. See RFR, p. 16.
10. 18 March 1966 revision of §142 of the Penal Code of the RSFSR; see RFR, pp. 159–61. Although we give references only to the Penal Code of the RSFSR, the other republics have equivalent laws, often numbered differently.
11. LRA, §18.
12. *The Christian Century*, Chicago, 21 July 1965, p. 915.
13. BV 1, 1968, p. 64.
14. Occasionally Lutherans have been able to study abroad and there have been evening classes. See Bourdeaux, *Opium of the People*, London, 1965, p. 185.
15. RFR, p. 20.
16. *Ibid.*, p. 160.
17. *Ibid.*, p. 13.
18. LRA, §19.
19. RSFSR Penal Code §142, quoted in RFR, p. 160.
20. *Daily Telegraph*, London, 7 July 1966, p. 1.
21. *Posev*, Frankfurt-am-Main, 27 October 1967, p. 5; cf. *Posev*, 7 July 1968, p. 6.
22. LRA, §17; NKVD, §3.
23. LRA, §17; NKVD, §3; Penal Code, §142 (see RFR, p. 159).
24. LRA, §§27–29.
25. LRA, §§35–42; NKVD, §§60–65.
26. NKVD, §22.
27. LRA, §§12 and 21; NKVD, §31.
28. E.g. NiR, 10, October 1961, p. 89, lists six.
29. F. Fedorenko, *Sekty, ikh Vera i Dela* ('Sects, Their Faith and Practice'), Moscow, 1965, pp. 191–2.
30. RFR, pp. 159–60.
31. See, for example, Leon Lipson, 'Hosts and Pests: the Fight against Parasites', PC 2, March–April 1965, pp. 72–82.
32. See RFR, pp. 161–4.
33. *Gospel Call*, Pasadena, California, December 1967, p. 4; April 1968, p. 9, and May 1968, p. 5.
34. *The Tablet*, London, 22 June 1968, p. 634.
35. London, 1965.
36. London, 1965.
37. New York and London, 1968.
38. London, 1967.
39. Washington, D.C., 1967.
40. W. C Fletcher, *A Study in Survival*, London, 1965, p. 29. In the pages following there is a discussion of the text of this declaration.
41. *Bakinsky Rabochi* ('Baku Worker'), Baku, 19 June 1963, p. 4.
42. Pp. 12–16.
43. Fletcher, *Nikolai*, New York and London, 1968, pp. 184–202.
44. JMP 2, February 1960, p. 27.
45. Fletcher, *Nikolai*, pp. 200–2.

46. *Ibid.*, pp. 193–4.
47. See also RFR, p. 16.
48. *Ibid.*, pp. 20–21 and 190–210.
49. Julius Čibulka, 'Church without Freedom', *Kultúrny Život* ('Cultural Life'), Bratislava, 22, 31 May 1968; translation in RCDA, Vol. 7, 11–14, June–July 1968, pp. 106–8.
50. Fletcher, *Nikolai*, pp. 195–7.
51. BV 6, 1966, p. 51.
52. *Russia Cristiana*, Milan, 73, January 1966, pp. 13–27, and 74, February 1966, pp. 24–36.
53. Nikita Struve, *Christians in Contemporary Russia*, London, 1967, pp. 311–20.
54. *Russkaya Pravoslavnaya Tserkov* ('The Russian Orthodox Church'), Moscow Patriarchate, 1958, p. 83.
55. Struve, *op. cit.*, p. 303.
56. RFR, p. 14.
57. SCUS, pp. 11–12.
58. But see Struve, *op. cit.*, pp. 310–11.
59. N. Yudin, *Pravda o Peterburgskikh Svyatinyakh* ('The Truth about the Holy Places of St. Petersburg'), Leningrad, 1962, p. 8.
60. MO, 37, 1, 1967, p. 1.
61. KmP, 8 June 1966, p. 4. Cf. KmP, 4 June 1965, p. 4.
62. See, among many examples, KmP, 3 June 1966, p. 4; Pr, 5 September 1966, p. 3; Izv, 23 September 1966, p. 4; SZh, 11 January 1967, p. 4; Pr, 28 February 1967, p. 4; *Nauka i Zhizn* ('Science and Life'), Moscow, 1, January 1968, pp. 89–96.
63. *The Times*, London, 18 November 1966, p. 8.
64. See RFR, pp. 127–30.
65. Cf. RFR, pp. 18–19, 58, 85–90, 92, 107, 112, 119, 152. See also the new Marriage and Family Law, VVS 27, 3 July 1968, p. 409.
66. Pr, 8 April 1968, p. 2; Pr, 18 April 1968, p. 2; Pr, 27 July 1968, p. 1.
67. See RFR, pp. 164–82, supplemented by *Posev*, 27 October 1967, pp. 6–7.
68. *Dialog s Tserkovnoi Rossiei* ('Dialogue with Religious Russia'), Paris, 1967, pp. 87–113. A short extract is given on pp. 263–4.
69. Pp. 185–6.
70. RFR, pp. 105–13.
71. BV 6, 1966, p. 50.
72. *Kampf des Glaubens*, Bern, 1967, pp. 75–142; *Dialog s Tserkovnoi Rossiei*; *Zashchita Very v SSSR* ('Defence of the Faith in the USSR'), Paris, 1966.
73. Levitin, *Dialog s Tserkovnoi Rossiei*, pp. 9–13.
74. For a fuller exposition of this theme, see the article by Peter Reddaway, 'Freedom of Worship and the Law', PC 4, July–August 1968, pp. 22 and 28.
75. *Posev* 3, March 1968, pp. 2–3.

CHAPTER I

1. SMo, 29 January 1960, p. 4.
2. Pr, 18 November 1961, p. 11.
3. *Partinaya Zhizn* ('Party Life'), Moscow, 2, January 1964, pp. 22–26. Cf. Pr, 2 March 1964, p. 2, for a commentary.

Notes

4. §227 of the Penal Code of the RSFSR. See RFR, p. 13.
5. Cf. NiR 6, June 1966, pp. 4–10, where illegal action against a believer is admitted. The case is discussed in RFR, pp. 96–97.
6. NiR 6, June 1966, pp. 7–8.
7. *Sovetskoye Gosudarstvo i Pravo* ('The Soviet State and Law'), Moscow, 1, January 1965, pp. 42–45.
8. *Pravoslavny Tserkovny Kalendar* ('Orthodox Church Calendar'), Moscow Patriarchate, 1946, pp. 58–60.
9. JMP 8, August 1961, pp. 15–17.
10. Pr, 6 December 1959, p. 4.
11. NiR 1, January 1968, pp. 57–58.
12. Krasnov is Levitin's pen-name.
13. Thirty new roubles. A new rouble is officially worth just over a dollar.
14. Duluman transferred here from Odessa in 1947, he tells us in his essay, 'How I Became an Atheist', in V. I. Golubovich (ed.), *Pochemu My Porvali s Religiei* ('Why We Broke with Religion'), Moscow, 1958, p. 12.
15. I.e. a month.
16. *Grani*, Frankfurt-am-Main, 65, 1967, pp. 157–62.
17. Where the Moscow Theological Academy is situated.
18. *Grani* 66, 1967, pp. 234–7.
19. NiR 2, February 1962, pp. 35–36.
20. *S Krestom na Sheye . . . Reportazh iz Monastyrya* ('Cross around Neck . . . Report from a Monastery'), Moscow, 1963.
21. NiR 10, October 1965, p. 14.
22. Now Metropolitan Nikodim of Leningrad and Novgorod.
23. *Messager de l'Exarchate du Patriarche Russe en Europe Occidentale* 38–39, 1962, p. 69.
24. *Posev* 5, May 1968, p. 54.
25. The Executive Committee of the World Council of Churches met in Odessa in February 1964.
26. SCUS, pp. 10–13.
27. Popular name for the period of terror during the purges of the 1930's, called after N. I. Yezhov, head of the Security Police.
28. *Vestnik* 82, 4, 1966, p. 6. Twelve full names and addresses are given at the end of the document.
29. Not to be confused with Metropolitan Antony (Bloom) of Surozh.
30. Or the Russian Orthodox Church in Exile.
31. *Posev*, 5 February 1965, p. 1, quoting TASS on Moscow Radio, 19 December 1964.
32. JMP 3, March 1967, pp. 2–3.
33. *Soviet Weekly*, London, 4 February 1967, p. 5.
34. JMP 2, February 1960, p. 27.

CHAPTER 2

1. JMP 12, December 1962, p. 16.
2. So the published text. 'For not belonging' would make better sense. It was precisely in June 1927 that Metropolitan Sergi did a *volte face* and pronounced his compromise with the state.

3. *Vestnik* 81, 3, 1966, pp. 13–17 (text fragmentary and slightly emended for inclusion here).
4. The Russian form of Job.
5. It looks as though Archbishop Iov had seen through the way the Soviet Government was exploiting the church's peace campaign.
6. If such letters were sent, they could well have been from local communists.
7. 100,000 new roubles.
8. Izv, 8 July 1960, p. 6. Cf. NiR 7, July 1960, pp. 36–43, for a longer version by the same author, together with a photograph of Archbishop Iov and his residence.
9. These sums must be divided by ten for the present-day equivalent.
10. SRo, 21 June 1960, p. 4. Cf. SRo, 20 July 1960, p. 4, which claims that public opinion deplored the leniency of the sentence.
11. JMP 11, November 1967, p. 10.
12. I.e. new roubles (the change was made at the beginning of 1961).
13. NiR 8, August 1962, p. 27. Cf. other arrests listed in *Russia Cristiana* 73, January 1966, pp. 13–27.
14. *Posev*, 7 January 1965, pp. 9–10. For official Soviet confirmation, see *Pravda Ukrainy* ('Ukrainian Truth') Kiev, 1 October 1965, p. 3.
15. Unpublished document.
16. Unpublished document.
17. Unpublished document.

CHAPTER 3

1. KmP, 22 October 1959, p. 3.
2. Struve, *op. cit.*, p. 201.
3. NiR 9, September 1961, pp. 22–31.
4. As far as is known, this has not reached the West.
5. Levitin, *Zashchita Very v SSSR*, pp. 10–31.
6. *Pravda o Pskovo-Pechorskom Monastyre* ('The Truth about the Caves Monastery at Pskov'), Moscow, 1963, pp. 47–49, 73, 75.
7. Levitin, *Zashchita Very v SSSR*, pp. 32–62.
8. Followers of Leonti Gritsan. See Walter Kolarz, *Religion in the Soviet Union*, London, 1961, pp. 370–71.
9. Medical centre.
10. Every police station in the USSR has one of these, usually in the basement. Conditions are worse than in a normal prison and food is served once a day only.
11. Cf. NiR 6, June 1966, pp. 5–6.
12. This is strong support for the contention that world public opinion can influence Soviet internal policy towards the churches.
13. P. 7.
14. 29 March–8 April 1966.
15. *Vestnik* 84, 2, 1967, pp. 39–69.
16. Levitin, *Zashchita Very v SSSR*, pp. 63–87.
17. JMP 11, November 1965, p. 14. Cf. a similar account relating to the Caves Monastery at Pskov in JMP 10, October 1965, p. 5.

M

18. JMP 12, December 1966, p. 38. Cf. the visit by a group of Americans in 1967 – JMP 11, November 1967, p. 12.
19. NiR 2, February 1962, p. 37.
20. KmP, 7 February 1962, p. 2.
21. See Chapter 1, Note 25.
22. SCUS, pp. 11–12.

CHAPTER 4

1. *Literaturnaya Gazeta* ('Literary Gazette'), Moscow, 23 August 1956, p. 1.
2. *Literatura i Zhizn* ('Literature and Life'), Moscow, 21 February 1960, p. 2.
3. In the Ukraine.
4. JMP 4, April 1961, pp. 30–31.
5. In the Urals.
6. SRo, 1 June 1961, p. 4.
7. In the Ukraine.
8. KmP, 14 June 1961, p. 2.
9. NiR 7, July 1961, p. 48.
10. *Novy Mir* ('New World'), Moscow, 11, November 1962, pp. 122–3.
11. *Istoria SSSR* ('History of the USSR'), Moscow, 5, September–October 1967, pp. 200 and 202.
12. In Belorussia.
13. Izv, 10 March 1968, p. 4.
14. Pr, 8 April 1968, p. 2.
15. Vologda region.
16. Pr, 18 April 1968, p. 2.
17. The 23rd Party Congress of the CPSU, 29 March–8 April 1966.
18. Unpublished document.
19. JMP 4, April 1966, p. 6.
20. The name after the councils for the Orthodox Church and the sects were united in January 1966.
21. There is a play upon words here. 'Bear' is *medved* in Russian.
22. P. 4.
23. He retired 'for ill health' in July 1966 – JMP 8, August 1966, p. 1.
24. Izv, 30 August 1966, p. 4.
25. See RFR, pp. 14–16 for documentary confirmation.
26. Not in the Kirov region.
27. *Vestnik* 83, 1, 1967, pp. 29–64. Bishop Ioann's death is recorded in JMP 1, January 1967, pp. 38–39.
28. *Posev*, 3 March 1967, p. 7.
29. Unpublished document; but see *New York Times*, 4 July 1968, p. 2.
30. *Encounter*, London, 3, March 1965, pp. 8–9.

CHAPTER 5

1. *Liudina i Svit* ('Man and the World'), Kiev, 7, July 1967, pp. 32–33.
2. *Trud* ('Labour'), Moscow, 20 September 1966, p. 2.

Notes

3. KmP, 6 June 1963, p. 2.
4. KmP, 25 August 1961, p. 2.
5. KmP, 19 January 1964, p. 4.
6. SZh, 14 June 1962, p. 4.
7. See Chapter 1, Note 25.
8. Children receive communion in the Orthodox Church.
9. SCUS, pp. 7–8.
10. 1963 (internal evidence gives late 1963 as the date of this document).
11. *Posev*, 8 May 1964, p. 3.
12. Unpublished document, unsigned and dated only '1966'.
13. Of the Russian Orthodox Church in Exile.
14. Cf. the reform Baptists: RFR, pp. 34–37.
15. *Vestnik Zap.-Yevropeiskoi Yeparkhii*, Geneva, 1–2, 1967, pp. 10–12.
16. *Posev*, 7 January 1965, pp. 7–9.
17. These lay Christians bring up this point more than a year before Frs. Eshliman and Yakunin made it one of the central issues in their letters.
18. P. 5.
19. Found on the defendant (stated in the omitted part of the document).
20. So far, there has been no confirmation of this information in other sources.
21. *Posev*, 7 January 1965, pp. 4–7. Part of the manuscript, including the signatures, is reproduced photographically here.
22. *Lvovskaya Pravda* ('Lvov Truth'), Lvov, 18 August 1964.
23. *Ibid.*, 18 November 1964.
24. Spelt thus in the original.
25. NiR 6, June 1965, pp. 43–45.
26. *Grani* 63, 1967, pp. 97–110. The opening (not translated here) gives the date of writing as April 1959.

CHAPTER 6

1. Stroyen, *op. cit.*, p. 125.
2. *Ibid.*, pp. 121 and 124.
3. RFR, pp. 159–64.
4. *Kommunisticheskaya Partia i Sovetskoye Pravitelstvo o Religii i Tserkvi* ('The Communist Party and the Soviet Government on Religion and the Church'), Moscow, 1959; *O Religii i Tserkvi* (*Sbornik Dokumentov*) ('On Religion and the Church [Collection of Documents]'), Moscow, 1965.
5. SVSQ, Vol. 10, 1–2, 1966, pp. 67–76; also in Struve, *op. cit.*, pp. 404–17. Cf. NiR 6, 1968, p. 10, for the first overt reference to Eshliman and Yakunin in a published Soviet source.
6. Alexi, Patriarch of Moscow and All Russia, *Slova, Rechi, Poslania, Obrashchenia, Doklady, Stati* ('Pronouncements, Speeches, Missives, Addresses, Reports, Articles'), Moscow Patriarchate, 1948, p. 98 (note by Eshliman and Yakunin).
7. I.e. part, not the whole, of the monastery.
8. Bishop Feofan, *Tolkovanie Pastyrskikh Poslani Sv. Apostola Pavla* ('Commentary on the Pastoral Epistles of St. Paul'), Moscow, 1894, p. 293 (note by Eshliman and Yakunin).

9. Boris Talantov traces all the present ills of the Russian Orthodox Church to the false step which he alleges Metropolitan Sergi took in 1927: *The Times*, 7 April 1969, p. 7.
10. A similar demand was made by the reform Baptists: see RFR, pp. 34–37.
11. SVSQ, Vol. 10, 1–2, 1966, pp. 77–107.
12. JMP 12, December 1965, p. 3. Translated on p. 239.
13. SVSQ, Vol. 10, 1–2, 1966, pp. 108–11.
14. MO 35, 3, 1966, pp. 51–55. The translations of this and the following documents from this source are from the unpublished Russian original.
15. *Ibid.*, pp. 55–56.
16. *Ibid.*, p. 56.
17. *Ibid.*, p. 57.
18. *Ibid.*, pp. 57–59.
19. *New York Times*, 9 June 1966, p. 47.
20. RCDA, Vol. 5, 15–16, 15–31 August 1966, pp. 127–8. The present version has been re-translated from the original.
21. At this point follows the biography of Bishop Afanasi, which was printed on pp. 65–9.
22. *Vestnik* 81, 3, 1966, pp. 5–12.
23. *Observer*, London, 27 November 1966, p. 13.
24. Letter to the author.
25. *Vestnik* 82, 4, 1966, p. 3.
26. *Ibid.*, pp. 18–19.
27. *Ibid.*, p. 19.
28. JMP 3, March 1953, pp. 11–12.
29. *Ibid.*, pp. 19–20.
30. JMP 12, December 1965, p. 3.
31. As far as is known, the texts of these have not reached the West.
32. *Vestnik* 86, 4, 1967, pp. 61–65.
33. *Ibid.*, pp. 74–80.
34. 1721–1917, the years during which the reforms of Peter the Great were operative.
35. *Vestnik* 87, 1–2, 1968, pp. 8–9.
36. *Ibid.*, pp. 9–14.

CHAPTER 7

1. The first Patriarch of modern times, elected just after the Revolution.
2. The schismatic movement of the 1920's.
3. A prominent leader of the movement.
4. NiR 5, May 1960, pp. 32–37.
5. I.e. the 1920's and 1930's. Published in *Novy Zhurnal* ('The New Journal'), New York, 85, December 1966, pp. 141–78; 86, March 1967, pp. 159–220; 87, June 1967, pp. 198–244; 88, September 1967, pp. 138–69. The list of articles quoted proves that we have seen only a small part of Levitin's output.
6. Solomon Mikhoels ran the Jewish theatre in Moscow and was murdered on 12 January 1948 (see *Grani* 68, pp. 106–18).
7. *Posev*, 7 January 1967, pp. 5–7.

8. Stroyen, *op.. cit.*, p. 121. Parishes must be registered, but not priests.
9. Levitin, *Dialog s Tserkovnoi Rossiei*, pp. 108–9.
10. This and other passages have led some Western scholars to claim that this document is a KGB forgery. Pending further evidence, we include it here so that the reader can make up his own mind. Levitin refers to it on p. 290.
11. Levitin, *Zashchita Very v SSSR*, pp. 88–101.
12. In an accompanying document, dated 17 October 1966 (*Posev*, 7 January 1967, p. 5), it is stated that there is a military establishment located near by.
13. *Posev*, 7 January 1967, p. 5.
14. A text which has not reached us.
15. Rafael de Riego y Núñez (1785–1823): Spanish revolutionary. Tadeusz Bulgarin (1789–1859): Polish émigré in St. Petersburg who gave evidence against the Decembrists. Nikolai Ivanovich Grech (1787–1867): pseudo-liberal journalist and writer. Alexander Ivanovich Herzen (1812–70): founder of the émigré journal, *Kolokol* ('The Bell'). Kondrati Fyodorovich Ryleyev (1795–1826): poet hanged after the Decembrist Revolt.
16. The integration of the Uniates of the Western Ukraine with the Russian Orthodox Church (forcibly carried out by the KGB, with the connivance of Russian Orthodox Church leaders).
17. NiR 10, October 1966, pp. 25–26.
18. Pp. 25–55.
19. See Fletcher, *Nikolai*, p. 200.
20. Actually 13 May 1966, according to MO 35, 3, 1966, p. 57.
21. Levitin obviously lacks full information here.
22. The reform Baptists have, however, demanded the right to set up their own Sunday Schools. See RFR, pp. 126–30.
23. VVS 12, 1966, p. 220.
24. Former premises of the Moscow Patriarchate, from which it has now been expropriated.
25. *Russkaya Mysl* ('Russian Thought'), Paris, 7 July 1966, pp. 4–5.
26. Evidently Levitin's memory is faulty here. The name in the earlier account of the talk is Shitikov (see p. 265).
27. Levitin gives it the old familiar name of 'Peter'.
28. Pp. 4–6.
29. See Bourdeaux, *Opium of the People*, pp. 209–10.
30. This did not appear in 1966–68.
31. Alexander Vasilievich Sukhovo-Kobylin (1817–1903). Playwright.
32. Chief character of Sukhovo-Kobylin's first play, *Svadba Krechinskovo* ('Krechinsky's Wedding'), 1855. It is a satire on bureaucracy.
33. The editorial office of JMP is in the Novodevichi Monastery, Moscow.
34. Premises of the Moscow Patriarchate.
35. *Posev*, 23 September 1966, pp. 3–4, and 1 October 1966, pp. 3–4.

CHAPTER 8

1. *Stimme der Orthodoxie*, Berlin, 2, February 1963, pp. 15–19. Translation from *Current Developments in the Eastern European Churches*, Geneva, 19 April 1963, pp 2–3.

2. 'The Smiths' – so called from the former trade of the district.
3. *Posev*, 1 October 1966, p. 3.
4. School begins with the first form at seven.
5. Archbishop Yermogen's views on this are fully expounded in *Vestnik* 86, 4, 1967, pp. 75–77.
6. See Stroyen, *op. cit.*, p. 121.
7. *Ibid.*, p. 131.
8. *Vestnik* 83, 1, 1967, pp. 7–28.
9. 30 August 1966, p. 4.
10. PC 4. July–August 1968, pp. 102–4.
11. JMP 8, 1961, p. 6.
12. Unpublished document.
13. Argentina.
14. JMP. 8, August 1961, pp. 6–17.
15. Mr. Khrushchev's chief 'ideologist'.
16. These words were written after the trial of the writers Sinyavsky and Daniel, but before its consequences for intellectuals could be fully assessed. The next paragraph shows that in fact Fr. Shpiller is realistic about the nature of the tasks ahead.
17. *Rossia i Vselenskaya Tserkov* ('Russia and the Universal Church'), Brussels, 4 (70) 1966 and 1 (71) 1967, pp. 57–84.
18. *Istina*, Paris, 2, 1967, pp. 133–35.

EPILOGUE

1. London, 1967.
2. The fourteenth-century builder of Russian monasticism.
3. St. Yermogen, murdered by the Poles in 1612.
4. The suffix '-shchina' is attached pejoratively to a personal name to indicate bad times or circumstances connected with that individual.
5. Unpublished document – but see *The Times*, 7 April 1969, p. 7.
6. In 1964.
7. Cf. RFR, pp. 42–46.
8. I Cor. 5:13.
9. Unpublished document – but see *New York Times*, 4 July 1968, p. 26.
10. Cf. the document written by Kamenskikh himself recording verbatim some of his conversations with the seminary authorities: *Vestnik* 89–90, 3–4, 1968, pp. 68–76.
11. *The Times*, 12 December 1967, p. 11 and *Church Times*, London, 29 December 1967, pp. 1 and 16.
12. 'National Labour Union' – a Russian émigré organization.
13. RCDA, Vol. 7, 15–16, 15–31 August 1968, pp. 123–36 (a different translation).
14. The writers Alexander Ginzburg and Yuri Galanskov, imprisoned in January 1968.
15. *Vestnik* 89–90, 3–4, 1968, pp. 77–79. Cf. *Posev* 11, November 1968, pp. 10–11.
16. *Posev*, 12 December 1968, pp. 13–14.
17. *Vestnik* 81, 3, 1966, p. 22.

Index